HELPING THE CLIENT

HELPING THE CLIENT
A Creative Practical Guide

fifth edition

John Heron

SAGE Publications
Los Angeles • London • New Delhi • Singapore

© John Heron 2001

Fourth edition first published 1990. Reprinted 1991, 1993
(twice), 1995, 1997, 1998, 2000

First, second and third edition © John Heron and published in
1975, 1986 and 1989 respectively by Human Potential
Research Group, University of Surrey

Reprinted 2002, 2003, 2005, 2006, 2007

SAGE Publications Ltd
1 Oliver's Yard
55 City Road
London EC1Y 1SP

SAGE Publications Inc
2455 Teller Road
Thousand Oaks, California 91320

SAGE Publications India Pvt Ltd
B 1/I1 Mohan Cooperative Industrial Area
Mathura Road, New Delhi 110 044
India

SAGE Publications Asia-Pacific Pte Ltd
33 Pekin Street #02-01
Far East Square
Singapore 048763

British Library Cataloguing in Publication Data

A catalogue record for this book is available
from the British Library

ISBN 978-0-7619-7288-4
ISBN 978-0-7619-7289-1 (pbk)

Library of Congress catalog record car number 2001131814

Typeset by Mayhew Typesetting, Rhayader, Powys
Printed and bound in Great Britain by Biddles Ltd,
King's Lynn, Norfolk

CONTENTS

PREFACE TO THE FOURTH EDITION

This book is in effect the fourth, revised and enlarged, edition of my Six Category Intervention Analysis, now given a new title. The three previous editions were published in 1975, 1986 and 1989, respectively, by the Human Potential Research Group at the University of Surrey. The book has been the basis for a developing programme of six category training there from 1975 to the present.

I must emphasize that this work has two aspects. The core of it deals with personal counselling, and this in some depth; hence its value for counsellors, counselling training programmes and counselling supervision. At the same time, its comprehensive repertoire of interventions means that it can be adapted and selectively applied to a broad range of occupational groups. Thus, it has been widely used in diverse settings and has become accepted as an important ingredient in, or the basis of, interpersonal skills training for continuing education programmes in medicine, nursing, social work, business management, teaching in secondary and higher education, police, youth and community work. One of its central uses is the training of trainers and facilitators in these professions.

I am grateful to Dr James Kilty, Nicholas Ragg and John Mulligan for their many valuable contributions to the earlier editions; to Sue Jones of Sage Publications for proposing important additions and revisions to this edition; to John Mulligan and Meg Bond for their continued commitment to the development of the six category approach through the Human Potential Research Group at the University of Surrey; and to all the participants in my Six Category Training Workshops over the years, in so many places, whose interest and deep involvement have provided the stimulus for the creative unfolding of the model.

I also wish to acknowledge the influence on the text of many schools of human development – eastern and western, ancient and modern – that have nourished my thought and practice. These influences have become thoroughly assimilated into my writing, and though I have not wished to labour the text with references, I am fully aware of my great indebtedness to a host of luminous others.

A great deal of experience and reflection are condensed into this fourth edition. I would recommend that it is dipped into as a reference book, when particular sections have special relevance or appeal. Sometimes I have put volumes into a diagram or a few basic points on a page.

John Heron
October 1989

PREFACE TO THE FIFTH EDITION

This fully revised edition incorporates several changes and additions. Their purpose is to usher the book into the new millennium.

I have improved the description of a number of interventions throughout the book, and added and edited text in relevant places to deepen the underlying view of human nature.

There is an extended account of emotional competence in Chapter 2, of whole personhood, and of transference, in Chapter 3. In Chapter 7, I have included an account of negative emotional states to complement the section on positive emotional states. There is a detailed new section on primary theatre, or charismatic expression, in Chapter 8. There is also a new section on deep choice in Chapter 9. And I have indicated the relevance of Chapter 9 to the emerging practice of coaching.

There are two new chapters. Chapter 15 is about methods for teaching interpersonal skills, and gives more practical back-up to the preceding chapter on six category training. Chapter 16 presents a peer self-help approach to developing the kind of emotional competence and house-cleaning needed for effective helping: it describes the theory, practice and working techniques of co-counselling.

I have updated the references, especially about relevant research methods, and added some new ones.

The six category approach continues to be used for interpersonal skills training by a wide range of professions and institutions in various parts of the world. I am appreciative of this developing commitment, particularly in relation to the University of Surrey, which through the Human Potential Research Group has now been running Six Category Training Workshops continuously since they were launched there in 1975.

John Heron

CHAPTER 1

INTRODUCTION

The six category analysis of counselling interventions in this book was originally inspired by the diagnosis and development matrix of Blake and Mouton (1972). This offered five kinds of interventions that 'characterize what applied behavioral scientists do as they work with people in organizations'. Their five kinds are: cathartic, catalytic, confrontation, prescriptive, principles/theories/models. I have altered this scheme to make it more comprehensive by adding two further types of intervention – informative and supportive; also to make it more internally coherent by regarding their principles/theories/models as a sub-species of the catalytic type of intervention.

What is now offered, therefore, are six basic intervention categories, which I have developed in ways that are quite independent of Blake and Mouton's monograph. Their focus is primarily on interventions in organizational life by organizational development consultants. Mine is primarily on one-to-one interventions from practitioner to client. It was actively developed in 1973 and 1974 when I was running courses for experienced general practitioners training them to become trainers of young hospital doctors entering general practice (Heron, 1974). We evolved a set of behavioural categories that was relevant, when appropriately applied, both to the role of trainer and to the role of doctor. It then became clear that it had universal application, and it has since provided the basis for interpersonal skills training in a wide diversity of social roles. The model has undergone revision and extension several times between 1973 and 2000.

In the rest of this chapter, I shall first have a look at the notions of practitioner and client; secondly, consider the concept of an intervention; thirdly, briefly outline the six categories; fourthly, make some introductory general points about them; and finally, identify valid interventions.

PRACTITIONER AND CLIENT

What I mean by a 'practitioner' here and throughout this book is anyone who is offering a professional service to a client: so the term covers equally doctor, dentist, psychiatrist, psychologist, counsellor, psychotherapist, nurse, complementary therapist, creative therapist, social worker, voluntary worker, probation officer, police officer, management consultant, tutor, teacher, trainer, lawyer, architect, bank manager, accountant, and many, many more.

What I mean by a 'client' is the person who is freely choosing (in most cases) to avail him- or herself of the practitioner's service, in order to meet some need which they have identified. The service will meet a need in relation to the client's person and personal life, or physical body, or possessions, or affairs (legal, financial and other), or in relation to some combination of these.

Between practitioner and client there is a mutually agreed voluntary contract implicit in the relationship: the client chooses the practitioner and the service, and the practitioner chooses to accept the client. There is a formal differentiation of roles between them. And there will usually be a fairly clear understanding between them as to what the practitioner's remit is. However, this primary account of the roles can usefully be extended in two further directions.

In the first extension, the terms 'practitioner' and 'client' can be applied in formal, occupational settings, where two people in the same organization are relating in terms of their work roles, and where one person is intervening in relation to the other. They may be on the same level of the system, such as manager and colleague; or on different levels such as supervisor and subordinate, foreman and worker. The interventions may be about work, about discipline, or even about personal matters that have a bearing upon work. The structure and norms of the organization, and the job descriptions of those involved, will normally provide a tacit contract, an understanding of the extent of the practitioner's remit.

In the second extension, the terms 'practitioner' and 'client' can usefully be applied to non-formal, non-professional settings, whenever one person is adopting, in terms of some tacit or explicit agreement, an enabling role for another. This temporary enabling relationship may be from friend to friend, lover to lover, spouse to spouse, parent to child (or vice versa), colleague to colleague, or stranger to stranger. But in every case, one person is the listener and the facilitator; and the other person is the talker, the one who is dealing with some special issue that needs the time, attention and service of another human being.

These two extensions give the six category system very wide application: to any human situation where there is a formal or an informal enabling relationship, or a formal working relationship, going from one person to another.

The central enabling relationship, in my view, is to service the personal development of the client. This is the primary thrust of this book. So it is first and foremost for the personal growth facilitator, the counsellor, the psychotherapist, and any practitioner such as nurse, doctor or complementary therapist whose work includes personal counselling.

It is important to stress, however, that this six category analysis is equally applicable to counselling where personal growth is not the prime aim, as in career guidance, or other problem-solving approaches. And it has been in use for many years as a general interpersonal skills training model in medicine, nursing, social work, business management and counselling, teaching in secondary and higher education, police, youth and community work. In relation to the many other fields of application, any practitioner, whether plumber or stockbroker, can get a great deal out of the book by selective reading and a bit of imagination in transferring the application of the relevant interventions to their own domain of service.

Chapter 12 gives examples of how the system can be used in several different professional contexts. Application of the six categories to academic tutoring is also dealt with in my *Behaviour Analysis in Education and Training* (Heron, 1977a).

INTERVENTION

What I mean by an 'intervention' is an identifiable piece of verbal and/or non-verbal behaviour that is part of the practitioner's service to the client. Throughout this book, my accounts of the different interventions refer mostly to the practitioner's verbal behaviour, occasionally with some reference to manner and timing. The non-verbal accompaniments of verbal behaviour are, of course, critical in determining how the verbal behaviour comes across to the client. But such matters, I believe, are best dealt with in a Six Category Training Workshop. Some important physical – that is, body to body – interventions are covered in the cathartic section.

It is possible to give an account of verbal behaviour in three different ways:

1 *Verbatim*: You can give an example of the actual form of words that is typically used in the intervention: for example, the practitioner says to the client 'What are your feelings about George?'

2   *Linguistic*: You can give an ordinary linguistic description of the form of words that is to be used in the intervention: for example, the practitioner asks the client an open question.
3   *Intentional*: You can define the intervention in terms of its intention, that is, in terms of what its point and purpose are, what the practitioner wants to achieve by it: for example, the practitioner invites the client to explore and express his or her attitude to a colleague.

I use all these three types of account in the text, but I use the third one – defining an intervention in terms of its intention – by far the most. And usually, but not always, I leave it to the reader to get a sense of what form of words, and of what particular words, to use. I think this is best. An account of the intention of an intervention takes us to the heart of the matter.

The right form of words will follow from grasping the intention of the intervention in *responding appropriately to a given situation*. There is not just one way of stating an intervention: it can have many verbal forms. So in the text I do not give many examples of the actual words to use. This is because I do not wish in any way to confuse an intervention with a verbal formula, a particular set of words. For an intervention is a person to person intention that can have many variations of verbal form, and the right variation depends on who those persons are and what is going on between them.

Many interpersonal situations between practitioner and client are similar, and so require similar interventions with the same basic sort of intention. But each of these similar situations is also in some respects quite unique, and the intervention in it needs a distinctive choice of diction, grammar, timing and manner of speech.

I want to emphasize the importance of the grammatical form of an intervention and the choice of the actual words used in it. Both can be critical in getting the intention manifest with real finesse. But I think these things, once again, are best dealt with in a Six Category Training Workshop, in which the use of role play can simulate the unique properties of real-life situations, and so provide a context for the choice of words. My purpose in this book is to clarify basic intentions.

THE SIX CATEGORIES

In the main body of the text, each of the categories is dealt with at some length, with a longer definition, a general preface, then a list

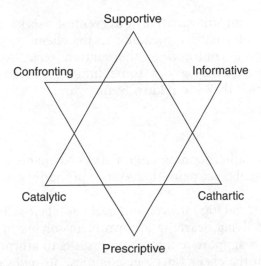

Supportive

Confronting

Informative

Catalytic

Cathartic

Prescriptive

FIGURE 1.1   The six categories of counselling intervention

of interventions that belong to that category. In the few paragraphs below, I give an initial short definition of each category.

The six category system deals with six basic kinds of intention the practitioner can have in serving his or her client. Each category is one major class of intention that subsumes a whole range of sub-intentions and specific behaviours that manifest them. So with six kinds of genus and many species within each genus, the system has great flexibility and power to cover a very wide range of client needs and practitioner roles, and to cover them with *practical intent*.

It is also accessible for professional use and professional training: people are quick to get the hang of it and get into action. This is because it focuses on the intention, the purpose, of interventions; because the six major types of intention picked out are close to the grain of the needs and interests of human beings; and because the genus–species hierarchy enables a large number of interventions to be organized under a very few simple and basic concepts. And at the same time, as we have seen, it gives scope for practitioners to explore variations in their use of language in order to make each intervention more effective in, and more suited to, its context. The six categories are shown in Figure 1.1.

Authoritative

1 *Prescriptive*: a prescriptive intervention seeks to direct the behaviour of the client, usually behaviour that is outside the practitioner–client relationship.

2   *Informative*: an informative intervention seeks to impart knowledge, information, meaning to the client.
3   *Confronting*: a confronting intervention seeks to raise the client's consciousness about some limiting attitude or behaviour of which they are relatively unaware.

Facilitative

4   *Cathartic*: a cathartic intervention seeks to enable the client to discharge, to abreact painful emotion, primarily grief, fear and anger.
5   *Catalytic*: a catalytic intervention seeks to elicit self-discovery, self-directed living, learning and problem-solving in the client.
6   *Supportive*: a supportive intervention seeks to affirm the worth and value of the client's person, qualities, attitudes or actions.

The first three I call authoritative because they are rather more hierarchical: the practitioner is taking responsibility for and on behalf of the client – guiding his or her behaviour, giving instruction, raising consciousness. The second set of three I call facilitative because they are rather less hierarchical: the practitioner is seeking to enable clients to become more autonomous and take more responsibility for themselves – by helping to release the emotional pain that blocks their personal power, by eliciting their self-directed learning, by unfolding their spiritual potential, by affirming their worth as a unique being.

The authoritative interventions are neither more nor less useful and valuable than the facilitative ones. It all depends on the nature of the practitioner's role, the particular needs of the client, and what the content or focus of the intervention is (I discuss this again in Chapter 4 on prescriptive interventions). It is the specific, concrete context that makes one intervention more or less valuable than another – nothing else.

However, some broad cultural observations can be made. Traditional education and training have rather overdone authoritative sorts of intervention, and have often omitted altogether the facilitative sorts. Similarly with many traditional kinds of therapy. This does not make authoritative interventions *per se* bad, it just makes them look bad, because they degenerate when they are used to the exclusion of facilitative ones.

Conversely, some innovative contemporary approaches to education and therapy rely too much on facilitative interventions to the exclusion of authoritative ones. They have thrown the positive power of authentic hierarchy away with their rejection of the negative power of oppressive hierarchy. So then their facilitative approach starts to degenerate, because it is used to the exclusion of healthy kinds of authority.

Three basic kinds of political value underlie the everyday use of the six categories: the values of hierarchy, of co-operation, of autonomy. Hierarchy manifests when the practitioner decides for and on behalf of the client; and co-operation, when practitioner and client reach a decision by mutual consultation. Autonomy is manifest when the practitioner facilitates the client deciding for him- or herself. Some balance between these three usually makes for good practice. What kind of balance depends again upon the total context – what sort of practitioner, what sort of client, and so on.

Balancing authoritative and facilitative interventions is all about the proper exercise of power: the practitioner's power over the client, the power shared by practitioner and client with each other, the autonomous power within the client. My own view is that these three forms of power need each other – always in due measure and ever-changing ratios – to keep healthy.

GENERAL POINTS

Many points are discussed in the prefaces to the category sections. Most of them are to do with the particular category under discussion in that chapter. Some of the issues raised in the context of one category have implications for all the others. So I refer the reader to these prefaces for a lot of conceptual and practical guidelines for the application of the categories. Below I make some general points not covered in these prefaces.

The six category system is a practical working hypothesis, not a dogma. It is in principle open to being checked and rechecked, amended and modified, by personal experiential inquiry, by testing it against the evidence provided by using it in action. There is nothing sacred or unchallengeable about the number 'six', nor about the way the whole thing is conceptually put together.

However, it does seem, after more than 26 years of application in many different professional contexts, that the six categories are exhaustive of the major sorts of valid intervention any practitioner needs to make in relation to their clients. This is a big claim, and it is made with paradoxical intent: both to establish confidence in readers, and at the same time to urge them to read the previous paragraph once again so that they continue to be vigilant in inquiry. What is certainly not being claimed is that the list of interventions under each category is exhaustive. I would only say that in each case it is comprehensive. But there are, no doubt, more entries to be made.

Another important claim, also to be checked, is that the six categories are independent of each other in the sense that each has its relatively pure forms which cannot be reduced to the form of any other category. There are also, however, significant areas of overlap between the categories: informative interventions that are confronting, prescriptive interventions that are catalytic, and so on. The major overlaps are identified in the text. And where such overlaps occur, the intervention is classified under that category which covers its primary intent.

There is no real value hierarchy among the categories. No one of them is in principle good or bad in relation to any other. In the abstract they are of equal value. They can only be comparatively evaluated in use: the practical context alone determines whether one category is better or worse than another. The category ethic is entirely situational.

Nevertheless, I would say that in general terms the catalytic category has a key functional role. It is the linchpin of any practitioner service that sees itself as fundamentally educational in the widest sense of encouraging the client's personal power in living, learning and growing.

So in the main text that follows, it is the living-as-learning theme brought out in the preface to the catalytic section, and in the interventions of that section, that is the functional pivot of this manual, both conceptually and practically. Central, too, is the map of the client's psychological field, no. 7 in Chapter 9.

There is a very important sense in which the supportive category has a key moral and spiritual role in use; for all the categories depend, for their validity in action, on a supportive attitude of mind and being in the practitioner, that is, one that respects the value of the client and of his or her autonomy. All the categories, when in service to the client, need to overlap with this kind of tacit support.

I should say a brief word about transmutative methods. They do not constitute a seventh category of intervention. For they are really forms of client self-help, so when introducing them to the client, the practitioner is working in the catalytic mode. I have listed some of them in Chapter 8 in the context of a discussion about the relationship between, and the differences between, catharsis and transmutation. But strictly speaking, they belong to catalytic interventions (Chapter 9), in particular to catalytic interventions nos. 9 and 18.

As I have said, the focus in this manual is mainly on one-to-one practitioner–client relationships where there is a full or partial concern with the client's personal development. Of course the interventions are also relevant to the interactions between group leader and any one group member. For facilitating small group discussions, the catalytic tool-kit contained in no. 6 in the catalytic interventions chapter is particularly useful – see especially no. 6.14. But for a wider discussion of the options open to the facilitator of a group *qua* group, see *The Complete Facilitator's Handbook* (Heron, 1999).

The six categories *per se* and the sorts of interventions that fall under them do not entail any particular theoretical perspective coming from any school of psychology or psychotherapy. Indeed, they could be used as an analytic tool to compare and contrast the therapeutic practice of different schools. However, in presenting some parts of this manual and some interventions, I have clearly let my own theoretical and practical perspective manifest itself – with its influences from humanistic, transpersonal and archetypal psychologies; from Cassirer, Plotinus and many other thinkers. I think it is more interesting to present the whole thing within the organizing power of a certain perspective. But the reader can quickly re-arrange things in accordance with their own perspective.

In learning to use the six categories, a person is not learning to use a particular method of counselling, but is rather acquiring a set of analytic and behavioural tools to shape his or her own method of practice. Indeed, the trainee is developing and extending basic human skills. It is not a question of starting from scratch with some whole new system. Many of the listed interventions simply name and describe behaviours which trainees will realize they have already been using. To have them thus identified increases confidence and command in their use. Other listed interventions will be new to the trainees – and enable them to extend their range of human functioning.

The skilled practitioner is, in the ideal case, someone who (a) is equally proficient in a wide range of interventions in each of the categories; (b) can move elegantly, flexibly and cleanly from one intervention to another and from one category to another, as the developing situation and the purposes of the interaction require; (c) is aware at any given time of what intervention they are using and why; (d) knows when to lead the client and when to follow the client; (e) has a creative balance between power over the client, power shared with the client, and the facilitation of power within the client.

VALID, DEGENERATE AND PERVERTED INTERVENTIONS: VALIDITY

A *valid intervention* is one that is appropriate to the client's current state and stage of development, and to the developing practitioner–client interaction. To say that it is appropriate, is to say that: (a) it is in the right category; (b) it is the right sort of intervention within that category; (c) its content and use of language is fitting; (d) it is delivered in the right manner; and (e) it is delivered with good timing.

A *degenerate intervention* is one that fails in one, and usually several, of these respects, because the practitioner lacks personal development, or training, or experience, or awareness, or some combination of these.

A *perverted intervention* is one that is deliberately malicious, that intentionally seeks to do harm to another person.

The main body of the text, starting with Chapter 4, deals with valid interventions, so far as their basic intention is concerned. There is an account of degenerate and perverted interventions in Chapter 13.

The overall validity of the six category system is a matter of lived inquiry. It can be regarded as a working hypothesis for each practitioner in their professional life, using first-person action research, in which the practitioner develops practical knowledge through self-directed inquiry into his or her own actions. For more on this see self-monitoring (Heron, 1977a), reflection-in-action (Schon, 1983), experiential research (Cunningham, 1988), action inquiry (Torbert, 1991), radical practice (Heron, 1996). The six category system can be adopted by a group of practitioners meeting at regular intervals as a co-operative inquiry team to review and revise the use of the categories in their ongoing professional work with clients. For details and examples of this type of inquiry, see Heron (1996), Heron and Reason (2000), Reason (1988, 1994). For an overview of participative forms of research in general see Reason and Bradbury (2000).

CHAPTER 2

PREPARATION FOR HELPING

I wrote in Chapter 1 that the term 'practitioner' can be applied to anyone offering a professional, occupational service to a client or customer, to anyone at work intervening in relation to someone else at work, and to anyone in an informal setting who is in a supportive enabling interaction with another person. This gives the six category system a very wide range of use; and I wish to say more about the various kinds of application and what sort of preparation a person needs to function well in using them.

I define 'helping' as supporting and enabling the well-being of another person. There is clearly something odd about turning human helping into a profession, with training, accreditation, status, case conferences and institutional politics. Does the wise flow of love from person to person require all this apparatus of paternalism? There are, I think, some simple and basic points to be made in answering this question.

GRACE, CHARACTER AND CULTURE

People who help people move by the grace within the human spirit. This grace is the primary source of effective helping behaviour. Its presence and expression are entirely independent of professional training: it can inform and be enhanced by the latter, but can also be obscured, suppressed and distorted by it.

This helping grace seems to have five key attributes: warm concern for and acceptance of the other; openness and attunement to the other's experiential reality; a grasp of what the other needs for his or her essential flourishing; an ability to facilitate the realization of such needs in the right manner and at the right time; and an authentic presence. This combination of concern, empathy, prescience, facilitation and genuineness is, I believe, the spiritual heritage of mankind. It can manifest among the tutored and the untutored alike.

But it will manifest in terms of the norms, values and belief-systems of the prevailing culture. Hence the form a person gives it is a function of their having been educated within a culture, whether that education is in part formal, or entirely informal through the process of socialization. Some people who are untutored may be very effective helpers, within the limits of their socialization; just as some people who are formally tutored in professional roles may be so within the limits of their professionalization.

What makes the effective helper is, then, an interaction between inner grace, character and cultural influence. Inner grace is a spiritual endowment and potential which everyone has. Character is what persons make of themselves in the light of this endowment and in response to their culture. The way these three factors influence each other will determine whether or how the capacity for helping emerges.

EMOTIONAL COMPETENCE

One of the primary aspects of character needed for effective helping is what I have called elsewhere (Heron, 1992, 1996, 1997) emotional competence, which I present in more detail in the next sub-section. For helpers, this means that their own anxiety and distress, accumulated from past traumatic experience, does not drive and distort their attempts to help.

Since we have no education and training in emotional competence in our culture – which if it were present would enable people not to displace their past distress into helping – the occurrence of distress-free helping is problematic and uncertain. So while many people, tutored and untutored, in formal and informal roles, may frequently have the psychological space for effective helping, equally the wish to help may suddenly be obscured and taken over by unaware, distressed compulsions – which I discuss again in Chapter 13.

There are three levels of emotional competence. The first is the zero level, when a person's helping is always contaminated by hidden, distorted emotion and has an oppressive, interfering and inappropriate quality. The second – mentioned in the previous paragraph – is when a person does help in an emotionally clear and clean way at some times, but also slips over at other times into compulsive, intrusive 'helping' *without realizing that he or she has done so*. The third level of emotional competence is when a person makes this kind of slip much less often, knows when it has happened and can correct it; and above all has done the kind of personal psychological work on past distress that gives the person this command. In my experience, the second of these levels is widespread in our culture.

So there is also a lot of misshapen, compulsive helping around, among the tutored and the untutored, the professionals and the laity. Hence the main preparation for helping, in the community at large, is the widespread dissemination of emotional competence through child-raising practices, socialization and general education at all levels. Emotionally educated people will be able to work on their distress and suffering, and to take charge of it enough to liberate their helping from it.

Much of this kind of preparation, certainly among adults, can be done through the training of peer self-help groups, in which people learn to prompt and support each other's self-direction in emotional house-cleaning. Co-counselling training and practice is a good example of this kind of bedrock preparation, which can usefully be undertaken by every well-intentioned citizen of the community (for an overview of co-counselling see Chapter 16; also http://www.dpets.demon.co.uk/cciuk).

MORE ON EMOTIONAL COMPETENCE

Emotional competence is one of the hallmarks of the self-creating person (p. 29). It means that a person who has it is able to manage their emotions awarely in terms of the basic skills of control, expression, catharsis and transmutation, plus one or two others.

Our society is emotionally repressive. It has no working concept of the wounded child, no pervasive methods of emotional education and training. Child-raising, socialization and early education have only one guiding norm about emotions: learn to control them in order to be socially acceptable. This norm is tacit only: there is no explicit training in how to control emotions, no real clarity about what it means, only a general supposition that it is too obvious a social necessity to discuss. It does not differentiate between healthy control and unhealthy repression. All too often the prescription to control emotion is misapplied and it then degenerates into suppression, repression, denial and the eventual return of the repressed in distorted form.

The result is that society has no way of dealing with the excess of distress emotion that children build up. Up to the age of 5, with a peak after the first stage of language mastery at about 3 years old, children holding on to an excess of distress will readily displace it into all kinds of acting out behaviours – disruptive, demanding, clinging – both to try to relieve some of the pressure and to try to find some pretext for discharging the underlying pain.

If you interrupt the acting out, firmly but also very awarely and supportively, emotional discharge of pain will immediately occur with an intensity that bears no relation to the issue involved in the little bit of displacement that preceded it. Old-style discipline put a stop to the displacement, but in a punitive way that acted out the parents' own repressed distress: in demanding that the disruptive behaviour cease, it also angrily demanded that the child's under-lying emotional pain be repressed and denied.

New-style discipline also stops the disruptive displacement behaviour, but in order to allow the child to release the distress emotion that is producing it. Interrupting the distorted behaviour needs to be done in a manner that is free of any parental irritation or anger. It may occasionally involve holding – in a way that is deeply affirmative of the child's being – as full-throttle catharsis proceeds. A distressed child will seize this opportunity to sob, scream, kick, tremble from anything between a few minutes to 20 minutes. All this time, the parent gives abundant supportive attention, gently affirming in words the child's self-healing. When the emotional release of pain reaches its clearance point for that occasion, the parent gives the child a warm and appreciative hug. The child will dance off to enjoy its world and its restoration to positive emotion.

A child that has been holding onto a lot of distress – because of some enforced period of parental deprivation, or for whatever other reason – will need to go through this whole process possibly many times. It is as if the organism measures out the release in manageable phases and at appropriate intervals. When the next chunk of material is ready to be discharged, it will distort beha-viour in some ritualistic manner; the parent interrupts the distor-tion and the release proceeds to a further point of clearance. Few parents have the nerve to do this. Their own repressed hurt child within is projected onto the child without: the inescapable result is that the repression of the child within the parent is imposed on the living child without.

The wounded child is, in our kind of society, a universal phe-nomenon. Its underlying emotional pain is repressed. The adult sustains the repression throughout life, achieving only limited release of the denied distress in the context of permissive intimacy and through laughter, dreams, post-orgasmic catharsis, the cathar-sis of drama, music and poetry, response to nature, and sport and religion. Some of these experiences may also be transmutative of hidden distress. The pain that is untouched by all this distorts behaviour.

For some this means neurosis and psychosis. For all it means unaware displacement: rational and sensitive responses to situ-ations are all mixed up with compulsive, distress-distorted, maladaptive responses. And people do not know which is which; they slip unawarely from one to the other. This is because significant amounts of displacement behaviour are socially legitimated; they have become conventionally acceptable. Within the professions they have become correct professional interventions. So rational teaching is mixed up with compulsive teaching, rational medicine with compulsive medicine, rational priesthood with compulsive priesthood, and, in general terms, rational helping with compulsive helping; and the professionals cannot differentiate one from the other.

This is a vast social pathology, a vast malaise. It cannot be regarded as a therapeutic problem, other than in the short-term individual case. It is an educational issue. We need concepts of child-raising and of education at all levels that foster the progressive development of emotional competence, in the same way that at present we foster the development of intellectual competence.

Emotional competence means many things.

- It validates both positive emotions and distress emotions.
- It sees the catharsis of distress emotion as evidence of self-healing, not as evidence of breakdown.
- It differentiates distress emotion as such from the disturbed, distorted forms it acquires after it has been repressed and denied.
- It knows the difference between the catharsis of distress which occurs when repression is dismantled, and the displacement or acting out of distress which is the result of repression still being in place.
- It can distinguish between catharsis as such and dramatization or pseudo-catharsis, which is the last vestige of acting out as repression falls away.
- More generally, it means the management of emotion in terms of the creative expression of positive emotion, the aware non-suppressive control of all kinds of emotion when appropriate, the catharsis of distress emotion at appropriate times and places, and the complementary process of the transmutation of distress emotion.
- These four basic intrapsychic skills are supplemented by being able to identify, own and accept emotions of all kinds, and to switch and redirect emotional states.
- In everyday living, emotional competence means being able to spot the restimulation of old emotional pain and to interrupt its displacement into distorted behaviour. So old hurt-laden agendas are not projected, not transferred, into current situations.

- Behind this there is general insight into the main elements of early traumatic experience and its influence on adult behaviour.
- It means being able to spot institutionalized and professionalized forms of displacement, and to find ways of replacing them with more rational, flexible and adaptive behaviours. This is a crying need in all the helping professions. So the doctor abandons the repeat prescriptions of psychotropic drugs and cultivates an ability to handle psychosocial disorders. The academic relinquishes 60 minute lectures and develops more skill in facilitating self-directed learning. The priest stops preaching sin and acquires competence in enhancing spiritual self-esteem.
- It means being able supportively to confront other people who are unawarely acting out their denied distress in negative and disruptive forms of behaviour. The confrontation does not shirk the behavioural issue: it deals with it straight and true. At the same time it does not attack, invalidate or abuse the person who is being confronted about the issue. The uncompromising feedback is fundamentally respectful.
- It means enjoying and expressing positive emotions.
- And noticing when these are clouded over by distress to a degree that requires taking some time out for catharsis and/or transmutation.
- It means cultivating celebration and self-esteem as a foundation of emotional life.

For an overlapping account of emotional competence and its criteria, see a work by Denis Postle (Postle, 1991). And for the closely related notion of emotional intelligence, see Goleman (1995).

KINDS OF HELPING AND TRAINING

What are the main kinds of helping? They are:

- Giving informal support to friends, neighbours, relatives, colleagues in times of change or crisis.
- Offering the service of special technical expertise through a professional role such as that of lawyer, bank manager, accountant, architect, engineer.
- Offering physical, social and cultural services through the helping professions of medicine and complementary therapies, nursing, social work, education, policing and many others.

- Offering organizational service through skilled communication and interaction in the workplace.
- Offering psychological services for personal growth and development, through both short- and long-term counselling and psychotherapy.
- Offering spiritual services through the roles of transpersonal practitioner, priest, shaman, seer, spiritual healer.
- Offering mutual support in organized peer self-help groups for life management and personal development, such as co-counselling, mentioned just above.

The first four types of helping, all of which include various forms of human relations and counselling skills, can benefit greatly from intensive short workshops in which the six category model is adapted and used selectively to meet the needs of participants.

The fifth type of helping, overlapping with some aspects of the sixth, and deploying the full range of interventions given in this book over a period of time for an individual client, requires extensive preparation and training, as in a 2-, 3- or 4-year course. And there are now an abundance of such courses, of diverse persuasions, available in this country, Europe and the USA. On all such courses, six category training can be integrated into the curriculum and used for building up practitioner skills. Such courses should also include sustained personal growth work for the trainees, in order to develop their emotional competence. A full discussion of the issues involved in six category training, and an outline of a 5-day workshop, are presented in Chapter 14.

Co-counselling, an example of the seventh kind of helping, is a grass-roots and people-based alternative to professional psychotherapy and counselling and puts the emphasis on training clients to be self-directing in the use of interventions, and in choosing one of three basic contracts that define the extent of counsellor interventions. It will have increasing relevance as educational and training models of acquiring emotional competence replace outmoded therapeutic models. For further details, see Chapter 16.

In all this discussion of preparation and training, it is important to get a good balance between professionalization and de-professionalization. An excess of the former means two things: the professional role is used both defensively and oppressively; and the professionals claim an excessive degree of expertise and will delegate none of it to the laity – whom they officiously claim to protect.

Nothing is worse, or more absurd, than such over-professionalization in the field of human helping (House and Totton, 1997).

De-professionalization in this field means demystification of the helping role, an acknowledgement that many of its basic human skills can be acquired by many people in relatively short training programmes, for reasonably effective use in the first four kinds of helping given above. The basics of emotional competence needed for all kinds of helping can be acquired through training in peer self-help personal growth methods, such as co-counselling, already mentioned.

THE PARADOX OF PRESENTATION

Finally, all helpers wisely acknowledge their human frailty, and realize that any unbridled claim to competence is a defence against owning such frailty. This raises a small paradox about the presentation of the interventions in this book. I have sought to describe them with precision and clarity, but in the process the practitioner included in them – appearing throughout in the second person singular as 'you' – may come over by the sheer accumulation of such accounts as someone of superhuman insight and ability.

This effect, produced by a comprehensive repertoire of interventions each of which has been carefully modelled, can be countered by realizing that there is always a gap between the model and the reality. The clarity of contour and symbol in the map is quite other than the earthy, fractal grain of the territory. The model is only a guideline in the mind, it is not a precise blueprint or programme for behaviour.

Behaviour is situational, idiosyncratic and above all practical – knowing how to respond to present reality. There is always a gap – a necessary and important gap – between knowing how to do something in deed, and describing how to do it. Human skills are maculate skills, enriched by earthy granulation: they are more basic and worthwhile than the immaculate descriptions that service them.

So I recommend that the reader exercise creative latitude in selecting, modifying and adapting the numerous interventions as they are described in this book.

CHAPTER 3

CLIENT CATEGORIES AND STATES

I wrote in the previous chapter that the central enabling relationship, in my view, is to service the personal development of the client; that such service is the primary thrust of this manual: and that it is first and foremost for the personal growth facilitator, the counsellor, the psychotherapist, and any practitioner such as nurse, doctor or complementary therapist whose work includes a good deal of personal counselling. But if you want to help your client develop as a person, this means that your interventions will be guided by some broad criteria that indicate what a developed person is. I call these criteria client categories.

CLIENT CATEGORIES

You will not want to impose these on your client, that is, use them without your client's knowledge. Your client has a right to know what the categories are before embarking on any series of sessions with you, so they need to be stated in simple, accessible form on your professional brochure. They are the basis of your client's contract with you.

Without these categories, your interventions will be fumbling about in the dark. They are higher order intentions, long-term client outcomes, ideals that illumine the more immediate interaction. They nurture and guide the facilitation process. Everyone will have their own version of these ideal outcomes (for example, Egan, 1990). Here is mine, devised to correspond to the six practitioner categories. Since persons only develop in association, each client category is given an individual and a social form.

1 Self-direction and co-operation

A person makes choices based on a commitment to their own beliefs and values; and does so in co-operative relations with other persons similarly autonomous. This is not the personal autonomy of an isolated Cartesian ego, but personal autonomy that is embedded in intersubjectivity, in a dynamic web of relationships and interconnectedness (Spretnak, 1995).

2 Informed judgement and open communication

A person thinks independently on the basis of relevant information; can communicate their thought clearly to other persons and be open to others' views and opinions.

3 Self-development and social change

A person is actively committed to ways of developing their potential – physical, energetic, emotional, mental, psychic and spiritual; and to the creation of social forms within which this new growth can develop and be shared and expressed.

4 Emotional competence and interpersonal sensitivity

A person is open to and aware of their own emotions; can control, express, discharge or transmute them as appropriate; and is sensitive to the emotional state and needs of other persons.

5 Self-awareness and social perception

A person has insight into their own psychological processes; and understands the social process around them.

6 Celebration of self and others

A person takes pleasure in their own being and in the being of other persons.

It is instructive to bring practitioner categories and client categories together, although it is also misleading to do so:

*   You, the practitioner, are *prescriptive* in a way that enhances *self-direction and co-operation* in the client's life.
*   You are *informative* in a way that enhances *informed judgement and open communication* in the client's life.
*   You are *confronting* in a way that enhances *self-development and social change* in the client's life.
*   You are *cathartic* in a way that enhances *emotional competence and interpersonal sensitivity* in the client's life.
*   You are *catalytic* in a way that enhances *self-awareness and social perception* in the client's life.
*   You are *supportive* in a way that enhances *celebration of self and others* in the client's life.

It is misleading to bring practitioner categories and client categories together like this, because there is, of course, no rigid

FIGURE 3.1   Relations between practitioner categories and client categories

and exclusive correspondence between the practitioner and the client categories: any one of the former may enhance any one of the latter. The catalytic category has functional pride of place because it is probably used the most and has the most influential spread over all the client categories, from self-direction to self-awareness and celebration.

The confronting category too can have wide application, but will not be used so frequently. Figure 3.1 shows some of the more obvious connections. No doubt every possible connection could be made in one context or another. The arrow above *supportive* indicates its basic role as an attitude of mind underpinning all the other practitioner categories.

The client categories provide an overshadowing ideal, a vision of the person as a flourishing autonomous and co-operative being, in circumstances that support such fulfilment. But this in actuality is far from being the case. The client is struggling to become a person, to emerge into full-blown self-direction and inner freedom. So we need a more complete account of personhood and its different states. I reproduce here some ideas from my *Cosmic Psychology* (Heron, 1988), elaborated in *Feeling and Personhood* (Heron, 1992).

PERSONHOOD

By a person, I mean the soul manifesting in alert, aware action: a being celebrating their self-determination in conscious deeds. A person emerges through their expressed intentions. 'I choose, and become a distinct person.' Through electing to do something the

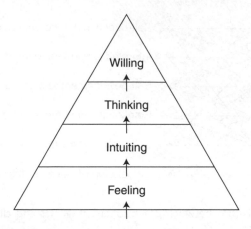

FIGURE 3.2　The psychological modes of the person

potential person becomes actual. Hence the person is a self-generating being. The sum total of my past acts constitutes the person I have become today. Within limits set by the fields of influence to which the everyday self is open, I am shaping my personality, making myself through my daily choices.

The person is a seamless whole, an interacting system which in simplified form has four psychological modes of being: 'willing' is the diamond apex whose facets are cut by the aware discrimination of 'thinking', which is made wise by the holistic receptivity of 'intuition', and grounded in the participation in life of 'feeling'. This can be represented crudely by a simple pyramid or triangle, as in Figure 3.2.

The pyramid, as arrowhead, is pointing towards deeds: the four psychological modes converge upon enterprise and endeavour. From our felt participation in the world, we open intuitively to grasp a total situation, then discriminate thoughtfully in order to act within it. Personhood is consummated in active agency in co-operative relationships with other active agents (Heron, 1996; Macmurray, 1957).

Through feeling and intuition we are grounded in the world, we indwell it. This receptive 'participation mystique' makes the human being, especially the small child, very vulnerable to the influences that surge through their physical, social and psychic environments. And so the emergence of personal autonomy – the full-grown exercise of discriminating choice – is a hazardous business.

I now develop this simple model further in the the next two sections.

FEELING AS THE GROUND OF PERSONHOOD

The distinction between feeling and emotion is quite fundamental, but general confusion abounds. In ordinary usage, 'feeling' is frequently used as a synonym for 'emotion'; it is also used as a synonym for almost all mental states from bodily sensations to subtle intuitions. In more considered usage, philosophers and psychologists have used the word 'feeling' or 'felt' to indicate how we apprehend the world. So William James says that it is 'through feelings we become acquainted with things' (James, 1890); and other philosophers talk about the felt qualities of the world. Kolb (1984) also allocates feeling to the apprehension of concrete experience. But none of these people says what this feeling is that enables us to apprehend things. The word is used, it seems quite aptly, but the meaning is left tacit, a concept shrouded in experiential vagueness.

My view is that while emotion is to do with the fulfilment or frustration of our individual needs and interests in the forms of joy, surprise, anger, grief and so on, 'feeling' is a term I reserve for the capacity of the person to participate in wider unities of being, to indwell what is present through attunement and resonance. Through feeling I become at one with the content of experience, and at the same time know my distinctness from it. This is the domain of empathy, indwelling, participation, presence, resonance, and suchlike (Heron, 1992: 16).

Lawrence Hyde made a clear distinction between the more intense, agitated character of emotion and the creative aspect of feeling by which 'we place ourselves in communion with what we find outside ourselves'. He variously called this empathy, heterocentric evaluation and identification with the being of things 'in the mode of love' which at the same time enhances our own sense of identity (Hyde, 1955). Suzanne Langer made a similar distinction, in her case between emotivity and sensibility: the former is to do with individual differentiation, and the latter relates us to wider wholes (Langer, 1988).

Koestler (1964) came close in his distinction between self-assertive emotions and participatory emotions, but the notion of feeling was never separated out from the latter. Empathy, from the German *Einfühlung*, feeling into, has been with us for a long while; but it has generally been defined as a projection of self into the state of the other, whereas, with Hyde, I would define true empathy as *feeling with*, that is, as participative communion with the other.

My point about feeling, as I have defined it, is that it does not have to be discovered. You do not have to make a special psychological journey to find it. Nor does it have to be pulled like a rabbit by meditative magic out of an internal hat. It has only to be noticed as an integral part of everyday living as a distinct being in a multiple world. It is through feeling that we meet our different worlds and engage in resonant transaction with them.

Feeling is a necessary condition of ordinary perception. It attunes us to the manifold of beings that perceptual imagery clothes. We do not know that our imagery is imagery of anything, unless our participative feeling tells us of our distinctness-in-union with what there is. The subject–object split which comes from the conceptual layer in perception – the restless seeing of things as objects of different named sorts out there separate from us – may cause us to disattend from the grounding level of feeling our world, to such a degree that it seems to disappear from consciousness. But the felt acquaintance is always necessarily there.

It is feeling that distinguishes between dreams and waking life, because by its nature it is attuned to the differentiation of being into different kinds and levels of particular. So feeling authorizes intuition to understand dream images as portrayals of our inner life, and as distinct from the perceptual world of life awake. Feeling, in short, enables us to engage with and participate in our various experiential realities, to differentiate them from each other, and to know that we are distinct from any one of them even while being in a unified field with it.

This capacity for feeling is the ground of personhood, is that in which all other psychological functions are latent and out of which they emerge. Suzanne Langer, coming from the perspective of scientific biology, had a similar view: 'The thesis I hope to substantiate', she wrote, 'is that the entire psychological field – including human conception, responsible action, rationality, knowledge – is a vast and branching development of feeling' (Langer, 1988: 9).

From my perspective, feeling is the guiding entelechy of personhood, the formative principle and potential which can be evoked to shape our inner development. It is a profound and immediately accessible spiritual principle, the manifestation of divine life immanent within the psyche. I must refer the reader to *Feeling and Personhood* (Heron, 1992) for further details to enlarge this summary account of a comprehensive theory.

THE UP-HIERARCHY MODEL OF THE WHOLE PERSON

I see the whole person as compounded of four basic psychological modes – the affective, the imaginal, the conceptual and the practical (feeling, intuition, thinking and willing – in the first simple model of personhood above, Figure 3.2). Each of these is composed of two polar and interdependent functions, a participatory one which makes for unitive interaction with a whole field of being, and an individuating one which makes for experience of individual distinctness (Capra, 1983; Das, 1953; Koestler, 1964, 1978; Langer, 1988). Stating the participatory first and the individuating next, the affective functions are feeling and emotion, the imaginal are intuition and imagery (imagery includes perception, extra-sensory perception, memory and imagination), the conceptual are reflection and discrimination, the practical are intention and action. Reflection and discrimination correspond to Piaget's formal operational and pre-operational thinking (Flavell, 1963).

In terms of whole person dynamics, I think there is a basic, ground process going on in which the affective mode as feeling has all the other modes latent within it, and they emerge out of it in what I call an up-hierarchy form. An up-hierarchy works from below upwards, like a tree with roots, a trunk, branches and fruit. It is not a matter of the higher controlling and ruling the lower, as in a down-hierarchy, but of the higher branching and flowering out of, and bearing the fruit of, the lower.

So the human psyche functions as an up-hierarchy grounded on feeling, the capacity for resonance with being and participative attunement to other beings. Out of the affective mode emerges the imaginal mode, including the imagery of imagination, memory and perception. From the imaginal proceeds the conceptual mode, the domain of thought and language; and this is the basis for the development of the practical mode, the level of intention and action. Figure 3.3 depicts the up-hierarchy with the participatory and individuating modes at each level.

Especially significant for learning is the view that the patterned fields of the imaginal mode are the source of all subsequent conceptualization. Hence the importance for the student of dwelling in the imaginal mode before explicit conceptual work, in order to make the latter easier and more fruitful. This view has been thoroughly worked out in *Feeling and Personhood* (Heron, 1992), and I refer the reader to this for the details.

STATES OF PERSONHOOD

Personhood manifest in any full sense is an achievement: its creation admits of degrees. In some respects behaviour may be oppressively subject to external influence and the person is still in a

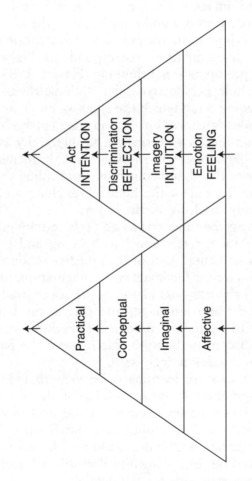

FIGURE 3.3 The up-hierarchy of psychological modes

potential state; in other respects it may flow from real freedom of informed choice, and here the actual person is manifest. In truth, there are as many different mixes of potential and actual person-hood as there are people. But certain broad types of mix can usefully be identified (Heron, 1992). In the first three below, the person is more potential and embryonic than actual, although less so as we go through them.

1 The deranged person

Behaviour is erratically and chaotically subject to psychic, psycho-social and physical influences, into which the individual has little or no insight and over which they have little or no control. They do not see that their autonomy is being buried by the invasion. Personal awareness is overwhelmed by alien forces. Voluntary choice is minimal and severely restricted. Yet there are occasions when this disintegration of the self may be a prelude to its eventual reorganization on a higher and more complex level, including spiritual opening (Grof, 1998).

2 The compulsive person

Behaviour is in certain ways rigid, maladaptive and repetitive. The person can see that their autonomy is oppressed by these restricted ways of being, but has little insight into their origins or into how to get rid of them. Most of us are compulsive in some areas of our behaviour, slipping in and out of distress-driven victim, oppressor, rescuer and rebel roles. The problem lies in buried, out-of-date mechanisms of emotional survival, which repress the psychological pain of early trauma. The repressed material returns to distort our behaviour into unaware, symbolic re-enactments of our past predicaments. Figure 3.4 summarizes the psychosocial pathology, and its self-locking vicious circle. However, in non-compulsive areas there may be greater or lesser scope for autonomous choice, depending on the degree of the next item.

3 The conventional person

Behaviour unreflectively conforms to the prevailing norms and beliefs of the wider culture, and of the smaller social groups within it, to which the person belongs. The person may have some, little or no awareness that such conformity constrains really autonom-ous behaviour; but the more conscious they are of the hindrance, so much the less is their compliance unreflective. Further, the

FIGURE 3.4   The psychosocial pathology of compulsive behaviour

person may be conventional in some areas of behaviour while autonomous in others. And a person may convert sensible conventional behaviour into autonomous behaviour without changing its external form, because they can see the point of it and can make it their own.

Some compulsive behaviour is also conventional behaviour, since some conventions are irrational compulsions writ large as social norms. Other compulsive behaviour is non-conventional but tolerated, such as drunkenness within limits. And yet other compulsive behaviour is unconventional, and may further be regarded as deviant or anti-social.

Some irrational and maladaptive conventional behaviour is not compulsive as I have defined it, but simply a matter of deep ignorance and social inertia. And some conventional behaviour is a matter of rational social coherence, even though people may still adhere to it through unreflective conformity.

In the second group of different mixes of potential and actual personhood, autonomy is no longer embryonic – it is born. The person is more actual than potential: significant voluntary choice is now being exercised. But there are increasing degrees of freedom and self-determination, of the emergence of the person, involved in the following group.

4 The creative person

Behaviour is genuinely autonomous in some major area of human endeavour: parenthood and the family; friendship, relationship and intimacy; education; social and political action; the professions; the arts; the sciences and the humanities; economics, commerce and industry; agriculture; and so on. Such people have values, norms and beliefs to which they are internally committed, and to which they give systematic, creative expression in one or more of these domains of action. Their choices transcend unreflective conformity to the prevailing beliefs, norms and values of these domains.

Creative people change their own behaviour only in so far as it is part of that domain of culture where they are being autonomous.

5 The self-creating person

Autonomous behaviour now becomes reflexive. Self-creating people become self-determining about the emergence of their self-determination. They consciously take in hand methods of personal and interpersonal development which enhance their capacity for voluntary choice, for becoming more intentional within all domains of experience and action. This means at least three things.

- *Unravelling.* They are at work on restrictions that come from their past, dealing awarely with the limiting effects of early trauma and social conditioning. The individual is committed to dismantle compulsive, and unreflectively conventional, behaviour in every area of living.
- *Receptivity.* They attend carefully to the deliverances of the receptive mind, the background field of daily consciousness. To become aware in exercise of choice and personal power, means to open more fully to intuition of, and feel participation in, the different realms of being. We need to resonate with the background to act appropriately in the foreground. Outgoing action is balanced with attentive passivity. The person both listens and speaks, notices what is there and creates what is different.
- *Relationship.* Forms of association with other persons become paramount, on the principle that free choice only emerges fully in aware relationship with other free persons. It then becomes clear that autonomy is interdependent with two other basic values of social life, co-operation and hierarchy.

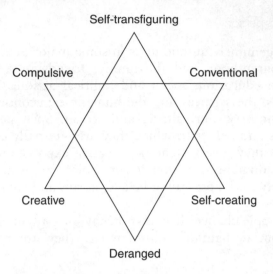

FIGURE 3.5   The six states of personhood

6 The self-transfiguring person

Autonomy now reaches out to uncover latent powers within the soul, to open fully to the depths of feeling and intuition, and to extend ordinary consciousness into realms that were seemingly buried within it, and beyond it. The person freely chooses, as an extension of their self-determination, to unfold the inner spiritual self, with its access to universal consciousness, to archetypal powers and their transmutative energies (Heron, 1998). The six states of personhood are diagrammatically displayed in Figure 3.5.

In the creative, the self-creating and the self-transfiguring states, the person is progressively engaged with deepening forms of *first person action research* (see p. 241, Chapter 15). And the ground motivation for all this appears to be an aspiration to participate in ever wider unities of being as a distinct, creative and autonomous person.

Most counselling will not be concerned with deranged, or so-called psychotic, states, but with people who awarely choose the various helping services detailed in Chapter 2. So it will deal with the five other states, actual or potential in most people, shown in Figure 3.6. This pentagram, as a symbol of a standing person, shows that a developing person is grounded in their compulsive and conventional states. Indeed, the autonomy of the creative person is born out of reflection on conventional states; and one of the first tasks of the self-creating person working on their own

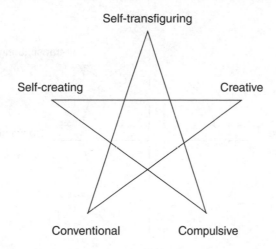

Self-transfiguring

Self-creating

Creative

Conventional

Compulsive

FIGURE 3.6   Actual or potential states of personhood in most people

development is to unravel the compulsive attitudes and behaviours that were adopted as defence mechanisms in early life.

To change the metaphor, and use an organic one, the conventional dimension provides the social ground, the compulsive dimension the loam, out which the plant of the creative person can grow, bearing self-creating leaves, and the bloom of self-transfiguration. The dark side of human nature is a complement to the light: the growth process reclaims energy from the undeveloped parts that had hitherto been rejected and denied. The dross is integrated and transformed, a *continuous* source of unfolding, creating a developing whole being, not a perfect one. To use a weaving metaphor, the warp of the compulsive and conventional, interlaces the woof of the creative and self-creating, dimensions of personhood, forming the fabric of our being, which can be shaped into the garment of self-transfiguration.

Finally, to use a geometric metaphor, and an ancient symbol, the horizontal bar of the compulsive and conventional, is at right angles to the vertical bar of the creative and the self-creating. From the point of intersection, the circle of self-transfiguration can expand, as in Figure 3.7.

Referring back to the six client categories given at the start of this chapter, numbers 1 and 2 relate to the creative person, and numbers 3, 4, 5 and 6 to the self-creating person. All of them are further enhanced in the process of self-transfiguration.

People who seek the services of a practitioner to work on their personal development are usually those who have a certain

FIGURE 3.7   The cross and the circle as a symbol of states of personhood

measure of autonomy in their lives, that is, in my terminology they are to some degree creative; but they still feel restricted by conventions and compulsions which cause frustration and unhappiness. They need to extend their autonomy into more creative living, and go deeper to become self-creating, and perhaps, self-transfiguring.

CLIENT DEGENERATIONS IN THE WORLD

By these I mean 'degenerations' in living when a person gets stuck in varieties of conventional and compulsive behaviour at work and at home. The signs of these will crop up in what the client says and how they behave within the session with you. Stated baldly, they look like this – as negatives of the six positive client categories given earlier:

1 Other-direction and collusion

A person makes choices unreflectively, conforming to social role steteotypes and conventional norms; and colludes in decision-making with others who do the same.

FIGURE 3.8   The four compulsions in their manifold context

2 Limited belief and dogmatic communication

A person thinks uncritically in terms of received, prevailing views; is prone to bigotry and irrational prejudice; and communicates with others in an intolerant, dogmatic mode.

3 Self-restriction and social stasis

A person is unknowingly compulsive as victim, oppressor, rebel and rescuer. They switch around among these four distress-driven roles, in internal relations within the self, in face-to-face relations with others, in organizational life, in the context of spiritual domains, and in relation to their environment on the planet. They are locked in by defensive avoidance of self-creation, and are without intentional social commitment. Figure 3.8 depicts the four compulsions in their manifold context.

4 Emotional incompetence and interpersonal insensitivity

A person is closed to their own emotions; represses their emotional distress, displacing it unawarely on themselves and others; and is insensitive to the emotional state and needs of other persons.

5 Self-rationalization and social misperception

A person has no insight into their own psychological processes; rationalizes or justifies their predicament in inappropriate ways; and similarly misunderstands the social process around them.

6 Self-denigration and invalidation of others

A person engages in persistent self-deprecation, is wedded to guilt and inadequacy; and blames and criticizes others.

The first two of these are typical of the unawarely *conventional* person; the last four of the distresss-driven *compulsive* person.

CLIENT DEGENERATIONS WITHIN THE SESSION

The client chooses to seek your services for the purpose of change and growth, yet that very intent will set up periodic reactions of resistance and avoidance. There are three basic forms of this resistance, I believe.

1 Conventional inertia

This kind of resistance is found in the purely *conventional* state of the person, when there is no strong distress-driven compulsion running into it as well. It is social nescience about some kind of belief and behaviour: an ignorance of the issues, disinterest in learning about them, and a lack of motivation to make any changes.

Such inertia holds a lot of limiting, inadequate social beliefs and practices in place in the client's attitudes as revealed in the sessions. Conventional inertia resists the development of the *creative* state of the person, as defined earlier. It blots out huge areas of sexual, social, economic, political and ecological awareness. Dealing with it has been woefully neglected in traditional psychotherapy and counselling.

2 Compulsive defensiveness

This sort of resistance characterizes the *compulsive* state of the person, and is more restrictive and congealed than conventional inertia. The client has survived the psychosocial traumas of early life by denying, repressing and defending him- or herself against a lot of emotional distress – grief, anger and fear. This defensiveness becomes, in a session, a resistance to the *self-creating* process of unravelling the limiting effects of childhood pain. It takes certain typical forms: a person may move around between all of them, adopting different ones at different times.

- *Submission.* Clients become dependent and powerless, seeking advice and insight from you, having no sense of their real needs, interests and identity. They may try to be a 'good' client, following your suggestions for work in the session. But the following behaviour is a way of remaining entirely closed up and cut off from their own emotional state. The client is internally shut down, an inner victim. He or she may also have strong compulsive and repressive guilt emotions, imposed improperly long ago, which continue to control inner attitudes and external behaviour.

- *Flight.* Clients go off into verbal fugue: a flight into irrelevant talk about themselves and their life, talk that keeps circling round and round, well away from the hidden pain. The talk manufactures pseudo-problems, it dramatizes the client's life without dealing with it, or it is too intellectual and analytic, or is persistently superficial and safe, dealing only with minor issues. The person is locked into compulsive and misguided self-help, an inner and ineffective rescuer.

- *Attack.* Clients displace the anxiety of hidden emotional pain against you. Any suggestion you make about ways of working within the session is actively resisted, with lurking hostility and resentment. Every proposal you make about their lives outside the session is subjected to 'Yes but'. You are accused and blamed for your way of being, for what you have and have not done in the sessions. Clients try to inveigle you into situations that can then be converted into bouts of recrimination. They unknowingly displace on to you the repressed distress held for bad parent figures from their past: this is negative transference (see below). The person is stuck in the role of either the compulsive oppressor, or the compulsive rebel.

3 Transpersonal contraction

This kind of resistance stands in the way of unfolding the *self-transfiguring* state of the person. Clients have the illusory belief and feeling that their everyday selves are somehow separate from the world, from things and other people, from other dimensions of being, and from universal consciousness-as-such.

Their ordinary consciousness is focused anxiously on everday choice and on the beliefs that service such choice. It contracts around these individual-centred concerns with a rigid, unyielding separatist illusion. It is closed to the unitive vision, the sense of dwelling in the whole, in its subtle and pervasive energies. The person is at the edge of transpersonal work, embarrassed, incredulous and sceptical, contracted, driven, fearful and reluctant to let go.

WAYS OF WORKING ON CLIENT RESISTANCES

1 Be informative, then prescriptive

Raise consciousness about any one of these three sorts of resistances as and when they first arise, by giving a brief, simple, theoretical explanation of how they function. Then invite the client to make a contract to practise spotting them and interrupting them.

2 Be confronting

When clients get tangled up in any one of them, give direct feedback about it, in a supportive manner, so they can get some insight into their way of resisting inner growth and change.

3 Be cathartic

Use the full range of basic cathartic interventions to help clients dismantle *compulsive* defensiveness and release the underlying emotional pain. Re-enacting and discharging past trauma through psychodrama is basic in helping clients to set themselves free from past chains, and learn the rudiments of being *self-creating*.

4 Be catalytic

Use structured exercises to practise new forms of awareness and behaviour: role-plays to break out of *conventional* stereotypes into more *creative* responses; transmutative exercises (see Chapter 8) to enter *self-transfiguring* states.

5 Be supportive

Value clients in the way you use the other categories; respect your clients' defences, honour the need for them as a form of survival, before encouraging their dismantling; affirm and celebrate clients' work for change and growth.

This account is minimal and merely introductory. It makes sense to work on conventional inertia, when it shows up clearly in the sessions, before compulsive defensiveness. In some areas, the two may interlock, so you move to and fro between them. It seems to me to be wise to deal with compulsive defensiveness before dealing with transpersonal contraction, otherwise self-transfiguring practice may have the effect of putting a spiritual gloss on the repression of childhood distress.

In a sustained series of personal growth sessions with a client, the tendency to negative transference, as defined below, will persist until its chains to the afflicted past are uncovered and released. Issues to do with handling this are an important part of long-term training. However, issues of transference are not part of a therapeutic mystique available only to the initiated. On the contrary, they are properly part of everyone's basic emotional education. The tendency to project, unawarely, unresolved past distress into present relationships is universal, and people can help each other out of the morass, as we have repeatedly seen, in co-counselling work sustained over time. So here is a little more about it.

TRANSFERENCE

When transference occurs, the client unconsciously transfers to the practitioner, from the hurt child within, hidden and repressed feelings about a parent or some other important authority figure from the past.

1 Positive transference

The client projects on to you the frozen need and longing for the good parent he or she never had. This may lead to submissive forms of defensiveness, such as dependency, following and permission-seeking in relation to you. A positive transference can be put to work and used to motivate learning and growth for a period. But sooner or later the client needs to withdraw – and be helped to withdraw – the projection, see it for what it is, and assume the attitudes of their own authentic adulthood.

2 Negative transference

The client unawarely projects on to you the distorted fear and anger about the bad parent he or she actually had. This can result in aggressive defensiveness that attacks you, such as active resistance, denigration, sabotage, rivalry, attempts at seduction. A negative transference always tends to make growth and learning more difficult as long as it is in place. Where it is particularly strong, you may need to work intensively with the client, so that he or she can identify the projection and withdraw it, after being helped to release some of the underlying distress.

The use of psychodrama within an identification check (see p. 256) is an effective way of raising awareness about, and withdrawing, positive and negative transference.

3 Acute transference

The client may temporarily undergo an acute transference, positive or negative, at some early stage in the relationship with you. It causes him or her to slip into defensive behaviour for a while, but as things proceed, and with a little facilitation, he or she moves out of it quite readily.

4 Chronic transference

This fastens relentlessly on to you, and will need special and sustained attention to resolve. It may be positive or negative.

5 Universal transference

The process of unaware projection of emotions that belong to the past, on to some one or more persons in the present, is one of the most persistent phenomena in all social life. It goes every which way, not just from the client to you, but from the client to all kinds of other people in his or her life. It is not just rooted in buried emotions about parents and authority figures. Any kind of repressed distress about anyone from the past can be unawarely projected on to some present person, who is thus unconsciously appointed to be the current scapegoat for past ills. This blind scapegoating is also a defence against facing and owning and dealing with the hidden pain. Hence a strong projection will not want to let go of its victim, and may powerfully resist being seen for what it is. The deeper the hurt, the more relentless is the projection. You may need to help your client deal with this phenomenon in the wider reaches of his or her life, both as perpetrator of it and victim of it.

6 Counter-transference

The unaware projection of hidden distress from the past may also proceed from you to your client. This is so-called counter-transference. Once your facilitation gets tangled up with your own blindly projected distress, it degenerates. It submits to manipulation by the client, or colludes with the client, or takes flight from the client's distress, or verbally attacks and blames the client. The dynamic of the practitioner–client relationship rapidly goes down the drain. One basic indicator of good practitioners at work is that they keep relatively clear of their own past unfinished business while on the job. This is one of the most important criteria of their emotional competence (see p. 12; Heron, 1992; Postle, 1991).

7 Spiritual transference

The self-transfiguring person, unfolding the inner spiritual self, may start off this process by becoming a follower of, and ascribing spiritual authority to, some religious tradition, teacher and text. This is an unaware projection onto an external source of the authority within his or her own soul; and the transference inevitably limits and misrepresents that internal authority. Sooner or later this projection will be withdrawn and the individual take his or her stand on the witness of the inner life and light, the discernment and intentionality found through opening to the divine enthroned deep within (Heron, 1998: ch. 2).

CHAPTER 4

PRESCRIPTIVE INTERVENTIONS

Prescriptive interventions explicitly seek to influence and direct the behaviour of the client, especially, though not exclusively, behaviour that is outside or beyond the practitioner–client interaction. Even when directive, they don't encroach on the self-determining competence of the person, and are presented with a timing and in a manner that fully respects their autonomy. The trouble with inappropriate, compulsive or excessive use of them is that they turn the client into a practitioner-directed being rather than a self-directed being. This has been a classic problem for child-raising, education and the helping professions. Nevertheless, they clearly have their place in many sorts of practitioner–client role-relations.

In what follows, I shall outline first a perspective on the issues to do with prescribing; secondly, a simple map of the context of prescription; thirdly, an account of levels of prescription; fourthly, a set of prescriptive agendas; and finally, a list of prescriptive interventions.

ISSUES ABOUT PRESCRIBING

There are two main issues about proposing behaviour to other people, and the second is more basic than the first.

1 *How to prescribe*: whether directively or consultatively; whether using some special type of prescription; at what level to prescribe; and in relation to what agenda to prescribe. Details on all these matters are discussed below.
2 *Whether to prescribe at all*: as against facilitating clients to be self-directing and to choose a course of action for themselves. This is a fundamental issue for every kind of practitioner.

In counselling for personal development, where the whole thrust is to elicit and enhance client self-direction in living, it is usually inappropriate for the practitioner to prescribe *courses of action*. But it may be appropriate from time to time to commend *attitudes of mind*. So it is important here to take into account the different levels of prescription, discussed below.

Prescribing courses of action is much more appropriate where the practitioner – such as an accountant, architect or doctor – is providing some technical service for the client, and where adopting a course of action depends on specialist knowledge. But here too it is important that full attention is paid to whatever client self-direction can contribute to the issues.

Supportive and crisis counselling, for those who are heavily disadvantaged, traumatized, in shock, in the midst of dramatic change, may also involve prescribing courses of action until the clients concerned have come through the worst of the storm and can take hold of the rudder again.

THE CONTEXT OF PRESCRIPTION

What type of prescription to use, what its agenda and level is, whether to use a directive (i.e. non-consultative) prescription, or a consultative prescription, or whether to use a catalytic intervention to elicit the client's self-direction instead – all these choices depend upon the following aspects of the context:

1 Practitioner–client roles

The role-relations of, for example, probation officer and probationer, doctor and patient, counsellor and client, trainer and student, consultant and client, police officer and suspect, provide differing contexts for judging what sort of prescription to use, or whether to use prescription at all.

2 Focus of intervention

This is the agenda, the issues the client is currently addressing. The basic distinction here is between technical matters and personal matters. As discussed above, it is more appropriate to be prescriptive about technical matters and to elicit self-direction about personal matters. But there is no hard and fast rule, since all the parameters need to be taken into account together.

3 Client state

This includes age, degree of knowledge or ignorance, level of awareness and stage of development, emotional state, physical state, external circumstances.

4 Practitioner state

This includes degree of professional experience, beliefs and values as a practitioner, competence and training (flexibility over a wide range of interventions), level of awareness and stage of development, freedom from counter-transference material, physical state, time available with the client.

LEVELS OF PRESCRIPTION

Although the intervention list later on talks about prescribing behaviour, it is important to remember there are in fact three levels at which prescriptions can be made. From now on I shall refer to the practitioner in the second person, as 'you'.

1 The level of beliefs, norms and values

At this level you, the practitioner, are prescribing *ways of thinking* about internal or external situations (that is, relation to self or relation to outer world). Such ways of thinking include beliefs about the client's self or situation, also principles and values that can guide choices about aims or actions. You are not prescribing goals for behaviour or behaviour itself. You may prescribe to clients ways of thinking about their lives:

- In every sort of situation.
- Only in certain sorts of situation.
- Only in one sort of situation.
- Only in one particular situation.

2 The level of goals

Here you are prescribing goals for behaviour, as distinct from prescribing behaviour itself. The goals may be short-term, medium-term or long-term. They may relate to internal behaviour or to external behaviour.

3 The level of behaviour

You are prescribing behaviour as such, either internal or external. Internal behaviour is to do with the mental regulation of thoughts, emotions and choices; it includes all forms of consciousness training, including meditation methods. External behaviour is to do with action through the body in the physical and social worlds; it may also be to do with action through the psi or ka body in the other reality (as in out-of-the-body experiences). The prescription may cover a class of behaviour for recurrent use, or one particular behaviour for use in one particular situation.

In using this map of levels, the issue is, first and foremost, whether to prescribe to the client, or whether to make a catalytic intervention and to elicit self-direction from them so that they make up their own minds about what to do. This is always the central political issue when working with people. And the question of level is relevant to this issue. For while the three levels are all about prescribing, they differ in their degree of other-direction. Proposing to a client that they adopt a certain perspective on a critical situation, a way of construing it or thinking about it (level 1), is less other-directed than proposing goals to move towards from it (level 2), or particular behaviours to adopt within it (level 3).

PRESCRIPTIVE AGENDAS

What I mean by a prescriptive agenda is the content area of a prescription, the grounds on which it is made. Each of the following content areas can be dealt with by different types of intervention, given later in the list of interventions.

1 Moral agendas

You propose certain behaviour to the client on moral grounds. This intervention is lethal when it degenerates (see under 'Prescriptive degenerations' in Chapter 13). The moral grounds will involve an appeal to one or more basic principles, that apply to the person's situation, to do with justice, benevolence, truth-telling, promise-keeping, making reparation, and so on.

2 Prudential agendas

You propose certain behaviour to the client on the grounds of enlightened self-interest. This, of course, includes behaviour that is self-nurturing, recreational and pleasure seeking.

3 Psychosocial agendas

You propose certain behaviour to the client on the grounds of some principle to do with individual and/or social psychology. It may be to do with psychodynamic, psychosomatic, interpersonal, group dynamic, organizational, cultural or even global issues. It may also be to do with further education and training. This is a very far-reaching set of agendas, and covers much of the territory covered in personal counselling. But use prescription sparingly here.

4 Transcendental agendas

You propose certain behaviour to the client in the area of altered states, the extrasensory, the meditative, the spiritual.

5 Technical agendas

You propose some behaviour to the client on the grounds of technical information about the structure and processes or procedures of something. Includes advice given by their financial adviser, garage mechanic, solicitor, etc., on the basis of their specialist knowledge. This agenda also includes referring the client to some expert.

6 Physical agendas

A special case of the former. You propose some behaviour to the client to do with their body, such as taking a pill, taking exercise, adopting some diet, and so on.

Note that either the various 'grounds' mentioned above can be fully stated and made explicit, so that the prescription is given with its rationale; or the grounds can be implied by the behaviour that you propose.

PRESCRIPTIVE INTERVENTIONS

Prescriptive interventions about personal matters, if it is appropriate to make them, become less offensive the less attached you are to the value and importance of making them. But if you are too attached to the importance of not making them, you are also in trouble.

1 Directive prescription

Here you respectfully advise, propose, recommend, suggest, request certain behaviour to the client, but do not explicitly seek either their opinion of or assent to the proposed behaviour. It is essential, of course, that you are implicitly open to the client's dissent, and are no way compulsively attached to his or her compliance. The extreme version, legitimate in certain emergency situations, is when you instruct, demand, order or command the person to do this or that.

Hence there is a directive continuum, from the mild to the strong form of direction given. Five grades along this continuum, from mild to strong, are roughly conveyed by the following verbs: (a) suggest; (b) propose; (c) advise; (d) persuade; (e) command. But your use of this continuum is particularly vulnerable to client interpretation and distortion. Thus you may make it clear you are suggesting behaviour, yet this is taken to be something much stronger, such as persuading or even commanding. This may be to do with your role, status and prestige in their eyes; or with some kind of projection or transference. So you must make allowance for this possible effect.

2 Consultative prescription

Here you propose some behaviour and also ask the client's opinion of the proposal and whether he or she has any alternative ideas. You consider the client's view carefully, but you claim the right to make the final prescription, which may or may not take account of what the client has said.

Note that these first two interventions are higher order, or double counted, ones. I mean by this that all the different interventions below, from no. 4 onwards, can be put forward in either a directive or consultative way. With each sort of prescription, I comment on its relation with these two.

3 Prescriptive–catalytic gradient

Prescribing to the client stands over against the catalytic approach of eliciting his or her self-direction. There is a gradient from the prescriptive to the catalytic, and some practitioners by the very nature of their particular role need flexibility in moving up and down the gradient. They may need to be at very different points with the same person at different times and in respect of different issues; they may need to be at different places with different people in relation to the same sort of issue; and so on. This is often so for the medical practitioner. The gradient is shown in Figure 4.1.

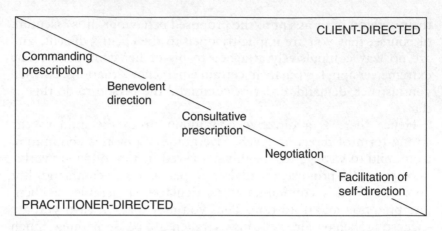

FIGURE 4.1   The prescriptive–catalytic gradient

3.1 Commanding prescription   You use the full authority of your role and in a commanding manner direct the client to do something, with no consultation before or after the command.

3.2 Benevolent direction   This is a benign and respectful proposal that the client do something, but still with no consultation before or after it. There is a continuum here from mild to strong: you can (a) suggest, (b) propose, (c) advise, (d) persuade.

3.3 Consultative prescription   You propose some behaviour, and also consult the client about it, eliciting their views – which you carefully consider. But you are responsible for the final prescription, which may or may not take account of these views.

3.4 Negotiation   From the outset you work in a collaborative way with the client on the decision, sharing and comparing views on the issues and the options. Together you work to agree on a final decision.

3.5 Facilitation of self-direction   At this, the fully catalytic end of the gradient, you are concerned only to facilitate the client in making up his or her mind in his or her own way in the direction that the client thinks is best.

4 Action research prescription

You propose that the client try out certain behaviour experimentally, as an experiential inquiry into this or that way of life, with a review of the behaviour and its outcomes at a later date. It needs a consultative format.

5 Homework prescription

This is closely related to the previous one. You propose that the client does certain things before the next session – at which he or she gives an account of how it all went. The proposed behaviours will relate to what the client is working on in the current session. It can be more directive.

6 Demonstrative prescription

You demonstrate to the client the behaviour you are proposing that he or she adopt. You show in action how to do it. Then the client goes off and does it autonomously. The proposal itself, of course, may be either directive or consultative.

7 Follow-the-leader prescription

You lead the way – you are not merely demonstrating but doing it for real – and propose that the client follow (for example, you propose that you both keep a diary of the sessions). Again, the proposal may be either directive or consultative, depending on the context.

8 Exemplary and tacit prescription

In your own real behaviour you provide a model for client behaviour, without making any explicit proposal that the client adopt such behaviour. Thus you may be self-disclosing, punctual, risk-taking, honest in ways that are both authentic in the situation, and offer a tacit model to the client.

9 Validating prescription

You recommend certain behaviour to the client by affirming that he or she has the special strengths and qualities needed to implement it, and by specifying what those strengths and qualities are. It is usually directive.

10 Support prescription

Where it is unreasonable to expect persons to be self-directing because of their state and/or circumstances, you make decisions for them and on their behalf and propose what they should do. It is usually directive, but can be consultative. It is often applied by the counsellor or social worker to the client's daily living between visits.

11 Charismatic prescription

You arouse, cohere, and motivate the will of the client with a charismatic command. It may be appropriate where the person is internally disoriented by agitation and distress. It is always directive.

12 Retrospective prescription

You comment on the client's past behaviour, on what he or she should or should not have done. In technical and specialist matters, practitioner comment of this sort may be essential for their learning. In personal matters, aiding the client's self-assessment may be better than prescribing, although there are exceptions. It can be directive or consultative.

13 Evaluative prescription

You evaluate, according to some criteria, a project or product of the client's. This is really a special case of the previous, retrospective, prescription. Here, their past behaviour is represented by a piece of work done, which you now assess.

The following batch of prescriptive interventions need to be labelled 'handle with care' since, in a peculiar way, they test the practitioner's authenticity. I believe that they can be used with integrity, depending as always on the context, but since they work to a greater or lesser degree with factors in the client that may be more or less unconscious, they can easily degenerate into manipulative control and practitioner power-play. See what you think of them.

14 Paradoxical prescription

You propose certain behaviour to the client and say you doubt very much whether he or she will have the resolve and/or the ability to do it. The unstated supposition of this intervention is that the client will be motivated by it to prove you wrong. It is always directive.

15 Contradictory prescription

You propose to the client in the same intervention two incompatible or contradictory behaviours. The supposition here is that the client will resolve the contradiction by opting for one of the two, or for an unstated third possibility. It assumes they will not tolerate cognitive dissonance. It is usually directive.

16 Counter-dependent prescription

You propose certain behaviour to an antagonistic client, with the unstated intention that the client's resistance will make him or her do the opposite. Counter-dependency means that the person is hostile and resistant to you, probably because of a negative transference. A negative transference means that the client is unawarely projecting onto you some repressed angry emotions that he or she harbours for some authority figure from the past. It is always directive.

17 Positive projection prescription

Where the client is in a state of positive projection or transference in relation to you, this projection is put to work to motivate the client to adopt your proposed behaviour. Positive transference means that the client is unawarely projecting onto you repressed longings for the good parent he or she never had. The proposal is made by you as loving 'good parent'. It is usually directive.

18 Quasi-hypnotic or symbolic prescription

You disarm the rigid, conscious mental set of the client by proposing behaviour that resonates symbolically with deeper, integrative processes of the client's mind. For example, if the client unawarely displaces unowned sexual agendas into talk of horse-riding, you may propose a riding expedition designed with symbolic touches that resonate with the expression and fulfilment of human sexuality. The rationale of the symbolism is unstated, implicit. It is usually directive.

19 Intentional negative practice prescription

You propose that the client do awarely and intentionally the unwanted behaviour that he or she does unawarely and compulsively. This is based on counter-conditioning principles from learning theory. The idea is that to do deliberately some negative act that is usually done unconsciously, will tend to eliminate it. Some spiritual teachers like it too: instead of trying to overcome limiting and restricting behaviour, attend to it with great awareness until it dissolves away in the light of Mind. It is always directive.

CHAPTER 5

INFORMATIVE INTERVENTIONS

Informative interventions seek to impart to the client new knowledge, information and meaning that is relevant to their needs and interests, in terms that the person can understand, and in a manner that enhances the person's need to participate in the learning process with self-directed activity. When overdone, as in traditional education, informative interventions can blunt the motivation for self-directed learning. When underdone, their absence disempowers people, leaving them in ignorance, the victims of professional or political exploitation and oppression.

In what follows, I give first a brief comment on the issues to do with giving information; secondly, a view on the objective–subjective dimensions of meaning; thirdly, an overview of informative agendas; and finally, a list of informative interventions.

ISSUES ABOUT INFORMATION-GIVING

There are two basic issues about giving information or meaning to the client.

1 *How much to give*: in terms of quality, and in terms of quantity. The first concern here is with the level or depth at which to pitch the teaching or interpretation; and the second is the amount of information to give.
2 *Whether to give it at all*: as against facilitating clients – through catalytic interventions – to find it, or their version of it, for themselves. Here we encounter the modern revision of thought about where the responsibility lies for the acquisition of information and meaning.

The shift that is occurring in certain critical fields is from telling people by talking at them, to encouraging them to find out for themselves. So educational reform encourages the move from too much imparting of information by the teacher, to the facilitation of self-directed learning and problem-solving in the student. Radical psychotherapies elicit client self-generated insight welling up spontaneously out of personal work, as against too many therapist-generated interpretations of the client's reality. And there is no doubt that this mutation towards autonomy of learning and meaning is healthy.

But there is nothing absolute about the shift. It is a matter of balance between the informative and the catalytic within the overall goal of enhancing client autonomy; and this balance, again, depends on the total context: the practitioner–client roles, the agenda of the interaction, the client's state and stage, the practitioner's state. All practitioners have to consider these parameters and work out their own sense of an appropriate balance for the given situation.

There are clearly some practitioner roles where the imparting of information is an essential part of the service. It is the doctor's job to give a diagnosis and an account of available treatments and their likely effects. But it is precisely in such roles that the enlightened practitioner will also want to elicit the client's way of construing the matter, and to create a dialogue with it.

OBJECTIVE–SUBJECTIVE DIMENSIONS OF MEANING

Public and objective information and meaning have general reference to the common or shared features of experience. And these you *can* impart to me, teach to me (although, of course, I can also find it out for myself in self-directed study). But the private and subjective meaning which, for example, I give to a particular experience, or set of experiences, or my personal development, or my life as a whole – this I can only discover for myself. I may be aided and facilitated by you in the process of discovery. But in the last analysis, the only truly illuminating insights about personal destiny are self-generated. If your interpretations start to awaken such personal insight – good. But if they oppress and inhibit it – very bad.

This means, of course, that all psychodynamic, developmental theories – which necessarily exist in the public domain – can only take the client so far: to the threshold beyond which insight from within reigns supreme. There is all the difference in the world between clients whose insight is self-generated, and those who repeat theory-laden interpretations which the practitioner has given them. A client whose insights are self-generated may, of course, have absorbed and digested all kinds of public theories. But what is important is that these are utilized and applied by the person's own idiosyncratic intuitive process. The insight comes from within, although the elements of which it is compounded may come from the public domain.

A related point deals with the distinction between disease and illness, where disease is defined as the observable and measurable disorder in my body, and illness is defined as my subjective experience of having that physical disorder. My *disease* is in the public domain: the practitioner can give meaning to it, give me information about it. But in the last analysis only I can see how to find meaning in, or give meaning to, or change the meaning of, my experience of *illness*. The practitioner can alert me to the task, arouse me and wake me up to it, facilitate my doing of it; but he or she cannot do it for me or to me.

INFORMATIVE AGENDAS

Any full-blown account of informative agendas would require a map of all forms of human knowledge and belief. Content areas can be sub-divided in several basic and overlapping ways. Thus: facts (and theories of facts), norms, values; physical, psychosocial, transcendental (including psi and the spiritual); particular, general, abstract; supposition, belief, knowledge. For the purposes of this book, the following simple distinction seems pertinent.

1 *Personal agendas*: the content of your intervention is personal to the client, is directly about the client's particular physical, psychological, social or transcendental situation.
2 *General agendas*: the content of your intervention is of general or background relevance, and is not directly about the client or his or her situation.

INFORMATIVE INTERVENTIONS

The art, then, is whether to *give* the information or interpretation, or whether to *elicit* it (see Chapter 9); and if giving it, when to give it, how much of it to give, and pitched at what level.

1 Practitioner rationale

You explain to the client what you the practitioner are doing or are going to do or have done in relation to them; and explain why you are doing it, will do or have done it. This is essential to the proper respect of the person, although clearly the context (as defined in Chapter 4, see p. 41) may legitimate exceptions. This intervention extends from medicine, through psychotherapy and education to any professional role.

2 Physical diagnosis and prognosis

You explain what it is you have found out about the client's body, and what the likely outcomes, and treatment options, are in the present state of knowledge. A moral imperative for the health professional, but as ever there are exceptions.

Prognosis is morally tricky: it depends on your belief-system what you regard, for example, as irreversible disease process. One kind of practitioner may tell a certain kind of cancer patient that death is inevitable, while another might tell the same kind of patient that self-cure is possible though by no means certain. It is irresponsible to err in either direction: statements of terminal finality can be as improper as those of ungrounded optimism.

Prognosis, as such, is purely informative; but in practice it leads over rapidly into some kind of prescription for treatment.

3 Personal interpretation

You interpret – that is, give a meaning to – the client's behaviour, or experience, or situation. Give too much meaning, however accurate, and the person becomes a cognitive puppet; give too little meaning and the client may improperly wallow in nescience. In addition, and more basically, this intervention stands in tension with its catalytic opposite – inviting people to find their own meaning in their own behaviour, experience or situation. There is always this choice between the practitioner giving, and the client finding, meaning.

Another important point is that some interpretations fall within the informative category, and other interpretations fall within the confronting category. Informative interpretations are interesting, illuminating and enhance awareness for the client, who is not defensive about their content. Confronting interpretations raise clients' consciousness about some attitude or behaviour of which they are defensively unaware; hence it is something of a shock to hear them. Informative interpretations, by contrast, are shock-free. I shall make this point again under the second item in the list of confronting interventions.

There are several kinds of interpretation:

3.1 *Simple ascription*   You ascribe a simple motive, intention or emotional state to what the client says or does. 'You sound very ambitious'; 'I think you really intend to see her'; 'You look angry'; 'I imagine you want to go'.

3.2 Psychodynamic   The meaning which you give to what the client says or does derives from some properly formulated psychodynamic theory. The interpretation is much more theory-laden than in 3.1. Thus the Transactional Analysis therapist may say 'It sounds as though your authoritarian parent (ego-state) is talking'. Everything depends on how sound the theory is; and even if sound, whether it accords with what is really needed. Too much of this sort of thing can leave a person cocooned in alien theory. It is important for raising consciousness about *compulsive* states of the person (see Chapter 3, p. 27).

3.3 Psychosomatic   This is the interpretation in which a physical symptom is attributed to some unowned emotional and mental state. This includes the Reichian type of psychosomatic interpretation as well as the conventional medical one. It is an open question how much any physical diagnosis can be extended to include a psychosomatic component.

3.4 Sociodynamic   The interpretation rests more on theories to do with group processes, with social and cultural phenomena. Thus you may relate the client's experience to prevailing norms and values, social and economic structures, social role expectations, issues of authority and power, gender stereotypes, political processes, doctrines of rights, and so on. This is often woefully neglected in classic psychotherapy. It may cover interpersonal, group dynamic, organizational, cultural (including ecological, economic and political) and global issues. It is important for raising consciousness about *conventional* states of the person (see Chapter 3, p. 27).

3.5 Transcendental   The interpretation invokes concepts to do with altered states of consciousness, other realities, psi and extrasensory perception, religious, spiritual or mystical dimensions of being. It can be used to raise consciousness about *self-transfiguring* states of the person (see Chapter 3, p. 30). This is the domain of psychic and transpersonal therapists.

There is probably some sort of cognitive hierarchy here. The use of later ones in the above list may modify the way earlier ones are used.

Finally, interpretations are often best offered with modesty: as an impression, or a subjective concern, or a phantasy, or a conjecture, or a hypothesis. This gives the client more intellectual scope to assess their merits, to accept or reject them. On the other hand, it is also important that the interpretations are not presented in a way that seems ill-considered, or superficial, or cavalier. Hence it may on occasion be fitting to support them with evidence and examples. And the last four in the above list presuppose a good grounding in relevant theory.

4 Psychosocial prediction

You may offer a view as to the likely future outcome, unfolding or development of some aspect of the client's current state, choices or situation. This is parlous territory, but it may be appropriate. The strictures of the previous paragraph apply.

5 Educational and growth assessment

You inform the client, on the basis of some assessment, what you think he or she needs in the way of new knowledge and skills and development – technical, verbal, emotional, interpersonal, intellectual, aesthetic, moral, or transpersonal. This is strictly an informative intervention, although it is clearly on the brink of prescription; in the same way that medical diagnosis is on the brink of recommendations for treatment.

6 Presenting relevant information

Apart from interpretation or assessment, you may give information, verbally in the session, that is relevant to the client. It may be general background knowledge – factual, technical, theoretical. It may have a more particular bearing on the client's situation, needs or interests. It may give a brief, simple theoretical account of the different states of the person and the three sorts of resistance, as described in Chapter 3 (pp. 25–36). It may be given on the practitioner's initiative; or it may be given in response to the client's question, or because he or she has clearly misunderstood something.

If, as in a tutorial, you are giving out any substantial body of information, then certain simple principles apply:

6.1 Attunement Empathize with the presence and attitude of mind of the listener, so that everything you say is shaped for them, related to their learning needs, existing knowledge and beliefs.

Talk out of this attunement, so that what you say and how you say it is existentially relevant. Build up on positive response cues of interest and involvement. Break off to deal with negative non-verbal cues of boredom, overload, incomprehension, scepticism, the need to question.

6.2 Overview   Give a brief advance account of the main areas you are going to cover.

6.3 Throw the basics into relief   Don't include too much in any one presentation; rather make only a small number of key points, which stand out clearly. Use non-technical language where possible.

6.4 Illumination   Illustrate each main point with examples and instances that are of relevance and interest to the listener. Amplify difficult concepts, restating them several times in different forms. Explain fully any technical terms that must be used. Use visual aids where possible. Avoid unnecessary redundancy of content.

6.5 Command of manner   Use tone and volume of voice, rate of speech, pauses and silences, inflection and emphasis, to enhance the content.

6.6 Recapitulation   Before closing, summarize the main points again, underlining any that are specially relevant.

6.7 Check for comprehension   Engage with the client about the content of what you have said, to see if he or she has understood, if there are queries, doubts, and so on.

6.8 Facilitate internalization   Encourage further discussion so that the client can assimilate the information, and integrate it with personal experience.

7 Feedback

You give clients informative, non-evaluative feedback on their performance in, for example, a role-play or piece of projected rehearsal. Or it may be feedback and comment on homework they have undertaken between sessions and have just produced or reported on. It is particularly useful to identify what has been unnoticed by them.

When the feedback becomes evaluative, discriminating between good and bad performance according to some criteria, then it overlaps with retrospective prescription (see Chapter 4 in the list of prescriptive interventions, p. 48).

8 Visual aids

You use extempore or prepared charts, drawings and diagrams, films and videos, to illustrate any of the above interventions.

9 Handouts

You give the client some written material with relevant information on it.

10 Referrals

You give clients details of people, books, meetings, courses, places, which provide the information or service they need.

11 Experiential modelling

By what you say and do in relation with the client, by your way of being, you are giving living, experiential information about human behaviour. This may be a central part of the informative aspect of the practitioner–client relation. It can be used as a basis for discussion between practitioner and client. It overlaps with exemplary and tacit prescription, and could lead over into demonstrative prescription (see the list of prescriptive interventions, p. 47).

12 Self-disclosure

You disclose information about yourself, your past or present personal experience, that may be illuminating for the client's situation. This is a particular kind of experiential modelling and, again, overlaps with exemplary or tacit prescription, for sometimes practitioner disclosure spontaneously begets client disclosure.

CHAPTER 6

CONFRONTING INTERVENTIONS

Confronting interventions directly challenge the rigid and maladaptive, attitudes/beliefs/actions that limit the client or unnecessarily disturb or limit others, and of which the individual is
defensively unaware – to a greater or a lesser degree. The interventions reach out to and are supportive of the person, while
throwing into relief that person's distorted behaviour, so that he or
she can become aware of it and get some insight into it. A confronting intervention unequivocally tells an uncomfortable truth,
but does so with love, in order that the one concerned may see it
and fully acknowledge it. It is a greater or lesser shock, therefore,
for the client to hear the content of the intervention, and to come
face to face with something about him- or herself that there was a
hidden investment in not noticing.

It is important to stress that this account of confrontation has
nothing to do with the aggressive, combative account that is sometimes applied to political and industrial disputes in our society. In
the six category version, confrontation is non-aggressive and non-
combative. Its manner is deeply affirming of the worth of the client,
however uncompromising the spotlight that is thrown on his or her
negative attitudes or behaviour.

In personal-development work, confronting interventions seek
to raise consciousness about conventional and compulsive states of
the person, and the three kinds of resistance, as described in
Chapter 3 (pp. 27–36).

In Six Category Training Workshops, most participants over
and over again, throughout the UK and in other parts of Europe,
when doing a self-assessment exercise on their two weakest categories, put down confronting interventions (alongside cathartic).
This I attribute to our culture's lack of education in handling
emotions. Any impending confrontation generates anxiety in the
practitioner. And this, in the absence of skill in handling one's own
anxiety, can lead to either avoidance or mishap, as we shall see. So
training in confrontation is vital.

What follows is divided into four parts, consisting of: first, an
account of some of the issues to do with confrontation; secondly,
a simple psychodynamic-cum-behavioural map of the process

of confrontation; thirdly, an account of some basic agendas of confrontation, the sorts of areas or issues which may call for a confronting intervention; and finally, a list of different kinds of confronting interventions.

ISSUES ABOUT CONFRONTING

There is a set of interrelated issues to do with the warrant for, the conditions of, the timing of, and the depth of, confronting interventions.

1 When does the practitioner have a warrant to confront the client?

Confronting is about consciousness-raising, about waking people up to what it is they are not aware of in themselves that is critical for their own well-being and the well-being of others. This makes confronting interventions presumptuous: I presume to judge what it is you are not aware of; I presume to judge that it would be in your interests to become aware of it; and then on an unsolicited basis I presume to appoint myself as the one to raise your consciousness about the matter.

Of course, it is not always quite as bald as this, for often the context of roles gives the practitioner an implicit warrant to engage in some degree of confrontation. Hence the psychotherapist has a warrant to confront the client about their defences, the medical practitioner about their unhealthy habits, the financial adviser about their improvidence. But even in these cases it is never quite clear how far the warrant extends and exactly what territory it covers. So if in doubt, make a contract with your client as to what your confronting remit is.

In the wider reaches of life it is still more ambiguous. For what sort of warrant for confrontation exists between lovers, between subordinate and boss, between total strangers on a train? This all makes life interesting and a challenge. It creates something of the warrior spirit. For many situations in life do present us with a warrant to confront. But if we get it wrong – by misjudging the situation or by adopting the wrong manner – we become bullies, bores, nags or prigs.

2 What are the conditions for effective confrontation?

First, your intervention needs to be on target in content, supportive in manner, poised in truth between the pussyfoot and the sledgehammer (see the next section). Secondly, the client, though

relatively unaware and defensive about the issue, is at a less conscious level ready and willing to hear about the issue and to do
something about it. And thirdly, there need to be opportunities in
the client's circumstances for doing something about it. Of course,
there are occasions when the individual seems nowhere near ready
to hear, but we have to have a go, because the effect of the
person's behaviour on others is becoming insupportable.

3 Timing

Thus, in the light of these conditions, the timing of a confronting
intervention is important.

4 Depth

And you need to get the depth right – raising as much into consciousness as is appropriate to the issue and the total situation, and
to the client's capacity to pay heed to it.

THE PROCESS OF CONFRONTATION

The key point about a confrontation as here defined is that it is
necessarily unsolicited. The client cannot ask for it precisely
because he or she is unaware of what it is that needs confronting,
or at least is unwilling to acknowledge it and deal with it. So
receiving it is going to be something of a shock to the client; and
one cannot be sure just how he or she will deal with this shock. All
this generates anxiety in the would-be confronter, who has to have
the nerve to be sure of him- or herself about the issue, as well as
facing up to the client's double-take. Such anxiety is perfectly
normal, part of the real present-time situation between confronter
and confrontee.

However, I believe it is more often than not compounded by
residual archaic anxiety, by which I mean old unfinished emotional business to do with a thousand confrontation agendas in
your, the practitioner's, past – most of which have probably never
been dealt with, particularly those in childhood. For the child is
too vulnerable, unskilled and insecure to confront its parents
about their repetitive mishandling. Hence there is a considerable
unprocessed, archaic legacy of fear and anger.

This double layer of anxiety, the present-time compounded by the
archaic, if you are unable to take charge of it, can skew the
intervention in one of two opposite ways: either you pussyfoot with
the client, go round the mulberry bush, dodge the issue, never square

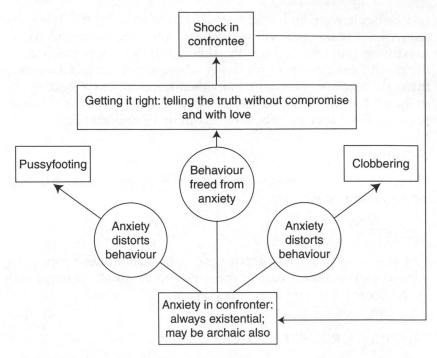

FIGURE 6.1   The process of confrontation

up to the real agenda and at worst simply avoid the confrontation altogether; or you sledgehammer the client, become aggressive and wounding about the issue, leaving the person unnecessarily hurt and defensive. Sometimes you may swing suddenly from pussyfooting to clobbering, feel guilty and swing back again. On the one side is the degeneration of love, and on the other side the degeneration of power; and in each case wisdom is missing.

If you can take charge of the anxiety, be aware of its two components, and keep the confronting intervention free of it, then you can get it right, be on the razor edge between love and power, and be both supportive and uncompromising. Some people often need quite a lot of training and re-training, with plenty of feedback, before they start to get the feel of this rigorous and powerful kind of love. Figure 6.1 depicts the issues involved in the process of confronting your client.

CONFRONTING AGENDAS

If we look across the whole spectrum of human interactions, then there are certain key issues and areas where it seems appropriate for people to confront each other lovingly. The trouble is, of course, that often they don't do it lovingly, but deviously, manipulatively, aggressively, evasively, collusively, and so on.

1 Shocking factual agendas

Strictly speaking, these agendas do not fall under the definition of confrontation given above, since they relate only to the non-culpable ignorance or unawareness of the client. Nevertheless, some of them are equally problematic for the practitioner. Examples are: telling someone they have a terminal illness, or need radical surgery; telling someone that a close relative or loved one has died; telling someone they are to be made redundant; and so on.

2 Intrapsychic agendas

These are the stock-in-trade of the psychotherapist and personal growth facilitator. They include the client's frozen needs and distresses of childhood, the denials and defences around these, the way they are acted out in compulsive victim/oppressor/rebel/rescuer roles, and so on. Included here also are current tensions and distresses which are not being owned and faced; and psychosomatic agendas.

3 Interpersonal agendas

These overlap with the intrapsychic. They include: unaware behaviours that unnecessarily disturb, hurt, frustrate others, or collude with, coddle, pamper, seduce others, or withdraw from, distance from, neglect and reject others; all kinds of relatively unaware distressed social interactions, such as the social acting out of compulsive victim/oppressor/rebel/rescuer roles.

4 Group dynamic agendas

These overlap with the intrapsychic and the interpersonal. They include issues in groups to do with: unaware contribution rates (high contributors excluding low contributors); unnoticed tacit norms; unaware competition and struggle for leadership; unnoticed role allocations and adoptions, including sexist ones; unaware avoidance of anxiety-arousing issues; unaware dependency or counter-dependency in relation to the group leader; and so on.

5 Organizational agendas

These overlap with the previous three. They include issues in organizations to do with the unaware handling of: leadership styles; decision-making; direction, negotiation, delegation; team work and team building; job definition and job satisfaction; appraisal and assessment; discipline, hiring, firing, promotion, redundancy; committee work; and so on.

6 Cultural agendas

These overlap with the four previous categories and include issues to do with rigid norms and values, rigid social structuring and allocation of roles in the wider society. They include restrictive attitudes and behaviour such as: patriarchy and rigid gender roles; authoritarianism and widespread subtle oppression in the professions and in the work-place; rigid stereotyping of children, the elderly, the physically ill, the mentally distressed, ethnic minorities, socio-economic classes; unaware political impotence and passivity in the street, in the neighbourhood, in the nation; unaware allocation of worker, manager, owner roles in the economic sphere; rigid party politics; nationalistic jingoism; and so on.

7 Global agendas

These overlap with the previous five. They include issues to do with: unaware collusion with the exploitation of, and expropriation of profits from, the underdeveloped poor world by the developed rich world; unaware disempowerment and despair about the nuclear threat and rising defence budgets, about the population explosion, world food shortages, environmental pollution, ecological imbalance, dwindling natural resources, the intransigence of nations; and so on.

Excluding shocking factual agendas, there is an ascending scale of six basic types of rigidity and unawareness here: the intrapsychic, the interpersonal, the group dynamic, the organizational, the cultural, the global. I think they all affect each other, but I do not think you can pick out any one and say it is the cause of any or all of the others. Each level has causes peculiar to it, as well as being influenced by the other levels. We all intermittently seem to need waking up on one or some or all of the levels.

It is interesting to look at these six levels in relation to the conventional and compulsive states of the person as these were

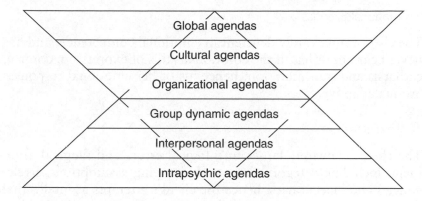

FIGURE 6.2 The relation between compulsive states and maladaptive conventional states of the person

defined in Chapter 3 (pp. 27–28). Now irrational and maladaptive conventional states may overlap with compulsive states but they can also exist on their own, simply as deep ignorance and social inertia. Figure 6.2 presents a model of this overlap: the upward pointing triangle depicts compulsive states, the downward one conventional states. The model proposes that the socially wider the agenda, the more scope there is for dealing with it by confronting maladaptive conventional states, by consciousness-raising education and training.

If this model is correct, then more emphasis in personal development work needs to be placed on working on maladaptive conventional states of mind about organizational, cultural and global agendas, without necessarily going into any catharsis of old, repressed emotional pain.

Taking another slice through the cake of limited human functioning, there is another set of six confronting agendas. Some of them, at any rate, seem to stem from lack of basic education, training and skills-building. The confronted client still has to undergo the shock of awakening to his or her deficit, because of a possible reluctance to face it and make it good.

8 Verbal-behavioural agendas

The client is unawarely deficient in verbal, conversational and social or interactive skills. The available repertoire of the person is too limited, hence maladaptive and problematic. This extends to practical skills of all kinds, technical and manual as well as human.

9 Emotional agendas

The client is unawarely deficient in emotional competence, and has never heard of or learnt the emotional skills of expression, control, catharsis and transmutation; hence his or her emotional responses are maladaptive.

10 Intellectual agendas

The client unawarely lapses into logical errors and illogical argument, including category shifts and changing assumptions, irrelevancies and inaccuracies; hence the client's attempts at intellectual dialogue are maladaptive. Intellectual agendas also include ideological ones: the rigid adoption of a belief-system without any critical grasp of the set of assumptions on which it is based; hence an inability to engage in any rational debate about it. And more generally, they include all forms of ignorance.

11 Technical agendas

The client lacks basic skills in some specialist area of practical competence, from plumbing to clinical medicine.

12 Aesthetic agendas

The client is unaware of aesthetic values and lapses into tastelessness, kitsch, decorative sentimentality, environmental crudity and ugliness, bad form. This is maladaptive since it reflects back into its originator's general behaviour. Beauty and order in one's immediate environment tend to influence positively the way one acts in that environment.

13 Contractual and moral agendas

The client has relatively unaware lapses about fulfilling contracts, keeping promises, telling the truth, being just in distribution and impartial in judgement, minimizing misery, extending loving benevolence, and so on. And this is all socially maladaptive in the most basic way. But then few people get an enlightened and liberating ethical education, which presents morality as a form of human flourishing, rather than as the oppression of duty.

14 Transpersonal agendas

The client lapses into nescience about the extrasensory, the other realities, the interconnectedness of all realities, the bliss-fields and the presence of the divine. The ultimate maladaptive somnambulism. (See transpersonal contraction, Chapter 3, p. 35.)

Finally, there is an agenda at the very forefront of practitioner–client interaction, but of course only some role-relations legitimate its use:

15   Immediate behaviour agendas

While talking with the practitioner, the client is unawarely producing any one or more of the following: eyes never make eye contact; breathing restricted or hyperventilated; body gesture/posture indicative of what is not being said, or mismatches what is being said; speech redundancies; volume inaudible; significant slips of the tongue; content of speech is indicative of what is not being dealt with; and so on.

CONFRONTING INTERVENTIONS

1 Raising consciousness about the agenda

This is the first, simple and obvious, and quite basic kind of intervention. It is easy to state, often difficult to do, because it has to be done in a clear and uncompromising but non-punitive and non-moralistic way. It involves at least five stages, although the whole thing needs to be handled with great flexibility and with sensitivity to the situation.

1.1 Identify the agenda   State what it is from among the fifteen I have listed above, or from any other formal or informal category system you use. So you may say 'I think there is some unfinished business from your past at work here', thus announcing a psychodynamic agenda.

1.2 Explain how it is you see the client falling foul of this agenda   This will involve negative feedback (as defined below) or educative feedback (see below). You give a very clear account of the unaware behaviour or attitude of mind, describing it exactly as it is – but without being punitive, moralistic or oppressive. You give the supporting evidence of your own eyes or ears, and of reports from others.

1.3 Explain why you think it is relevant and appropriate to raise this matter with the client in this way at this time   This is optional:

sometimes it is obvious why you are being confronting and so it is silly to explain it; at other times your apparent presumption may need full and adequate justification.

1.4 Give the client plenty of space to react to what you have said   You now give the person time to accommodate to the shock. Don't overtalk them, crowding them out of the way by premature follow through, displacing onto them your anxiety about what you are doing. They have to deal first with the shock of what you have said, and their emotional reaction to it. Only then can they deal with the content of it. You may ask how the person is feeling. You wait for the emotional response to unfold and work itself out: first shock, then grief, anger, fear, embarrassment or any combination of these. If the shock is too great or the client doesn't have time to deal with it, they go into compulsive submission or denial or blaming or pleading or some other defence.

You respectfully but firmly interrupt any of these defensive reactions. Hold your ground with uncompromising regard, both for the truth, and for the person of the client. Be ready for anything: you may need to be supportive, cathartic, catalytic, informative or yet again confronting, and in any order – to help the person come to terms with the confrontation, both in their emotions and in their understanding.

1.5 Follow through   You seek to help the person to identify the source of the unaware behaviour or attitude of mind, to find a way of dealing with this source, and to work toward some new and more fulfilling way of being.

If your article of faith is that everyone wants to get out of whatever cage they are in, it is best to do the whole thing on the gentle and laid-back assumption that you and your client will get honest, frank and open dialogue going about the agenda – which is only at root a way of avoiding the joy and challenge of living. Timing, as in every other kind of effective intervention, is everything. There is a time for consciousness-raising, and a time for leaving well alone.

2 Negative feedback

You feed back to the client impressions about what he or she is saying or how he or she is saying it or non-verbally conveying it, where these are impressions of conventional or compulsive states and resistances (see Chapter 3, pp. 27–36): some social ignorance and inertia, something restrictive, maladaptive, unaware, denied, defensive. They may be about transpersonal contractions (see Chapter 3, p. 35). The impressions may refer to past unaware behaviour. They may generalize across a whole lot of sayings and doings of the person. The feedback is non-punitive, non-moralistic. It is owned for what it is – your subjective impressions. It is not put forward as heavy-handed 'objective' criticism.

This intervention overlaps with 'Personal interpretation' given above under 'Informative interventions' and is the confronting version of it. So the feedback may cover simple ascription (for immediate behaviour agendas), psychodynamic interpretation (for intrapsychic and interpersonal agendas), sociodynamic interpretation (for group dynamic, organizational, cultural and global agendas). Somewhere in there there is also the psychosomatic interpretation, which gives meaning to a physical symptom in terms of some unowned emotional or mental state.

An interpretation is informative when it simply interests, illumines and enhances the awareness of the client, without the latter going into greater or lesser shock: the client has no resistance about, no unwillingness to face and acknowledge, the issue. It is confronting when they do go into shock, precisely because there is such resistance – conventional, compulsive or transpersonal – around the issue.

Practitioners can, however, make interesting misjudgements: they think they are being shockingly confronting, only to discover they have informatively illuminated. No doubt they projected what for them are or have been confronting issues, only to find that the client's reality is different.

3 Educative feedback

Here it is not so much that there is a resistant rigidity in the client's lack of awareness of an agenda, but a reluctance to accept his or her ignorance, to discover its degree and to realize that there is quite a task of learning ahead. You say that you get the impression from what the client is saying or doing, or has said and done, that there is some knowledge or some skill he or she has never acquired. You then go on to raise one or other of the agendas which I have called verbal-behavioural, emotional, intellectual, technical, aesthetic. Of course, there may be resistant rigidity, as well as simple reluctance, around some of these areas, where they overlap with agendas 2 to 7. Then educative feedback also becomes negative feedback.

4 Direct question

You ask a direct question aimed at what it is you sense the client is concealing, denying, avoiding, unaware of. 'When did you last say to X "I love you"?' Obviously the question can have a thousand forms, depending on what the issue is, but it always goes uncompromisingly to the heart of the matter. And it does this best when it has an experiential focus – that is, when it asks the person to say whether he or she has or has not had some experience or performed some action. The question gets them home to experiential base. Sometimes the client sweeps past the question, pretends to answer it but does not, is temporarily sunk or stunned by it. So repeat it quietly again . . . and perhaps again . . . then yet again. But this is also one of those interventions where you can misjudge it: you think the questioning is searchingly confronting, while the client finds it delightfully liberating.

5 Rattle and shake

You challenge, in a cognitive mode, the client's assertions or denials, by statements and questions about the evidence or contrary evidence for his or her view, its incoherence or inconsistencies, its implausibility or dubious assumptions, and so on.

6 Correcting and disagreeing

You correct the client's factually incorrect statements, and disagree with his or her opinions and views; and both of these in a way that seeks to raise consciousness, not put the client down.

7 Changing the diction

You seek to raise the client's consciousness about his or her disempowering way of talking by inviting the client to change diction, for example, from the language of constraint to that of choice – from 'I can't' to 'I choose not to', and so on.

8 From what to how

To help clients gain awareness that they live in an alienated self, cut off with inner pain from the expression of their real needs, you invite them to switch attention from what they are saying to how they are feeling, and how they are being in their body. The switch is from distracted analysis to immediate process and existence.

9 From then and there to here and now

For the same reason as in no. 8, you invite clients to switch from anxious preoccupation with the past or future to what they experience right here and now, what they here and now perceive, sense, want and need; and to own and express all this. This closely interweaves, of course, with no. 8.

10 Holding up a mirror

You raise consciousness about the immediate behaviour of clients by mimicking it back to them, piece by piece, as it occurs. But you do this with supportive attention, not in any kind of mocking or malicious spirit. This may be followed by verbal feedback; or may lead over into the cathartic use of this intervention.

11 Interrupt the record

When the client is unawarely going over old neurotic ground, talking out of congealed distress and negativity, you interrupt the talk by changing the topic, or by drawing attention to something in the immediate environment, or by validating what the client is invalidating, or by proposing an activity other than talking, or by radically changing your physical position in relation to the client or by touching, or by the use of the preceding kind of intervention (no. 10).

12 Disarming the body

You propose that the client move with his or her body in ways that contradict that person's psychological rigidities: this usually means opening and extending movements, such as the arms up and out. In this way, clients become more aware of their emotional armouring, because it normally keeps the body contracted in certain typical ways, and they can feel it resist being interrupted. This can lead into its cathartic use.

13 Appropriate anger

You seek to raise awareness about what the client is saying or doing by expressing to an appropriate degree the proper anger that it generates in you. This intervention degenerates massively if the anger is expressed to an inappropriate degree and/or is improper – that is, acts out your own past distress, or is simply misplaced because you have misunderstood them.

14 Discharge feedback

Some clients, in denying their hidden anger and rage, unconsciously and persistently try to provoke other people into acting out anger with them. If you are at the receiving end of this, you can both relieve your own tension and give strong non-verbal feedback to them, by going to a cushion in the corner of the room and pounding it vigorously with a prolonged roar. It is important that the roar is purely non-verbal and contains no words of criticism or abuse of them. You return to give loving attention to them and work with their reaction. You may give an interpretation of what has happened. This is only for the emotionally competent practitioner and the seasoned therapist-killer client. You do four things: interrupt their acting out, demonstrate real catharsis, step out of the impending battle to return with love, get some awareness through the back door of their dynamic.

15 Confronting validation

You affirm and validate those qualities or experiences of the client which he or she is busy denying or invalidating. The person is then face to face with his or her addiction to self-denigration.

16 Loving attention

You give prolonged, loving, absolutely silent attention to the client, while he or she is busy erecting, maintaining or lurking within his or her defences.

17 Self-validation

You invite clients to repeat several times unqualified appreciations of themselves. In this way they can become aware of the force of their compulsive tendencies to self-deprecation. It can be allied with no. 12 (above), especially holding the arms well out and up to the side. And it can lead over into its cathartic use.

18 Paradoxical confrontation

You call the bluff of clients. When they threaten to do something foolish, you discuss with them what method they will use. When they insist they do not want to work on some issue, you immediately drop it and turn to something totally different. By going fully with the defensive acting out, you paradoxically disarm it. This intervention requires good judgement, a cool nerve and no counter-transference.

19 Moral confrontation

You raise a contractual or moral agenda. This is where it is pretty clear from what clients have and have not said that they have not fulfilled a contract, have broken a promise, avoided the truth, told a lie, committed slander, generated unnecessary misery, been partial and unjust, and so on. So you take them through the procedures of no. 1 (above). This sort of confrontation has been so abused in the past – by being made moralistic, punitive and oppressive – that some practitioners think it should never be used at all. But moral principles are the most fundamental of all human principles and we need to find a loving way of raising them, where relevant, and of helping the person own and work through the genuine guilt that arises through their breach. A special case, of course, is where the moral breach is in the context of the practitioner–client relationship.

20 Factual confrontation

This form of confrontation is for dealing with shocking factual agendas (see above), especially such things as announcing to clients a terminal disease, or radical surgery, or the death of a friend, relative or spouse. It needs (a) statements to prepare them for the shock; (b) a simple and informative account of the facts; (c) time for them to assimilate the shock and the facts (perhaps alone or with some other person); (d) follow through at the informative, practical, interpersonal or emotional levels. Distress at the news, if not worked through, can lead to all kinds of behaviour distortions. You need to be careful not to work them over with talk that comes out of your anxiety, especially when the client needs time to assimilate the shock and the news.

21 Disciplinary confrontation

A similar format as for the previous intervention can be used for the disciplinary interview, in which a manager confronts an employee with some breach of organizational rules, or some unacceptable lapse in performance. It can also be used for the bad-results confrontation, in which under unilateral assessment the teacher tells the student that he or she has failed an exam – although all unilateral assessment systems can properly be called into question.

22 Transpersonal confrontation

You raise agendas to do with the extra-sensory and psi, with other realities and dimensions of being; and with the spiritual, religious, mystical, sacred aspects of living. Earthly existence, with its claims of biology and survival, is itself a sort of defence against all this, a cocooning screen. It hypnotizes and seduces and harasses and worries us into psi occlusion and spiritual nescience; and this effect is compounded by our relentlessly secular culture. The client may also have a lot of distress left over from the oppression of false and distorted religious teaching; and this puts a defensive rigidity around the whole area, including its authentic and positive potential. You can:

22.1   Raise their consciousness about how either or both of these defences seem to be operating in their case.

22.2   Give a transcendental interpretation (see informative interventions, no. 3.5, p. 55) of clients' experience which challenges their assumption that the whole area has nothing to do with them.

22.3   Ask a direct question (no. 4, above) aimed at the heart of the matter – for example, about their ESP or psi experiences, their experience of powers and presences, and other dimensions; and about their peak experiences and ecstasies, their encounters with the numinous and awe-inspiring. People often have experiential knowledge of what for defensive reasons they disavow at the level of stated belief.

22.4   Rattle and shake (no. 5, above) their disavowals by statements, questions.

22.5   Simply affirm and validate (no. 15, above) clients' potential for psi and spiritual awakening, to challenge their defensive, limited self-image.

This is a grossly neglected area in a lot of work with people. The result, presumably, of a collusive biological and cultural conspiracy – among schools of practitioners, and between practitioners and their clients.

Note that when confronting interventions are punitive, they fail since the client recoils with further distress, defences harden and attack or flight is soon under way. Confronting is effective when clients feel you respect them, however much their behaviour is being called into question.

CHAPTER 7

CATHARTIC INTERVENTIONS

Cathartic interventions help the client to abreact painful emotion, undischarged distress that is disabling and distorting his or her behaviour: anger is discharged in 'storming' sounds and movements, harmlessly directed; grief in tears and sobbing; fear in trembling and shaking; embarrassment in laughter. The interventions are pitched at a level of distress which the person is ready to handle in a relatively undisruptive way. They are followed through systematically so that available distress at that level is cleared. They enable the client to keep some attention free of the distress while discharging it. They give space for the expression of spontaneously generated insights – which are the real point and purpose of the release.

In personal-development work, helping clients to manage their own catharsis is to provide them with one of the basic keys of the self-creating person in unlocking compulsive states (see Chapter 3, p. 29). I have elsewhere presented a theory of catharsis (Heron, 1977b, 1992), and will not repeat it here. Cathartic interventions, along with confronting, are those the majority of participants in Six Category Workshops assess themselves weakest in. This is because our society is repressive of the emotions of grief, fear and anger, as in Figure 7.1.

We do not learn techniques of controlling the distress emotions of grief, fear and anger non-repressively, nor the techniques of releasing them through aware and intentional catharsis, or of transmuting them by spiritual practices. In short, we do not as yet have any education and training of the emotions. Hence, the inclusion of cathartic interventions as one of the basic six categories is itself a cultural phenomenon. Very many people need help with releasing the distress which society has conditioned them to deny and disown, but which they dimly sense is distorting their behaviour.

To give this help the practitioner needs emotional competence as defined in Chapter 2 (p. 15) and in-depth training in the use of cathartic techniques. It is also important to demystify these techniques and point out that many people not in the helping professions have acquired them, and the emotional competence to use

FIGURE 7.1   The social repression of distress emotion

them, through co-counselling training – a peer self-help personal-growth method (see Chapter 16).

While in my view catharsis is indispensable, it is not the only way of dealing with distress emotion. There is transmutation, which I consider in the next chapter. In addition, later in this chapter I review a range of ways of dealing with emotions (pp. 85–86); and catalytic intervention no. 8 (p. 141) relates to these.

In what follows, I will present: some issues about catharsis; a practitioner's map to outline some of the basic parameters of cathartic work; a map of client states of attention in and around cathartic work; an account of other positive emotional states; an account of negative emotional states; some cathartic agendas; a list of cathartic interventions; and, finally, some more on the practitioner's map.

ISSUES ABOUT CATHARSIS

1 The cathartic contract

There needs to be some kind of contract with clients about cathartic work. They are making a choice to do it, are not just having it done to them: they have the right to hold on to their defences as long as they choose. The context for an in-depth contract will be long-term counselling, co-counselling or a growth workshop. All but a few of the interventions in this chapter are for in-depth contract work, and require appropriate preparation and training.

2 Acute episodes

There are acute episodes when catharsis spontaneously breaks out, especially tears and sobbing. Practitioners of all kinds need to be ready for this and able to cope. For although it may not be part of the task of the tutor, or bank manager, or team supervisor, or police officer, to induce catharsis, it will certainly break out unbidden from time to time in some of their clients who are in extremis. Here the client needs permission-giving, acceptance and support: a tacit, very short-term contract that receives the release without in-depth work. The practitioner sees the catharsis through to a natural pause, then gently helps the client to bring his or her attention out of the distress. The interventions needed from the list below are few and simple: *giving permission* (no. 15), *validation* (no. 14), perhaps *light holding* (no. 34) and an informal version of *ending* (no. 41).

3 The cathartic continuum

There is a continuum of catharsis from the release of tension nearer the surface – in fresh, spontaneous talk, in yawning and stretching, and in laughter, to the deeper levels of sobbing, 'storming' and trembling. Every practitioner, of whatever kind, has cause to be supportive within some part of this continuum, in acute episodes. Figure 7.2 shows the two basic layers.

At the deeper levels, which kind of distress – whether grief, anger or fear – is the more buried, and which the more accessible, is highly idiosyncratic. It is specific to the client, his or her traumas and defences.

4 Depth, angle and timing of intervention

This is important: going in too deep, too steeply and too soon may render the client unable to handle the uprush of distress. The result is sudden shut-down and repression. Very occasionally, the result may be dramatization or acting out, rather than authentic discharge of emotional pain. Here again, good training counts.

5 Balance of attention, and insight

Important, too, is helping clients to keep some attention in balance outside the distress in order to have a place of strength from which

Nearer the surface	Release of boredom: fresh, spontaneous talk
	Release of fatigue: yawning and stretching
	Release of embarrassment: laughter
Deeper levels	Release of grief: tears and sobbing
	Release of anger: shouting and pounding
	Release of fear: trembling and shaking

FIGURE 7.2   The two layers of catharsis

to work on it; and prompting them to catch and verbalize the insight, the restructuring of awareness which follows catharsis, and which is the *raison d'être* of cathartic work.

6 Resistance

The main challenge for the practitioner is not one of overflow in which the cathartic process gets out of hand; but of resistance, of helping clients work through their defences (see Chapter 3, pp. 34–37).

7 Follow-through

Clients introduced to their own catharsis on a short workshop may welcome support and information on ways of continuing the healing process in other settings, whether in individual sessions, co-counselling or an ongoing group. Follow-through after an acute episode on the job is situational: it may or may not be appropriate.

THE PRACTITIONER'S MAP

There are three basic polarities to take into account, like three axes at right-angles to each other: leading and following; content and process; thought and feeling emotion. They apply to catalytic as well as cathartic work. They are shown in Figure 7.3.

1 Leading and following

You can lead, or you can follow, the client. When leading, your intervention comes out of your own hunch, hypothesis, therapeutic

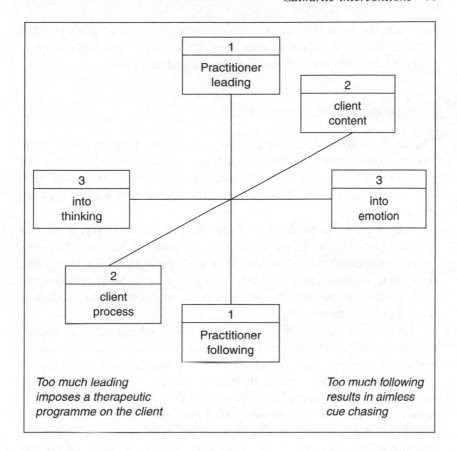

FIGURE 7.3   The practitioner's map

programme. When following, your intervention picks up on the immediately presented content or process cues – what clients are saying, or how they are saying it and how they are doing their breathing, posture and movement while saying it.

All leading and no following is to indoctrinate clients with a therapeutic programme and to ignore their immediate, living presence. This is scarcely facilitative of real growth. All following and no leading means both you and your client are hopping aimlessly from cue to cue; but it seems to me to be the lesser of two evils. What is best is a continuous interplay between the two. A hypothesis may select, develop or launch a cue; a cue may generate or change a hypothesis.

The client will produce many more cues than you can notice, although you can train yourself to notice more and more; and of the ones you notice there are only a small number which it is ever practicable to use. To attempt to work with every cue would belabour the person with excessive intervention. And since there is never a shortage of cues, you need to be sure you have a good range of hypotheses to illumine the abundance.

2 Content cues and process cues

The client will produce both content cues and process cues, inter-woven together, all the time. Content cues are embedded in *what* is being said: they include the meanings of the story being told, significant features of the storyline and significant imagery in the story.

Process cues are to do with *how* the person is saying it all, the paralinguistic features of tone and volume of voice, emotional charge and emphasis of voice; and with how they are breathing, restricting or moving their body while saying it. So you can work with content cues or with process cues, and can move back and forth between them.

The content cues will indicate what sort of events and images trigger certain distresses, and, when followed through, what earlier events originated these distresses. The process cues are signs of the distress itself distorting in minor but unmistakable ways the surface texture of verbal and non-verbal behaviour, although the person will usually be unaware of them. Too much content work can bury distress within the story; too much process work can discharge distress without any context. 'The story' here, of course, means the story of the client's life.

Another way of saying all this is that you can reach into the underlying distress through the mind of clients (words, meanings, story, imagery) or through their body (sounds, use of voice, breathing, posture, movement). And in each area they can be active or passive.

2.1 Client mentally active Recounting and exploring some past event, exploring associations, chains of linked memories and insights.

2.2 Client mentally passive Listening to you verbally evoke some event in the client's past (or in a group identifying with someone else working on some critical event).

2.3 Client physically active Deepening breathing, hyperventilating, exaggerating a gesture, engaging in some vigorous physical move-ment, making loud sounds.

2.4 Client physically passive   You apply pressure on tense areas; extend the client's limbs, spine, head and neck; touch energized points gently; or hold lovingly.

3 Emotion or thought

Clients can work in the domain of emotion or in the domain of thought. On the side of emotion, they are identifying, accepting, owning and above all discharging the distress. On the thought side, they are understanding the context of the distress, getting insight into its origins and its effects, re-evaluating their self-image and their perspective on their personal histories.

Discharge of distress, when followed through, spontaneously generates insight and re-evaluation. There is a restructuring of understanding set in motion by the release of the emotional pain, which had previously kept that understanding blinkered and occluded. So your role is that of midwife to the discharge while remaining attentive to those cues which indicate a sudden shift to the cognitive mode. Hence, there is a special class of process cue, the pensive cue, to do with a more reflective arrangement of facial expression and posture, which you need to watch for and pick up on.

MAP OF CLIENT STATES

Let us take the concept of the client's attention – that is, the active focus of his or her awareness. Then, simply considering its relation to the client's emotional distress, the following nine states are possible. Figure 7.4 represents them in graphic form. It shows the cathartic process at a central point in the transition from distress-bound states to free-attention states.

1 Shut down

The client's attention is sunk in his or her distress; it goes into congealed negativity. The person is shut down, submitting to pain. Until some attention is freed from the morass, there can be no catharsis.

2 Fascination

The client is fascinated by his or her distress, going on and on about the 'problem', analysing it, reporting on it, peering and probing and turning it over: a kind of inspection flight. Until this

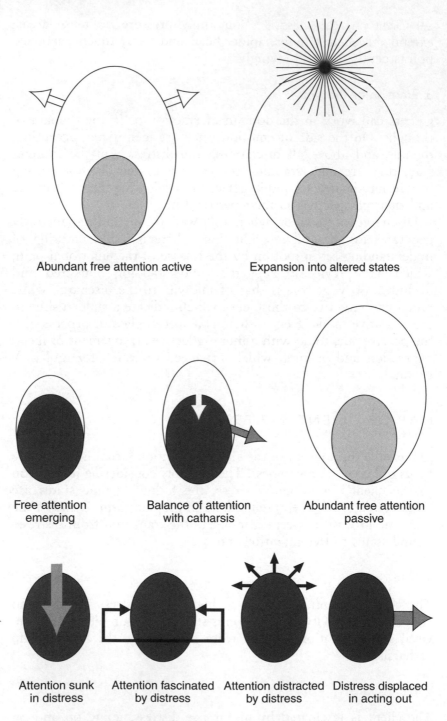

Abundant free attention active

Expansion into altered states

Free attention emerging

Balance of attention with catharsis

Abundant free attention passive

Attention sunk in distress

Attention fascinated by distress

Attention distracted by distress

Distress displaced in acting out

FIGURE 7.4   Map of client states

analytic collusion with the client's pain is interrupted, he or she cannot do cathartic work.

3 Distraction

The attention of clients is distracted and scattered by their distress. It goes off in directions irrelevant to the work in hand. Clients are in flight from their pain. They cannot cathart until they get their attention free of this distracting fugue.

4 Displacement

The attention of clients is caught in actively displacing their distress, in unawarely acting it out. They attack with their pain. They may be busy blaming or complaining or rebelling. Or they may be acting it in, displacing it against themselves, by invalidating themselves, their actions, their experiences. So they oppress other people or victimize themselves with their displaced distress. They cannot do cathartic work until this is interrupted or contradicted.

5 Attention emerging

The client has some free attention – that is, attention that is free from being sunk in distress, from being busy displacing it, from being distracted by it. Attention is liberated by recounting the positive content of past experience or by being open to the positive content of present experience. When enough attention is freed in this way, the client can begin to do cathartic work.

6 Balance of attention with catharsis

Some attention is free, outside the distorting effects of distress; and some attention is open to experience the distress as it really is, without distortion or denial. In this state, the client can discharge distress freely and fully. He or she is both in touch with it enough, and sufficiently disengaged from it, to release it.

Sometimes, the balance of attention can slip in some clients and the discharge degenerates into dramatization – a kind of hysterical production in a no-man's-land between discharge proper and thoroughgoing displacement or acting out. If there is more discharge than dramatization, it is probably best to let them get on with it. But if there is more dramatization than discharge, it is certainly best to interrupt it, get the balance back and start again.

Client states	Forms of defensiveness	Distress-driven roles
Attention sunk	Submission	Victim
Attention fascinated Attention distracted	Flight	Rescuer
Distress displaced	Attack	Oppressor Rebel

FIGURE 7.5   Relations between negative client states, defensiveness and compulsive roles

7 Abundant free attention, passive

The cathartic work has been done, awareness is enhanced, attention is liberated on a flood of spontaneous insight and re-evaluation.

8 Abundant free attention, active

The client is creatively engaged with projects, plans and enterprises. Every day is a new opportunity; every crisis a fresh challenge.

9 Abundant free attention, entering altered states of consciousness

Ordinary thought and perception yield to deeper and wider reaches of feeling and intuition A new dimension, the post-cathartic state, with its great openness to the present moment, is at the threshold of an expanded awareness − of feeling interconnectedness within a multidimensional cosmos − and of attunement to divine potential deep within the psyche.

The four negative client states at the bottom of Figure 7.4 can now be related to concepts used in Chapter 3, where I wrote of the defensiveness and distress-driven roles of the compulsive state of the person (p. 27). Figure 7.5 shows the connection. When people are locked into self-blame, they are both internal oppressor and internal victim, combining attack and submission, distress displaced with attention sunk. After a while, they may switch into compulsive self-rescue attempts.

POSITIVE EMOTIONAL STATES

Including catharsis, there are at least eight positive emotional states. Awareness of them gives you a comprehensive guide for working with your client's affect. When doing this work, you will be concerned to help your client acquire skills in the exercise of several of these states as well as catharsis. This will call for catalytic interventions too.

1 Identification

Clients know what emotional state they are in, can identify the emotions involved, can experience them, and own them as part of their reality.

2 Acceptance

Clients both identify/experience/own their emotions and accept them.

3 Control

Clients awarely control their emotional state, without either denying it or suppressing it, in order to accomplish some task, or interact appropriately with other persons.

4 Redirection

Clients awarely direct an aroused emotion into a channel other than its normal outlet. Thus, a person who is angry about an interruption of his or her activity may for good reason choose to direct the energy of the anger into some vigorous game.

5 Switching

Clients awarely choose to change an emotional state by switching attention off it and its context, and on to some other activity which generates a different emotional state. As a result of switching, one sort of emotion gives way to a different one. You can switch laterally, from an emotional state on the ordinary level of consciousness to another state on the same level; or you can switch vertically, from a state on the ordinary level to a state on a higher level of consciousness.

6 Transmutation

Clients awarely choose to sublimate and refine an emotional state so that it is internally transformed. This is the psychological alchemy of turning base metal into gold. A basic method is to reconstrue a situation, cognitively restructure it, so that you see it in a new light, which transforms your emotional response to it. Another is to hold the light of awareness intently and constantly within a negative emotional state, until its dross is transfigured.

It is important to underline the difference between redirection, switching and transmutation.

- *Redirection.* The emotion continues to be present, but its energy is given some alternative outlet to the one it would normally seek. So anger is redirected into competitive sport rather than let out in protest at whatever interference triggered it off.
- *Switching.* The emotion falls into the background because some other emotion is intentionally generated in the foreground. So the anger recedes because choosing to attend some quite different and good news creates exhilaration.
- *Transmutation.* The emotion internally changes its nature and becomes a different emotion. So anger, by the transformative, focused action of consciousness, becomes peace.

7 Catharsis

Clients awarely choose to discharge distress emotions – embarrassment, grief, fear, anger – through laughter, tears, trembling, high-frequency sound and movement. The painful emotion is released from the mind and body; and this generates spontaneous insight into origins and subsequent effects.

8 Expression

Clients awarely give verbal and physical expression to their emotions, to celebrate, affirm and bear witness to the joy and drama of their unique existence.

NEGATIVE EMOTIONAL STATES

There are eight, roughly corresponding, negative emotional processes:

1 Alienation

Clients are cut off from their emotional state and cannot identify what it is. Asked about their emotions, they will talk about their thoughts.

2 Suppression

Clients identify their emotional state only enough to subject themselves to instantaneous social inhibition.

3 Fixation

Clients are stuck in some emotional state, either fascinated by it in a morbid way or sunk in it with depressive inertia. Their awareness is a slave of the state and cannot (or, more properly, feels unwilling to make the effort to) move out of it.

4 Displacement

Clients' distress emotion is displaced unawarely into some action that is maladaptive, socially inappropriate and disturbing, or into some negative attitude toward the self. The distress emotion involved is usually also repressed.

5 Distraction

Emotional states fluctuate in a disoriented way because the client is being chaotically distracted by one stimulus after another, coming from some mixture of the mind and the external world.

6 Degradation

An emotional state is debased into a lesser or lower or more negative one, by the client indulging in it in a distorted way.

7 Dramatization

The client's distress emotion is displaced into pseudo-catharsis. The outlet has elements of the hysterical or the rigid. The distress slips out of the true cathartic channel, and distorts itself on the way out.

8 Repression

The client's distress emotions are pushed out of consciousness and their presence in the mind is denied. Then we have the return of the repressed in distorted form. Most of the so-called defence mechanisms are a combination of repression and no. 4, displacement.

Experiential learning (see Chapter 9, pp. 119–122), in its affective dimension, is concerned to help clients acquire skills in identifying all these negative processes, in interrupting them, and in transforming their energy and integrating it with positive processes.

CATHARTIC AGENDAS

These are the different sorts of distress material that the client may need to work on cathartically. We can look at this in three basic ways.

1 Kinds of distress

These include boredom, physical tension, embarrassment, grief, anger and fear; discharged respectively in spontaneous talk, yawning and stretching, laughter, sobbing, 'storming' and trembling (see Figure 7.2).

2 Times of distress

These refer to when the client was hurt. There is current distress to do with recent upsetting events; intermediate distress to do with upsetting events in past adult life; childhood distress; prenatal and birth trauma.

3 Causes of distress

The generic cause is interference with basic human needs and capacities. Species within this genus include: nature's interference – birth trauma, death, disease, natural catastrophes and so on; physical interference such as accidents; interpersonal interference, as from parents; social interference – the norms and values of oppressive institutions and the oppressive society.

CATHARTIC INTERVENTIONS

In what follows I separate out interventions that work with client *content* (nos. 1 to 24) and interventions that work with client *process* (nos. 25 to 41). Remember that in practice these two sorts of intervention continually weave in and out of each other, enhancing each other's effectiveness. Effective use, for the in-depth contract work referred to earlier, requires training and practice.

WORKING WITH CONTENT

Working with content means working with what the client is saying, with his or her stated difficulty, with meaning, story-line and imagery. The content may start out anecdotally evasive or analytically defensive; may evolve into talking *about* some real difficulty or problem area; and culminate in working *on* some traumatic scenario. In practice, working with content interweaves closely with working with process (see below).

1 From analysis to incident

You ask a client who is busy analysing a current difficulty or problem in his or her life to describe a specific, concrete critical/ traumatic instance of it. You gently persist until the client gets there. Then:

2 Literal description

You ask the client to describe the traumatic incident in literal detail, not analyse it or talk about it but summon the story-line through vivid recall of sights and sounds and smells, of what people said and did. Distress is lodged in imagery of all kinds, and is drawn up by its evocation. And to increase this effect:

3 Present tense account

You ask the client to describe the incident in the present tense, as if it were happening now. You keep the client to the texture of the scene, the imagery, in the present tense, perhaps going over it several times, and with discreet questions edge them to the distressed nub of the matter. Working with process cues (see below pp. 94–101) evident during the description will help a lot. Catharsis may occur at any point. What is certain is that the threshold of catharsis is lowering: the person is getting closer to feeling the distress.

4 Psychodrama

As the distress emotion comes to the fore through literal description of a critical incident, you invite the client to re-enact the incident – that is, to re-play it as a piece of living theatre: the client imagines he or she is in the scene and speaks within it as if it is happening now.

You ask the client to express fully in the re-enactment what was left unsaid, suppressed or denied at the time, and to say it directly to the central other protagonist (for whom you can usefully stand in). Catharsis can occur powerfully at this point.

This is original theatre: clients re-creating dramatic incidents from their own life in a way that enables them to abreact the painful emotion which they suppressed at the time. The past is often full of pockets of unfinished emotional pain which can be discharged by this simple and classic technique – the use of which requires good training.

There are two points of shift where clients typically resist because each shift gets closer to the distress: first, the move from analytic talking about a problem to literal description of an actual instance of it; secondly, the shift from this description of the scene to dramatically talking to someone in the scene. You will need gentle persistence in helping your client to break through at these two points of resistance. This kind of persistence needs to be both caring and quietly unrelenting.

5 Shifting level

If the psychodrama is about an incident later in the client's life, when he or she is making a charged statement to the central other, such as 'I really need you to be here', you quickly and deftly ask 'Who are you really saying that to?' or 'Who else are you saying that to?' At this point, at the heart of the psychodrama, the client can very rapidly shift level to a much earlier situation and become the hurt child speaking to its parent, and continue to use the same line but in relation to a more basic agenda. Often the catharsis dramatically intensifies as the deeper level is reached.

6 Earliest available memory

Instead of prompting the client to shift level while re-enacting a recent critical incident, you can simply ask for the client's earliest available memory of that sort of incident, and work on that with literal description and psychodrama. Depending on how it goes and how early it is, you may then get the client to shift level inside that psychodrama. Distresses line up in chains of linked experiences going right back to the start of life. However, there is no need always to shift level to earlier incidents. It may be appropriate to defuse the incident with which you happen to be working.

7 Hypnotic regression

When clients state a current difficulty, you invite them to lie down with eyes closed, and then count them down from 10 to 1 into deeper and deeper states of relaxation, and further into their past towards early incidents at the start of the chain linked with the current difficulty. They recount what memories surface. Follow through with psychodrama and/or process work.

8 Scanning

When clients state a current problem, you invite them to scan along the chain of incidents, all of which are linked by the same sort of difficulty and distress. They evoke each scene, then move on to the next, without going into any one event deeply. They can start with the earliest incident in the chain which they can recall and then move chronologically forwards; or they can move chronologically backwards from the most recent incident. This loosens up the whole chain and brings the more critical incidents to the fore to be discharged.

9 Imagining reality

When the content indicates that there is some trauma lodged in an incident which the client knows has happened but cannot recall (for example, circumcision), you can suggest that the client simply imagine the event without worrying whether it really was like that. Follow through with interventions nos. 2 to 4 above and process work. Hypnotic regression is another possibility here, of course.

10 Eschatological drama

When clients are talking about feeling cut off from other realms, from the sacred and the divine, you suggest that they talk directly to these realities, saying whatever they need to say. This can be very cathartic, with a re-evaluation of the relationship, leading into further transpersonal work.

11 Slips of the tongue

When a word or phrase slips out that the client did not intend to say, you invite him or her to repeat it a few times, and to work with the associations and/or process cues. This invariably points the way to some unfinished business.

12 Monodrama

The client is invited to play both sides of an internal conflict which may, for example, be between the claims of two different social roles, or more basically between the internal oppressor and the internal victim. There are two chairs, one for each side of the conflict, and the client moves from chair to chair, speaking the lines for each of his or her internal protagonists. This is certainly consciousness-raising, and can become rapidly cathartic if you work skilfully with the process cues on either side of the conflict.

13 Contradiction

The client is invited to use statements and a non-verbal manner that contradict, without qualification, self-deprecating, self-denigrating statements and mannerisms. In full contradiction, both statement and manner (tone of voice, facial expression, gesture – arms well out and up, posture) are self-appreciative and unqualified. In partial contradiction, the client's statement is self-deprecatory but his or her manner is totally self-appreciative: it is the irony of this that is cathartic. In double-negative contradiction, both statement and manner are exaggeratedly self-deprecating: the caricature implodes into catharsis.

Contradiction challenges head on the external invalidation and oppression which the child has internalized to keep both its distress and its positive potential suppressed and denied so that it can conform and survive. You need to work deftly to help the person get it going in all its appropriate modes, verbal and non-verbal; then it rapidly opens up into laughter, followed, if you are quick on the cues, by deeper forms of catharsis.

14 Validation

At certain times, you can gently and clearly affirm clients, their deep worth, their fine qualities, their deeds, in a way that releases a lot of grief about the denial of all these fundamental truths in their childhood.

15 Giving permission

In early stages, clients often still feel the force of the old conditioning that tells them they are not allowed to discharge their distress. You can help this by gently giving them verbal permission and encouragement as they falter on the brink of release.

16 Freeing attention

When clients' talk indicates that their attention is sunk, caught up in verbally acting out or acting in, distracted or fascinated by their distress, you interrupt this to get some attention free and ready for balance by physical process work (see below pp. 94–101), describing the immediate environment, the use of contradiction, describing recent pleasurable experiences, moving around in or changing the arrangement of items in the room. Then see what is on top (next).

17 What's on top

When clients have got some free attention and are starting to get into balanced attention, you ask them 'What's on top?' – that is, what recent (or remote) experience comes spontaneously to mind, however irrelevant or trivial it may appear to be. Then work as in nos. 2 to 8, or it may be that the next one, no. 18, happens quite quickly.

18 Catching the thought

As clients are working (describing an incident, doing a psychodrama, during a pause in catharsis), a sudden thought comes to them, and they have switched briefly to the cognitive mode – some re-appraisal of an event, re-evaluation of its meaning, insight into its effects. They may let it go unless you spot its arrival via the pensive cue – the slight pause and sudden reflective look. The pensive cue alerts you to invite them to verbalize it – and own it. This fully expressed restructuring of awareness is the real fruit of the catharsis, not just the release itself.

19 Free association down the pile

As clients are working on, or describing, one event, another and often earlier one suddenly comes to their mind. Again, you may spot its arrival through the pensive cue and ask 'What are you thinking?' Unlike scanning (no. 8, above), which is directed association along an explicitly identified chain of distress-linked events, this is free association along a chain or down the pile of interlinked chains. This may lead to a primary working area for the session. Nos. 18 and 19 are basic.

20 Dreams

One useful way of leading your clients is to enquire about recent dreams or about repetitive nightmares. You can work with these just as you would with a real-life incident: literal description, psychodrama, shifting level, free association and so on. You can also invite your client – in order to grasp how the dream symbolizes the relation between different parts of his or her psyche – to become each main item or person in the dream in turn, and to let each one speak to the others and say what it wants. Pick up the accompanying process cues.

21 Quick asides

Sometimes associated material comes up as a quick aside, which is something clients say that seems to lie a bit outside the mainstream of what they are talking about. They also tend to sweep on past it as if it were not important. You pick up on the aside and invite them to go into it, associate to it and so on. This is invariably fruitful, but you will need a little persistence, if clients are defensively impatient and wanting to get on with their surface theme.

22 Lyrical content

When clients mention recall of a poem, a piece of music or a song, you invite them to recite it, hum it or sing it. This can be powerfully cathartic and full of associated material.

23 Seeking the context

When clients are deeply immersed in process work and in catharsis, you may judge it fitting to lead them into the associated content, asking them to identify and describe the event and its context, to verbalize insights, to make connections with present-time situations and attitudes.

24 Integration of learning

After a major piece of cathartic work that has generated a good deal of insight and re-evaluation, you prompt clients to formulate clearly all they have learnt, and to affirm its application to new attitudes of mind, new goals and new behaviours in their life now. At this point cathartic work finds its true *raison d'être*.

WORKING WITH PROCESS

Working with process means working with the full range of nonverbal cues, with how the client is talking and being – that is, with emotional tone and charge and volume of voice, with breathing, use of eyes, facial expression, gesture, posture, movement. (See also the overlap with catalytic interventions, Working with non-verbal cues, p. 133, where there is more on the pensive cue, among others.) Working with non-verbal cues will interweave with working with content. More and more non-verbal cues emerge, as clients get deeper into their story. So the practitioner is moving around creatively between client process and content. Here, again, I emphasize training and supervised practice.

25 Repetition with amplification and/or contradiction

Clients can never totally deny or contain their distress. It continually has brief outcrops in the surface texture of their behaviour, as if it is always struggling to get out, however defensively unaware of it they have had to become. And it also has a more constant grip on some of the muscular mechanisms of their behaviour and bodily being. There are four classes of cues that they can repeat, amplify and/or contradict.

25.1 Distress-charged words and phrases You pick up on these words or phrases not because of their meaning but because of their emotional charge. Indeed, the meaning may sometimes seem quite irrelevant to the work in hand. And you must distinguish between a normal expressive emphasis and a distress charge. It is words with the latter that you invite the person to repeat, perhaps several times, and perhaps louder, and even much louder. This repetition and amplification may start to discharge the underlying distress; or it will bring it nearer the surface and loosen up associated material – so you watch for pensive cues. It is particularly potent at the heart of a psychodrama, when the individual is expressing the hitherto unexpressed to some central other protagonist from their past.

25.2 Distress-charged mobility While clients are talking, and unnoticed by them, their underlying distress starts to move some part of their body: the feet and legs start a kicking or jerking motion; the hands and arms start a small stabbing, slapping, thumping, scratching, twitching or wringing motion; the pelvis and thighs start a small bouncing or rotating movement; the trunk, head and neck start swaying, bending, rotating; the head starts shaking or nodding; there is a sudden deepening of the breath.

You pick up on this mobility and invite the person to develop it and amplify it and follow it into the underlying emotion. When the exaggeration is well under way, ask them to find first the sounds and then words that go with the movement. This can rapidly undercut more superficial content they are busy with and precipitate earlier, more basic and even primal material. The effect is particularly powerful when you encourage your client to develop a sudden involuntary deepening of the breath into quite rapid deep breathing into the emerging emotion, with an accompanying crescendo of sound.

Picking up on distress-charged words and movements needs to be light and deft, with only a brief time gap between the cue and the intervention. The beginner's error is to have too big a time gap, and then to ask the client why they produced that bit of movement or said that word in that tone. 'Why?' questions like this are fatal: they inappropriately throw the client into the analytic mode, and interrupt the emerging energy of the distress, which will soon reveal itself and what it is about if the person is simply encouraged to get into action.

So for bits of distress-charged movement, the sequence is: get the action well exaggerated and energized, then find the sound that goes with the movements, then the words. Later on in the pauses invite clients to identify the context: who are they saying this to, what situation from their past are they re-enacting?

25.3 Distress-charged rigidity   The underlying distress temporarily locks some part of the client's body into a rigid state: the breathing becomes tight, restricted and shallow; the legs are rigid, the muscles locked; the thighs close tightly together; the arms are held tight to the sides of the body, or crossed tightly; the fists are tightly clenched, the arms rigid; the hands are firmly clasped; one hand or both hands tightly hold the head, or cover the eyes, or have fingers pressed over the mouth; head, neck and trunk lock together in one rigid posture; and so on.

Again, you invite the client to exaggerate the rigidity, get the distress energy right into it, then find some sounds and words that articulate it, then identify its context. At any point the rigidity may break up into mobile catharsis; or you may encourage the client, after some time in the exaggerated rigidity, to put energy into the opposite mobility, finding appropriate sounds and words – and this may loosen up the discharge. So a tight fist and rigid arm is first exaggerated into even greater tension, then converted into rapid thumping on a pillow. You will need to encourage your client not to throttle back the sound, and behind that the long-repressed words.

Whether the body cues are mobile or rigid, they may either match the content of what the person is saying, or they may mismatch it. So a clenched fist may accompany a statement of being irritated with someone, or a statement about having had a wonderful time with someone. In either case, amplify the body cue, then find the words within the action. In the case of a mismatch, experience shows that the body cue rather than the statement is telling the truth of the matter.

25.4 Chronic archaic-defensive cues   Cues in the previous three entries are intermittent: they crop up in and among the content of what the client is saying, they come and go, sometimes at a great rate of knots. But there is a class of process cue that is permanent, chronically entrenched in the client's behaviour. The class includes three species:

25.4.1 Chronic archaic-defensive tone of voice   The client persistently talks, whatever the content, with a tone of voice that pleads or complains or whines or self-effaces (this one may lower the volume too) or distances or irritates. The locked-in childhood distress is acted out through the tone and perhaps also the volume. This may extend into the chronic use of speech redundancies such as 'ums' and 'ers', 'you knows' and 'you sees', and stutters.

25.4.2 Chronic archaic-defensive posture and/or gait   The client stands or walks in terms of permanently distressed adaptation to an early oppressive environment – the stance or walk is embarrassed, self-deprecating, mincing, cautious, ready for flight, defiant or stubborn, or whatever other emotional posture the child adopted to survive.

As before, you can invite the person to exaggerate the tone (25.4.1), or posture or gait (25.4.2), get energy into it, then find out what it seems to be saying, and to whom and in what context – which will lead over into a psychodrama with more process work and, of course, catharsis. Or once amplified, the rigidity can be contradicted, and the contradiction, or opposite behaviour, can be amplified and worked with.

25.4.3 A third type of chronic archaic-defensive cue is more covert   It is a rigidity of muscular tone, a rigidity that afflicts the free and full use of a group of muscles, anywhere in the body – what Reich called 'character armour'. It is a more subtle, not so obvious, psychosomatic rigidity: it may be evident in defensive posture and gait, but only to the trained eye. Its purpose is primarily to maintain a constant inhibition of the physical expression of strong pockets of repressed grief, fear and anger. Again, you can propose that the client physically amplify and/or physically contradict this type of rigidity.

To amplify, the client can be invited to adopt a stress position – that is, to put a muscle group into sustained contraction, until the physical discomfort of doing so is strongly felt. If they go into the physical pain with deep breathing and sound, it may implode with catharsis of the underlying emotional pain.

To contradict, the client can be invited to hyperventilate – that is, to breathe deeply and vigorously with sound on the outbreath; to kick and thrash the legs, to thrash the arms, to thrash the pelvis, shake the head, all this with sound and when lying down on a mattress; to squat and pound pillows with the fists vigorously, with sound; to stand and tremble the whole body and jaw, with sound; and so on.

This activity needs to be sustained, and to get to the right frequency of vigour. It may then become strongly cathartic, or loosen up images and material that can be worked with in other ways. It can also be used as a kind of gymnastic retraining for catharsis, re-establishing muscular and behavioural pathways for the release of distress.

26 Acting into

This is just a special case of physical contradiction. The client is already feeling the distress, wants to discharge it, but is held back by conditioned muscular tension. You suggest that he or she acts into the emotion – that is, creates a muscular pathway for it, by vigorous pounding for anger, or trembling for fear. If they produce the movements and sound artificially, then very often real catharsis will take over.

27 Hyperventilation

Already mentioned (under 25.4.3 above), hyperventilation requires separate consideration. It involves rapid breathing, but this can become defensive if it is excessively fast or too slow. So there is a frequency which opens up the emotionality of the whole psycho-physical system, if it is sustained long enough. It can be used to lead the client into discharge from scratch, by working on basic character armour; or it can be used to follow a mobile body cue, especially a sudden deepening of the breath. To prevent tetany and excessive dizziness, have the client do it in many cycles, with pauses in between. When carried on for a sufficient period of time, this is a very direct and powerful route to primal and perinatal experiences, which may also be interwoven with transpersonal encounters.

28 Physical pressure

When the client is just struggling to get discharge going, or has just started it, or is in the middle of it, you can facilitate release by applying appropriate degrees of pressure to various parts of the body: pressure on the abdomen, midriff or thorax, timed with the outbreath; pressure on the masseter muscle, some of the intercostals, the trapezius, the infraspinatus; pressure on the upper and mid-dorsal vertebrae timed with the outbreath, to deepen the release in sobs; pressure against the soles of the feet and up the legs to precipitate kicking; extending the thoracic spine over the practitioner's knee, timed with the outbreath, to deepen the release of primal grief and screaming; and so on. The pressure is firm and deep, but very sensitively timed to fit and facilitate the client's process. Anything ham-fisted and unaware of what the client's energy is doing is intrusive. Physical pressure should be handled with great care and skill.

29 Physical extension

As the client is moving in and out of the discharge process, you can facilitate the release by gently extending the fingers, if they curl up defensively; or by gently extending the arms; or by drawing the arms out and away from the sides of the body; or by extending an arm while pressing the shoulder back; or by gently raising the head, or uncurling the trunk; and so on. All these extensions are gentle and gradual, so that the person can yield and go with them.

30 Surrender posture

Sometimes the full release of grief needs a surrender posture. If the client is kneeling, and grief is on the way up and out, gently guide his or her trunk forward until the head rests on a cushion on the floor, arms out to the side, palms facing up to either side of the head, fingers unfurled. After the intense sobbing subsides, raise the person gently up again to catch some thoughts and insights; then down on to the cushion again when another wave of grief comes through.

31 Vertical and horizontal

When doing body work with your client, start with standing positions, and as the process cues emerge, shift directly to work lying down. A well-timed change from the vertical to the horizontal can facilitate catharsis.

32 Relaxation and light massage

This is an alternative mode of contradicting physical rigidity. You relax the client and give gentle, caressing massage to rigid areas. Catharsis and/or memory recall may occur as muscle groups give way to the massage. Gentle and light oscillation, or rocking, applied to various areas will have the same effect.

33 Relaxation and self-release

This is yet another way of undoing physical rigidities that lock in distress. You relax clients and invite them to 'listen' for movement micro-cues within their muscles in every part of their body. The micro-cue is a continuous buried impulse to move against the distress-charged rigidity. It is normally blocked and suppressed by the rigidity. But if clients can heed and amplify the micro-cues and start gently to stir and move their body (and perhaps their voice) in unfamiliar ways, and increase the movement and sound, then they may break right out of the rigidity into catharsis.

34 Physical holding

You reach out lightly to hold and embrace the client at the start, or just before the start, of the release of grief in tears. This can gently facilitate the intensity of sobbing, and can be combined with aware pressure on the upper dorsal vertebrae at the start of each outbreath. Holding the client's hands at certain points may facilitate discharge. When discharging fear, the client can stand within your embrace, and your fingertips apply light pressure on either side of the lower spine.

35 Pursuing the eyes

By avoiding eye contact with you, clients are often also at the same time avoiding the distress emotions. You gently pursue their eyes by peering up from under their lowered head. Re-establishing eye contact may precipitate or continue catharsis.

36 Regression positions

When process cues suggest birth or prenatal material, you can invite the client to assume prenatal or birth postures, start deep and quite rapid breathing and wait for the primal experiences to rerun themselves. This may lead into deep and sustained cathartic work in the primal mode. If so, you need to keep leading the client to identify the context, to verbalize insights and at the end to integrate the learning into current attitudes and life-style. Regression positions may be less ambitious, like lying in the cot, sitting on the potty, sucking a thumb.

37 Holding up a mirror

You can lightly precipitate the discharge of embarrassment in laughter by mimicking, with loving, not malicious, attention the various self-deprecating and self-effacing behavioural cues the client is producing. If followed through deftly, with both content and process, this may pave the way for much deeper catharsis.

38 Use of water

All these varieties of process work may usefully be done when the client is immersed in water, or lying on a waterbed. The stimulus of water may precipitate prenatal and birth material.

39 Psychotropic drugs

Mescalin and LSD can be powerful abreactive drugs if the client is properly facilitated when under their influence (see Grof, 1976).

40 Transpersonal process cue

Sometimes the client spontaneously assumes a posture or makes a gesture that has transpersonal significance, like one of the consciousness-changing postures in oriental yogas. You can ask the client to repeat it, stay with it and develop it, perhaps finding the words that go with it. This may generate a good deal of insight and be incidentally cathartic. It may also be the start of trans-mutative work (see Chapter 8).

41 Ending a session

At the end of a cathartic session, it is necessary for you to bring the client back up out of cathartic regression into present time, by chronological progression at intervals of 5 or 10 years, by affirming positive directions for current living, by describing the immediate environment, by looking forward to the next few days, and so on. See also nos. 23 and 24 above for bringing out content issues during and after cathartic work.

MORE ON THE PRACTITIONER'S MAP

In the light of these cathartic interventions, I will elaborate the practitioner's map which I outlined earlier in this chapter. There are three axes which yield eight quadrants – eight basic modes in which you can work. When you lead the client, you are not basing your intervention on immediate client cues, but on your sense of a balanced programme of work. I only give one example in each quadrant.

1 Practitioner leading client content into emotion

For example, you propose, without immediate client cues, a chronological scan over some category of experience, to loosen up distress emotion in the chain of events. Your intervention proceeds from your own hypothesis or plan.

2 Practitioner leading client content into thought

For example, you propose, without immediate client cues, that the client rehearses the learning and insights acquired through the cathartic work of the previous session.

3 Practitioner leading client process into emotion

For example, you propose, without immediate client cues, that the client adopt a regression position for doing primal cathartic work.

4 Practitioner leading client process into thought

For example, you propose, without immediate client cues, that the client assume and cultivate a pensive posture and see what thoughts it generates.

5 Practitioner following client content cues into emotion

For example, you note that the imagery of the client's description is becoming more evocative of the scene, and you invite him or her to enter a psychodrama on the event.

6 Practitioner following client content cues into thought

For example, you hear the client verbalizing post-cathartic insights, and ask questions to facilitate a development of these insights.

7 Practitioner following client process cues into emotion

For example, you pick up on a distress-charged body movement and invite the client to amplify it into catharsis.

8 Practitioner following client process cues into thought

For example, you pick up on a pensive cue and ask the client to verbalize his or her thought.

CHAPTER 8

CATHARSIS AND TRANSMUTATION

An alternative to the cathartic release of distress emotion is the transmutation of it. This means that the distinctively agitated, hurting energy of the distress is changed and refined into the calming, peaceful energy of a positive emotional state. And this is done by a silent, behaviourally imperceptible rearrangement of the structures of consciousness.

Whereas catharsis can clearly be elicited and facilitated, so that we have cathartic interventions, this is not so with transmutation. It is an imperceptible, internal self-help method. If you suggest its use to your client, this is what I call a catalytic self-help prescription (no. 18 in the list of catalytic interventions in Chapter 9; see also no. 8 in the same chapter). Its use presupposes you have had preparation, training and grounding in transpersonal fields.

THE PROCESS OF TRANSMUTATION

What I mean by the 'structures of consciousness' is the way in which the energies of a person's consciousness are organized (or disorganized) by its resident imagery. And by 'resident imagery' I mean the store of images and meanings in terms of which a person experiences his or her world, and which inform sensation and perception, emotion and mood, belief and appraisal, intention and action. Resident imagery exists at different levels:

1 *The level of personal history*: the individual's encounter with his or her physical and social environment from birth (or conception) onwards; the level of personal memory images.
2 *The level of cultural history*: the way in which personal history is informed with the history of the culture within which the individual has been raised and educated; the cultural content of personal memory images. By 'culture' here I mean the whole range of institutions within a society, from the economic to the religious.
3 *The level of imagination*: the way in which both personal and cultural history are informed by music, art, drama, poetry,

fiction, fable, myth, metaphysics; the imaginative content of cultural and personal memory images.

4 *The level of archetypes*: the way in which the three previous levels are informed by primordial imagery in the scheme of things that provide the basic parameters of human experience; the archetypal content of imaginative/cultural/personal memory images. I use 'archetype' in a Neoplatonic not a Jungian sense. I will refer to work at levels 3 and 4 as *imaginal* work.

Now catharsis deals with the way in which the emotional energies of consciousness have been disorganized, turned into distress, by certain images, and the meanings with which they are imbued, at levels 1 and 2. It deals with this by discharging the disorganized energy, leading to a spontaneous re-appraisal of the imagery. So the client stays in those levels and does housecleaning and healing within them.

Transmutation also deals with the disorganized emotional energies in some of the resident imagery of levels 1 and 2. But it does so by reconstruing this imagery by means of imaginal work on it from levels 3 and 4. Figure 8.1 shows the two processes as complementary poles of a figure-of-eight flow of psychic energy.

When I say 'reconstrue' (or, as in the diagram, 're-vision' and 're-evaluate') resident imagery, I mean alter the perspective of meaning on it, so that the imagery means something different to me after it has been reconstrued. I appraise it in a new light. For after all, it is how I understand a scene that determines how I feel about it. If I see it primarily as frustrating some of my needs, then I feel anger; but if I construe the same scene primarily as fulfilling some of my other needs, then I feel excitement. Such reappraisal can be direct, explicit and conscious; or more indirect, tacit and subliminal.

Catharsis first releases the disorganized emotional energy of distress, which in turn leads to a spontaneous re-evaluation of the resident imagery with which it is associated. Cathartic re-evaluation manifests a spiritual process immanent within levels 1 and 2. Transmutation first re-visions, gets a new perspective of meaning on, the resident imagery, which in turn leads to a spontaneous internal reorganization of distress emotion into a less disorganized state, or even into positive emotion. Transmutative re-visioning manifests a transcendent spiritual process that works from levels 3 and 4 into levels 1 and 2. Catharsis and transmutation are complementary and polar opposite processes.

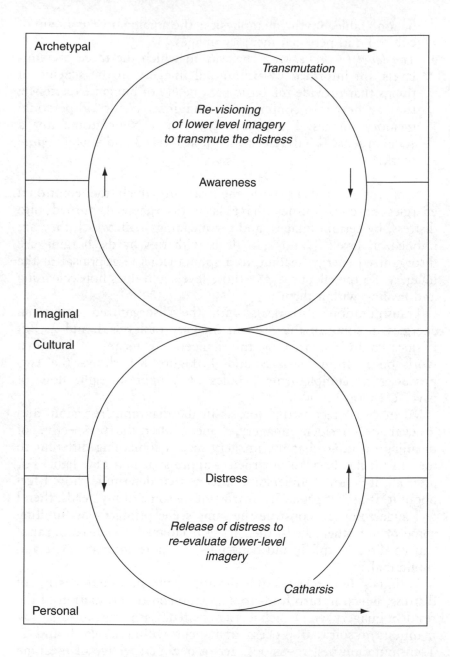

FIGURE 8.1   The complementary processes of catharsis and transmutation

Cathartic technique is a basic tool of the self-creating person, transmutative technique a basic tool of the self-transfiguring person. Both tools are needed in the process of human unfoldment.

TRANSMUTATIVE METHODS

These are all self-help methods, many of them involving purely internal mental processes. As practitioner interventions, they really fall within the next (the catalytic) chapter; see therein interventions nos. 8, 9 and 18, where you are enabling the client to work with emotions through the use of some self-discovery technique. However, these methods are not simply about working with distress emotions. Note that many of them are centrally concerned with developing the self-transfiguring state of the person. They are about deep levels of feeling, intuition, imagination, reflective contemplation and intention – which ground us in our inherent spirituality (see Chapter 3, pp. 23–25). For a comprehensive map of spiritual and subtle states, and of methods of spiritual transformation, see Heron (1998).

1 Active symbolic re-vision

Invite clients to make an art form to re-evaluate their traumas. At the level of imagination, they give symbolic form to any one or more of the distressed aspects of their life stories (with both personal and cultural content). This is not a literal re-creation as in psychodrama – which is a cathartic technique – but an imaginative restatement and reformulation, expressed in music, in painting and drawing, in drama, in dance and movement, in poetry or in biographically based fiction.

The assumption here is that the organizing power of the imagination at level 3, with its latent archetypal content at level 4, can reconstrue resident imagery at levels 1 and 2 so that its disorganizing effect on emotion is reduced.

2 Passive symbolic re-vision

Suggest to clients that they attend selected artistic events. It is the incidental function of a great deal of art, of which we are the spectators and/or audience, to have symbolic transmutative power. For we implicitly project our own agendas into the poem, drama, picture, music, dance, novel; and the more commanding the imaginative power over form and process in these creations, the greater their effect in reconstruing the resident imagery of our hidden distress agendas at levels 1 and 2, and in reorganizing the associated emotions into a more harmonious mode.

3 Imaginal work with core passion and vision

The client may have an imaginative vision of a certain possibility for his or her life which has hovered in the sidelines for a long time, kept in the wings by distressed attitudes. You can encourage the client to uncover, affirm, develop and above all realize this vision, this central passion, this life-dream. Once it is realized in living, then its formative presence, simply through the process of living it, can work to reconstrue some of the resident imagery at levels 1 and 2 and so transmute the negative energy of the distress associated with it. This formative potential of soul I also call 'the archetype of personal destiny' (see catalytic intervention no. 15, Chapter 9).

4 Imaginal restructuring of belief systems

Belief systems are acquired at levels 1 and 2, are organized around deeply ingrained perceptual imagery, and some are charged with distress emotion. This distress is the glue holding together negative and restrictive beliefs, which limit how we perceive ourselves, other people and the world. You support the client to use creative, active imagination to restructure these restrictive beliefs into an alternative system and re-educate his or her mind to perceive the world, to feel, think and act within it, in terms of the new system (Heron, 1992, pp. 148–9). This system, generated at levels 3 and 4, starts to reconstrue resident imagery at levels 1 and 2 and reduce its distorting effect on emotional energy.

5 Imaginal restructuring of self-perception

This is a particular application of no. 4. When clients have a lot of negative emotions about their self, as an alternative to discharging the distress of old external invalidations which they have since internalized, you encourage them to see their present state not as the distressed outcome of past oppression, but as the receptive opening for liberating possibilities streaming in from the future; or to see their shadow side not as something bad to be deprecated and cast out, but as a loam or humus to be positively accepted as a nutrient source of growth; or simply to focus in a sustained way on their strengths. This imaginal restructuring of one's negative self-image is intended to transmute the distress associated with it, whereas the use of contradiction (no. 13 in the cathartic list, Chapter 7) is intended to discharge distress emotion.

6 Imaginal restructuring of events

Perception of particular situations is at level 1, against the backdrop of level 2. When clients perceive a particular situation as distressing, an alternative to cathartic work on it is to invite them to reconstrue how they perceive the situation. They hold the distress awarely in mind, without trying to do anything directly to or with the emotion. Then, by an imaginal act at levels 3 and 4, they learn to see the situation in a new light: its imagery is cast in a totally different perspective of meaning. And this changes the organization of the emotional energy attached to the old perspective. Thus a situation first construed as a debilitating threat, can be re-construed as an invigorating challenge.

7 Reversing the image internal to distress

Distress emotion itself has an image internal to it: something dark, murky, turgid, agitated. Invite the client to take the focus of his or her attention right into the heart of the murky distress emotion, and hold it there as the image of a bright light bulb. If the client sustains this, gently but persistently for long enough, the distress image will be completely reorganized into one of clarity, and the distress emotion transmuted into positive emotion. The knack is to maintain inner alertness without becoming entangled. This is an ancient oriental method.

8 Archetypal imagination

The client can explore his or her own relation to archetypal images by an exercise in active imagination about interacting with them. You can guide and prompt the client through a conscious symbolic day-dream, a spontaneous, unscripted story of interweaving with images of wisdom, folly, birth, death, necessity, man, woman, love, light, darkness and so on. This will reconstrue lower level imagery and transmute its associated emotional energies.

9 Charismatic expression

This is a dynamic way in which the client can manifest their interaction with the archetypal parameters of human existence. You invite the client to engage in here and now creative improvisation, exploring their relationship with what there is – with being in its many modes and dimensions – through the archetypal meaning of posture, gesture, movement, sound and breath, and through the declaration of verbal assertions and metaphors. This improvisation may include elements from nos. 10 to 13 inclusive below. For more on charismatic expression see the section below, Primary theatre.

Such improvisation integrates the movement of immanent, indwelling spiritual life with the impact of dynamic archetypes, transforming lower-level imagery and transmuting emotional energies. A similar effect, though less powerful, is through traditional formalized and pre-designed systems of posture and movement such as Tantric mudras and Tai Chi. A halfway house between the improvised and the formalized is found in my workshops on charismatic training (for a full account see Heron, 1999: ch. 12).

10 Reflective contemplation

Invite the client to dwell reflectively in archetypal symbols such as mandalas, the tetragrammaton and others, to achieve a subtle transmutative effect. This reflective indwelling means allowing the symbol to resonate with associations and meanings within the depths of the mind.

11 Disidentification

Invite the client to invoke the archetype of his or her self as a principality and power of consciousness that is beyond the range and claims of distress emotions. 'My everyday self has distress emotions; I am not distress emotions; I am consciousness as such.' More generally, invite the client to trace his or her 'I' to its source in an absolute, ineffable awareness beyond all name and form. This transcendental perspective reorganizes lower-level imagery and emotional energy.

12 Cosmic identification

Invite the client to invoke archetypal knowledge of the universe as a vast interrelated system on many levels and with many dimensions of being, by declaring – in speech, gesture, posture and movement – an identification with this, that or the other entity, presence, principality or power. Again this perspective rearranges the resident imagery on levels 1 and 2, and reorganizes the energy of any distress emotion associated with that imagery.

13 Worship

Invite the client to open to ecstatic encounter with the transcendental Thou through praise, high prayer, numinous adoration; and in everyday life, to practise enjoying the presence of God/dess as the reality of interconnectedness, as the go-between divinity.

14 Concentration

Invite the client to hold attention focused for a long time on one image, whether physically perceived or mentally visualized, and to trace that image back to its original source in consciousness-as-such, thus entering a primordial perspective that reorganizes lower-level imagery and its associated emotional energy.

15 Witnessing

Invite the client simply to notice and watch and not identify at all with distress emotion, so that the imagery that generates it will be reconstrued enough for it to transmute. A less focused version of no. 7.

16 Switching

Invite the client to switch out of a situation or activity charged with the projected distress of one sort of resident imagery, and to move into another kind of situation or activity charged with the positive emotion of another kind of resident imagery. This may kick back some rearrangement to the abandoned area.

17 The transmutative process cue

Sometimes the client spontaneously assumes a posture or makes a gesture that has spiritual significance, like a mudra, one of the consciousness-changing postures in oriental yoga. You can ask them to stay with it and develop it, finding the words that go with it. This may be the start of transmutative work. More imperceptibly, there may be a significant pause: a silence that is luminous with spiritual overshadowing.

18 The transmutative content cue

Occasionally, the client may unintentionally say a word or a phrase, or cut a sentence short, in a way that reveals a sudden breakthrough into an altered state of consciousness. The slight and brief aperture will close again quickly, so you move deftly and invite the person to repeat and elaborate the words, expanding awareness into an extraordinary state through the unexpected gap.

PRIMARY THEATRE

'Primary theatre' is another name for 'charismatic expression', no. 9 in the above list. It is a spiritual practice based on the following assumptions:

- I have my own original relation with creation, with what there is.
- Revelation is now, in my immediate present experience of what arises at this time and place.
- Spiritual authority is within me.
- I can use posture, gesture, movement, sound and breath as an original language for exploring and expressing my relation with what there is.
- I can use verbal metaphors to elaborate that expressive language.
- My spiritual enlivenment is an ongoing process, starting now as I open myself to, and actively express, my intrinsic connectedness with what there is.
- I am included within, and am at the crest of, the living process of divine becoming.

This is a form of first person inquiry (Torbert, 2000) and a method of enlivenment. I respond to the spontaneous promptings of my indwelling spiritual life, giving dynamic form and voice to, and inquiring into, my immediate relation with what there is. I explore, reveal and affirm, in non-verbal and verbal ways, my primary, original participation in creation. Primary theatre works with the depth, breadth and height of participative feeling and participative intuition (Chapter 3, p. 22). It integrates (a) immanent spirit, the dynamic presence within, (b) transcendent spirit, and the archetypal world above, and (c) the here and now phenomenal world.

TAKING A TURN

I, your client, may take a turn, with your support and occasional prompting:

- Stepping out of and transforming ordinary, culturally conditioned ways of being.

- Originating authentic forms of posture, movement, sound and speech; liberating and reclaiming metaphor and analogy, the revelatory power of verbal symbols.
- Gifting you and other beings present, sharing with, revealing to, and interacting with you all.

In these ways I am engaged in:

- Releasing, expressing and celebrating personal presence and connectedness; remembering my original and archetypal self, rejoicing in who I am.
- Opening to being, cosmic presence, our go-between divinity.
- Opening to powers and presences, interrelating different levels of being.

DEGENERATE FORMS

Here are some degenerate forms of charismatic expression:

- Contracting the person into the alienated, distressed ego.
- Inhibiting personal presence, being constrained by embarrassment, and not wanting to embarrass others.
- Seducing the audience, showing off, hiding behind the props.
- Inflating the distressed ego.
- Conforming to imagined expectations, doing-it-right.
- Competing with actual or imagined other people present.

WORKING KNACKS

- Own, express and move out of embarrassment, fear, shame, avoidance, shut-down, competitiveness, copying, showing off, etc. When they are owned as included within the living process of divine becoming, they transform, dissolve and fall away.
- Explore the dramatic interface between the contracted ego and the expansive person.
- Explore fully symbolic use of posture, gesture, facial expression, eyes, movement, breathing, sound; and verbal use of metaphor, analogy, myth, story. Try things out. Explore acting into charismatic dance, sound, gesture, speech.
- Talk to, with or as, what there is in every respect without let or hindrance, or any part, aspect or dimension of it: people, culture, the audience, nature, the solar system, the galaxy, the cosmos, archetypal powers, presences, immediate experience, complementary realities, indwelling living presence, universal consciousness, the jewel in the heart . . .

- Let awareness go down into body being, the belly brain, the *hara*, centre of timing and spacing; and rather than being fully prepared in advance, let expression charismatically emerge, as in a spontaneous dance, with smooth transitions in and out of the flow, in and out of the session.
- Explore a within focus, or an interactive, connectedness focus.
- Be open to emotional processing as part of the ebb and flow.
- Take time, allow pauses, silences – for their own sake, and for gestation and emergence.

GROUP WORK

Here are some forms of primary theatre when working with a group:

- People take individual turns in a group or in pairs, each person exploring their unique relation with creation – verbally, vocally, in gesture, posture and movement. The audience gives full, supportive attention.
- One person takes an individual turn, and one or more members of the audience respond, either as discreet mirroring, or as a discreet response, or as full interaction.
- Group members are expressive together non-verbally, with vocal toning, gesture and movement. They may do their individual thing, resonating with each other side by side, or explicitly interact, as moved.
- Group members are expressive together verbally, each being a spokesperson for an archetypal power or a presence.
- Two people explore verbalized co-visualization, focusing on some entity within, or aspect of, creation, such as a planet within the solar system.

LEAN RITUAL

The group as a whole explores its original relation with creation, collaborating in the design and execution of a ritual. The leanest rituals are free of any explicit theology, that is, any language or artefacts which are loaded with ancient or modern religious beliefs. They are designed using only the primal metaphoric meaning of basic gestures and simple words and everyday objects such as flower, leaf, key, bell.

Thus the group may choose to stand in a circle with arms reaching upward and say 'above', then kneel to touch the ground and say 'below', then stand and cross their hands over the heart and say 'within', finally reach out to take the hands of those on either side and say 'between'. Or each person in turn may hold up a key to the next person saying 'This is a key', touch it from heart to heart, and pass it on. Innumerable versions of a lean ritual can be designed by a group open to the presence of being.

The group, through you and three or four members building on and modifying each other's proposals, will quickly get a feel for a well-rounded lean ritual. Have a couple of practice runs, with feedback, which may lead to one or two more changes.

Lean ritual generates a subtle sense of shared sacred space and creates a method for inquiring into the coming into being of such a space. Other rituals may awarely adopt and integrate elements drawn from a variety of sources, ancient and modern. These elements are always adapted and reframed for use in a context of independent inquiry.

BENEFITS OF PRIMARY THEATRE AND LEAN RITUAL

- Primary theatre practices are forms of enlivenment. They complement, and fulfil in outward action, the inward practices of attunement, such as high prayer and meditation, which are traditional forms of enlightenment. They may also lead over into such inward practices.
- They nourish us, and they empower us to bring the spiritual into our everyday life. Thus:
- They help develop charismatic presence and timing at home and at work and at play.
- They can be built directly into the the process of mothering and fathering, and of education at all levels.

CATHARSIS OR TRANSMUTATION?

There remains the important question of the relative weight to be given to either catharsis or transmutation in practice.

1 *Both are needed.* They work in complementary and mutually supporting ways.
2 *Exclusive use of either has distorting effects.* Thus, if you rely entirely on transmutation, there is the danger of deep-seated distress remaining denied, contracted and congealed, causing a distorted, dissociated or inflated kind of spirituality to develop. And if you rely exclusively on catharsis, there is the danger that frustrated spiritual energy will continuously inflate the

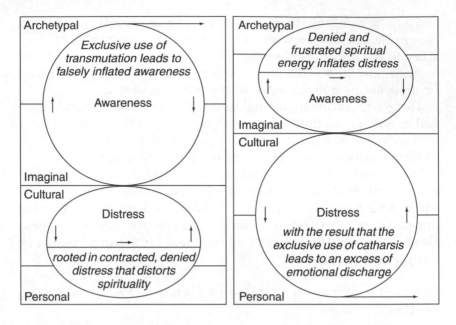

FIGURE 8.2   Distorting effects of the exclusive use of either transmutation or catharsis

cathartic process, causing an excess of emotional discharge. Figure 8.2 illustrates these two possibilities.

3   *Catharsis is important as the first step.* I believe that some things have to be worked through at their own level. You cannot entirely resolve unfinished business at one level by working at it from a higher one. Not all personal/cultural distress can be transmuted by imaginal/archetypal work; some of it simply has to be catharted at the level where it was laid in. So it seems a sensible idea to start with this; then it does not get forgotten or left behind or covered over with transcendental gloss. Catharsis and the very personal insight it generates establish and affirm human autonomy on a bedrock basis. It is a basic tool for the self-creating person.

4   *Transmutation is important as the second step.* Of course, it is going on all the time in minor ways: the imaginative content that informs any culture sees to that through drama, stories, films, rituals and so on. But it can become much more intentional in personal growth work. And it is important because, equally, I do not believe that you can deal with all personal/cultural distress at its own level by catharsis. To believe so is to get trapped on the cathartic treadmill, which is yet another version of the materialistic fallacy, the idea that everything has

to be worked through at the material level, with something bodily going on. So transmutative work both helps clean up the personal/cultural domains, while at the same time opening up wider vistas of imaginal, archetypal reality. It is a basic tool for celebrating the emergence of the self-transfiguring person.

CHAPTER 9

CATALYTIC INTERVENTIONS

Defined for general use, catalytic interventions seek to elicit self-discovery, self-directed living, learning and problem-solving in the client. Those in no. 6 below can be applied intensively in every helping role.

Catalytic interventions are central to personal-developmental work with people. Their purpose is to facilitate self-directed living, to help people become more responsible for who and what they are, to gain greater control over their lives. This means eliciting in the client learning about how to live: how to handle emotions; how to reduce the effect of past trauma and social conditioning; how to think and act in different ways in different sorts of situations; how to relate to other people; how to deal with exigencies and crises; how to plan a life-style; how to change and grow; how to enter altered states of consciousness, manage subtle energy, become spiritually attuned. In terms of the states of personhood described in Chapter 3 (pp. 25–32), the client is learning how to become a creative, or self-creating or self-transfiguring person, as distinct from a compulsive and conventional one. There is a considerable overlap between the content of this chapter and the recent emergence of coaching as a form of helping. There is an overview of coaching at the end of the chapter.

Catalytic interventions need complementing, in personal-growth work, with informative ones that offer ideas about human nature, processes of personal growth and descriptions of mental and behavioural skills. They also need supplementing with confronting and cathartic ones.

In what follows I shall outline first the experiential learning cycle; secondly, agendas for experiential learning; thirdly, a map of values; and finally, a list of catalytic interventions. For a very useful general purpose map of the client's 'psychological field', see intervention no. 7 below.

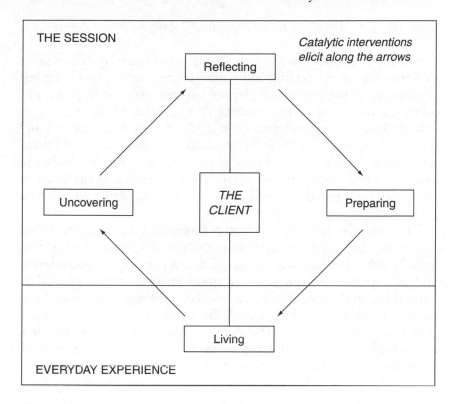

FIGURE 9.1 The experiential learning cycle

THE EXPERIENTIAL LEARNING CYCLE

In their session with you, the practitioner, clients can learn more about how to live by uncovering and reflecting on their past experience, and by preparing to take this learning back into living their future experience. They apply their new-found awareness in everyday action, expressing it by developing new skills. So they learn about living not only from times of reflection, but also by a continuous activity of practising how to feel, think and act in different situations. They can thus move between learning from living and living their learning. This is the experiential learning cycle and it is shown in Figure 9.1.

'Uncovering' in this diagram means recalling some experience in full, exploring one's emotions about it and one's understanding of what was going on. 'Reflecting' means pondering on the uncovered experience, getting insight into it, learning about oneself, others and the world through it. 'Preparing' means getting ready to take this learning back into living. For a more extended account of these three in different terms, see no. 7 below, and Chapter 12, p. 169.

Not many people see living as experiential learning. They see it as suffering, or as feeling guilt and blame, or as surviving, or competing, or the pursuit of pleasure, or the exercise of power, or doing their duty, or as many other things. None of these things is excluded from living as learning: it is all a matter of awareness and intent. Thus, seeing life as suffering is low in awareness and intent, whereas seeing life as learning how to suffer is altogether higher in awareness and intent; and similarly with seeing life as the exercise of power, compared to seeing life as learning how to exercise power.

The 'learning how to' adds the dimension of awareness and intent: it raises a person's life into the creative, and beyond that, into the self-creating mode. It establishes a perspective on suffering and power; it raises questions of good and bad ways, as well as competent and incompetent ways, of suffering and exercising power. In short, it raises questions of norms or standards for action, and of values for the ends of action. Being self-directed, living with awareness and intent means we are making internal choices about norms and values to guide our external actions.

AGENDAS FOR EXPERIENTIAL LEARNING

These agendas constitute a simple map to guide you around the basic territory when helping anyone to learn how to live. It is a map with three times five, i.e. fifteen, quadrants. There are three obvious areas of living – present, past and future – and for each of these areas there are five aspects to consider. The three basic areas are:

1 *Review of current experience*: you enable clients to talk out, resolve or ponder issues within the thrust of their current range of experience.
2 *Assessment of past experience*: you enable clients to assess whether they have learnt something, or what they have learnt, or how well they have learnt something, from past experience in this or that area of living.
3 *Planning future experience*: you enable clients to explore future possibilities for living, to decide with what else in the wide universe of human experience they could learn to engage in ways that might be interesting, fruitful and fulfilling.

For each of the above three areas, the practitioner can enable the client, as appropriate, to cover one or more of the following five aspects:

1 *Purposes of living*: What are clients living for? Is it for power, profit, pleasure, social service, self-realization? Do they have compulsive and conventional goals; or creative, or self-creating or self-transfiguring goals?

2 *Life-style*: How are clients going about realizing these objectives? What are the different facets of their life-style? Are they active or inactive, satisfied or dissatisfied, in the manifold areas of living, from their occupation and domicile, through intimacy, to political engagement and spiritual unfoldment?

3 *Resources for living*: What human support, what social and physical resources of different kinds, what potential within, have they marshalled in order to enhance their life-style?

4 *Life-plan*: How are they pacing themselves, and over what time scale, in relation to each strand in their current life-style? Are there any stages or steps for a given strand? And how are the strands integrated into a balanced and manageable mode of life?

5 *Constraints*: What are the limits and difficulties within the client and their situation, in respect of any one or more of the above four aspects; which of these limits appear to be alterable and how can they be changed; which of them appear to be immovable and how can things be modified accordingly?

The whole map is shown in Figure 9.2. By gradually enabling people to use more and more quadrants of this fifteen-part map, and initiating them into its use, you are facilitating their self-direction in living.

Sometimes you will follow clients who are already moving into some quadrant of the map; sometimes you will lead them into a quadrant whose relevance has not yet occurred to them. But whether following or leading, you only use the quadrant to facilitate self-exploration and self-direction. You do not use it to prescribe or to inform or interpret.

Living-as-learning means great awareness and intent. In this respect, the emerging self-directing person waxes and wanes. Sometimes the person innovates, developing and unfolding new learning; at other times he or she reverts to a steady state of habituation based on past learning. Living is rhythmic, periodic, with alternating phases of expansion and contraction, of momentum and inertia.

	Purposes	Life-style	Resources	Life-plan	Constraints
Current experience					
Past experience					
Future experience					

FIGURE 9.2   Map of experiential learning agendas

More radically, the learning person is embedded in a chaotic loam of nescience and disorder; or, to change the metaphor, is unripe in those areas not yet exposed to the sun of learning.

A MAP OF VALUES

Since, as we have seen, living-as-learning raises questions of choosing standards and values, you, the practitioner, in facilitating self-direction, are facilitating a person's choice of values. This is not simply inescapable, it is essential. But it means that you and the client need to form a community of value. You cannot conscientiously help someone to learn how to live a life that you regard as disvaluable. And equally, no one will be morally happy at being facilitated in terms of values of which they disapprove. So you need to get clear what values you stand for, and to tell the client what they are, so that both of you can find out whether you can do business together. Learning how to live is very much about choice. And in this domain, there seem to me to be four fundamental and interdependent values. They are the positive opposites, respectively, of the compulsive states of rebel, rescuer, oppressor and victim, mentioned in Chapter 3 (pp. 33 and 35).

1 *Autonomy*: I decide things for myself, in the light of norms and values which I have awarely chosen. Disvalues here include compulsive rebelliousness, affected eccentricity, anarchic individualism.
2 *Co-operation*: We decide things together for ourselves, in the light of decision procedures, norms and values which we have awarely chosen. Disvalues here include unaware conformity, peer collusion, peer pressure, messy democracy, compulsive rescuing.

FIGURE 9.3 A map of values set in their total context

3 *Active hierarchy (leading)*: I decide things for others on their behalf and in their interests, in the light of norms and values I have awarely chosen. The norms will include norms about whether or not it is appropriate to consult those on whose behalf I choose. Disvalues here include oppression, exploitation, cultivation of dependency in others.
4 *Passive hierarchy (following)*: I decide in the light of norms and values I have awarely chosen, to accept a hierarchical decision made for me on my behalf, by some other person or persons. Disvalues here include compulsive submission, powerlessness, unaware dependency.

These four kinds of choice can be applied in five different areas: within the person among parts of the self; in face-to-face relations with others; in organizations; in relation to the psychic and spiritual domains; and all this within the planetary environment. They supplement the client categories given on p. 33.

So, in the light of Figure 9.3, learning how to live is at least something about learning how to realize and balance in one's life the four sorts of choice, in the five areas shown. The map correlates,

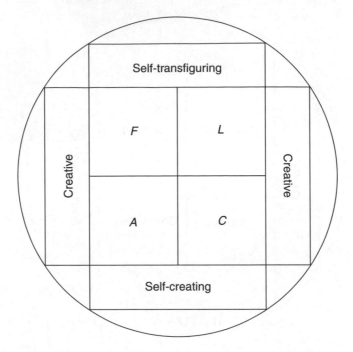

FIGURE 9.4   The four values and the three intentional states of personhood

too, with the three intentional states of personhood described in Chapter 3 (pp. 29–32), and this is shown in Figure 9.4.

There is one final thought about this map. Passive hierarchies are of two kinds. There is the passive hierarchy in the explicit social system of which we are a daily part, where we decide to accept decisions made for us on our behalf by administrators in this, that or the other association – from the social club to the state. Alternatively, we may decide not to accept the decisions they have made on our behalf, and then we are in the business of social protest and social change.

But there is also the passive hierarchy in the tacit universe, in the other reality, where we have a sense of *dharma*, a path, a way, an unfolding of events, and where we decide to wait on the emergence in this world of our part in a comprehensive programme that seems to have been devised in another.

Of course, passive hierarchies of this latter sort are notoriously problematic, since they can be confused with all kinds of deluded, superstitious and neurotic material; and if they exist, there may be nasty ones as well as nice ones. Nevertheless, it is clear that some people do make critical decisions in the light of this concept.

CATALYTIC INTERVENTIONS

In what follows, many interventions deal with living-as-learning. Some are all-purpose, for use in relation to past, present or future learning of any sort. Others deal with only certain aspects or areas. It is clear from the description of the intervention, or in some cases its name, which is which. The 'basic catalytic tool-kit' is provided by the first 11 interventions included under no. 6 below, eliciting self-directed learning. This is one of several entries which subsume a set or gradient of interventions.

The assumption underlying the many interventions that follow is that there is within the client an overarching *vision* of possibilities for his or her human flourishing; and an indwelling *ground* of dynamic motivation, which generates creative impulses about liberating behaviour in any and every situation. So the basic purpose of any catalytic intervention, when all is said and done, is to support clients in opening to the interaction between their vision and their creative ground.

1 Making a life-style map

You sit down with the client and together draw up a map which shows all the major aspects of living, including those in which the person both is and is not active. This map can then be a basis for a systematic review of current and past learning from living, and for planning future learning from living. It can include the following categories: domicile and cohabitation; occupation; career prospects; money and finance; social roles/class/status; education and training; professional and personal development; recreation, fun and pleasure; sexuality; gender; the physical body, health and hygiene; emotional and physical traumas; personal relationships – intimate, family of origin, parenthood, social, professional; support networks; verbal and social skills; pursuit of knowledge; political and social-change awareness and commitment; artistic appreciation and activity; psi and the psychic; spiritual aspiration and activity.

You can negotiate with the client a self-discovery trip around this map over several sessions, in relation to current, past or future experience. Is the person active or inactive in an area, satisfied or dissatisfied with the activity or with the inactivity; and is some kind of change wanted? To guide the self-discovery and help it be fruitful, you have at the back of your mind the experiential learning agendas map (Figure 9.2), with its various quadrants (see also no. 15 below).

2 Making a negative life-style map

If the client is surprised at the living-as-learning notion and has been living with relative unawareness, you suggest that they draw up a map showing the different sorts of things they have been living life as: such as social-role stereotypes, compulsive victim/rebel/rescuer/oppressor, and so on. You can help the person explore what it has really been like living life like this, and what motivations and aspirations emerge out of such an exploration. This intervention may, of course, also be intermittently confronting.

3 Making a map of one part of a life-style

If clients are going in depth into one area of their total life-style you can work with them to map out the major aspects of that area; or you can simply present them with a ready-made map and let them get familiar with it and modify or amend it. You help people use the map to deepen their self-discovery. The map itself may also be highly informative to the client; but its basic use is catalytic.

A sexuality map might include: sexual conditioning, sexual fears, inhibition and dysfunction; sexual phantasies; sexual likes, dislikes, secret wishes; sexual expression and fulfilment; masturbation; celibacy; fertility and procreation; menstruation; puberty, menopause, andropause; sexual attraction; sexual contracts; sex and speech; sex, love, affection and nurturance; sex and celebration; sex and spirituality.

Note that the point about all these maps is that they need to be used with great discretion. First, the map is never the territory. Secondly, the client's reality needs to be very much in the foreground, with the map in the background. It is bad news when a person's experience becomes subordinate to the map and is used just to feed it and fill it in. Sometimes it is best to produce the categories of the map piecemeal, as and when they seem to fit the reality the individual unfolds. Thirdly, the map is dispensable at any time, but the client's reality never.

The criteria for map-making are twofold. First, the categories of the map need to be comprehensive so that the whole field is covered. The catalytic power of the maps depends on their range in covering diverse domains of living, especially so when they are used to consider possibilities for future learning. Secondly, the maps need to make sense to the client, to include their own categories and constructs where relevant. People must feel at ease in using them to chart their self-discovery.

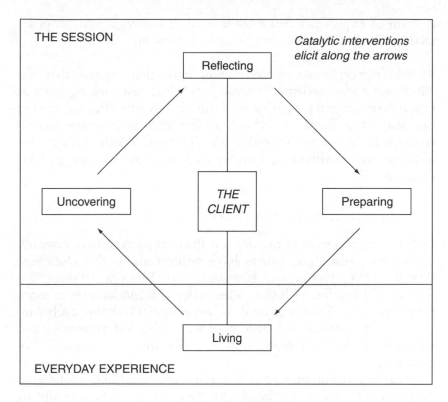

FIGURE 9.5   The experiential learning cycle

4 Using the experiential learning cycle

Whether clients are considering current, past or future experience, you can enhance their self-discovery by inviting them, through questions and other catalytic interventions, to think in terms of the experiential learning cycle. I reproduce again here the diagram from the introduction, in Figure 9.5.

In this cycle, the individual moves between experience and reflection, to and fro, with a two-way influence. After living a certain kind of experience, a person takes time out to uncover its nature, reflect on it, get some insight into it, and this in turn influences how the person prepares to go back into that same domain of experience (or in some cases, whether he or she does go back in). Each session with the practitioner is itself a reflection phase, a processing of current or past experience, followed by preparation for future experience. The impact of the reflection phase on preparation for future action is either conservative or innovative: if conservative, it confirms continuing on in the domain of experience being considered; if innovative, it proposes changes in that domain, or changes of domain.

4.1 First person action research   You may also suggest that the client uses the experiential learning cycle not just looking back at past behaviour and preparing for future behaviour after the session but also as a form of self-monitoring and first person action research in his or her everyday life (Torbert, 2000). This means noticing and modifying behaviour as it is going on (see p. 241, Chapter 15).

5 Using the co-operative inquiry model

Full-blown co-operative inquiry is a form of participative research on persons, and I and others have written about this elsewhere (Heron, 1996; Heron and Reason, 2000; Reason, 1988, 1994; Reason and Bradbury, 2000). When using this model, two or more people go several times around the experiential learning cycle (no. 4 above) in a formal and structured way, with full awareness and intent, in order to inquire systematically into some domain of experience.

Occasionally you may be able to point the client in the following direction. The client may be able to participate in relationships or enterprises with others, in ways that constitute an informal co-operative inquiry. So you have a group of people who are awarely and intentionally doing their living-as-learning together. They are consciously using, in a co-operative way, the experience–reflection cycle in their daily lives. They plan to live or work in a certain way for a period, and having done so they meet together to reflect on their learning. They then apply this learning in a new plan of action, and so on. In a full-blown co-operative inquiry, daily living-as-learning and formal inquiry become the same.

A more radical suggestion: you and your client can launch a co-operative inquiry into one or more aspects of your practitioner–client relationship.

6 Eliciting self-directed learning

We now come to a bedrock range of interventions that provide the behavioural basis of all your catalytic work, whatever the issue, the area or aspect of living-as-learning. They are all very simple and go together as a set of everyday working tools. Their purpose is to elicit the client's self-directed learning about living, or about specific topics, and to do so with the minimal behaviour from you. They enable you, if you use them well, both to be highly effective and to maintain a very low profile. So here is the 'catalytic tool-kit'.

6.1 Be here now This is the everyday mystical one. You are centred, present, with your awareness unencumbered, in the moment that is now. It is nothing to do with your talk or social behaviour; but it is all to do with how you are being. You are not distracted by concerns to do with the past or the future. You are fully aware of what is present, but not caught up in it or anxiously engaged with it. You are intensely *in* the moment, and yet not at all *of* it.

Some simple bodily adjustments can aid entry into this state: you can relax your breathing and deepen it a bit; you can let go of all unnecessary muscular tension in your posture; you can relax the anus; you can find a posture that feels both comfortable and attentive. But the state is not to do with your body, it is to do with inner alertness. To use a metaphor, you are awake to the moment, not distractedly dreaming it. You have presence and are grounded in your innate spiritual capacity for feeling the presence of what there is. Hence you can:

6.2 Be there now The previous state seems to me to be a precondition of all effective catalytic behaviours. One reason for this is to do with the mystical principle of the identity of the centre of being with the circumference of being. So to be here now is very much also to be there now. When you are attuned to your own centre, you are already very open to the other. Within the 'I' is found the divine reality of the unifying relation with the 'Thou' (Buber, 1937).

6.3 Giving free attention This is the extension from being here now within the self, to being there now with the other. When you are here now, you have abundant free attention, which is not enslaved by past, present or future content, and which can dwell with and energize your client. You have active and directed presence.

This is a subtle and intense activity of your consciousness mediated by gaze, posture, facial expression, sometimes touch. It has the qualities of being supportive of the essential being and worth of clients independent of anything they say or do; of being expectant, waiting for the potential fullness of the person to emerge in ways that are meaningful and fulfilling; of being wider and deeper than the content of their speech, encompassing all their body cues, their whole way of being and doing, their total living reality. It is also relaxed and a little laid back. It overlaps with *Being supportive* (p. 154).

6.4 Simple echoing   You echo back the last word, or the last few words, the client said before pausing. The words are echoed back just as stated, or perhaps slightly rephrased, and without any interrogative inflection (i.e. not as an indirect question), and without any inflection that carries some judgement or value-loading from you. Simple echoing is a way of conveying to people attention, interest and above all an invitation to develop the theme in any way that they find meaningful. So they can go on talking on their own chosen path, whereas any question, however open, leads them off in a certain direction.

6.5 Selective echoing   You are listening very fully and with fine tuning to the whole of what the client is saying. You then reflect or echo back something not at the end but from the middle of the client's talk, some word or phrase that carries an emotional charge or stands out as significant in its context. Again there is no interrogative inflection or any other kind of inflection on your echo. It gives space for the person who so wishes to explore more fully, and in any chosen direction, the hidden implications of the reflected word or phrase. Selective echoing is usually used to follow the speaker deeper into territory he or she already inhabits. But it can be used to echo something that leads the person into new territory.

6.6 Open questions/6.7 Closed questions   A simple but central polar pair of interventions. The open question does not have one correct answer, but gives plenty of space for the client to come up with several possible answers, for example 'What do you remember about your first school?' The closed question only permits of one answer, the right one, for example 'What was the name of your first school?' The distinction between open and closed is not an absolute one. Some questions are ambiguous, for example 'Do you believe in school?' – a person may hear this as open or closed. And there are degrees of openness (or closure), for example 'What do you remember about your first school?' is more open than 'What do you remember about the headmistress of your first school?'

   In general, open questions tend to be more catalytic than closed questions simply because they give more scope for self-directed exploration and discovery. But there is no hard and fast rule: it depends on the context and the timing. In any case, the skilled practitioner can ask both open and closed questions as and when appropriate, and can control the degree of openness on open questions.

Highly anxious practitioners, compulsive helpers, often have difficulty with mastering open questions: their anxiety contracts their questioning into the closed form. Hence, they may have harassed or anxious clients (or students) worrying about whether they dare give an answer in case they get it wrong.

Questions, whether open or closed, need to be client-centred, tuned in to the individual's reality, and not practitioner-centred ones that derive from your curiosity or determination to be proved right, and so on. And, whether open or closed, they can either follow where the client is going, or lead into new territory. They can also be used with confronting intent, about some defensive attitude.

6.8 Empathic divining   When a client says something that has an implicit emotion, thought or intention which is lurking between the lines and which is not fully expressed, you divine this unstated content and put it back to them. So if they say, in a certain context, and with a certain kind of tone and inflection, 'I can't say any more', then you may say 'It seems as though you are quite frightened'. You are divining that part of the speaker's attitude of mind that is just below the surface of what he or she is saying, and is affecting the way it is being said. It may be an emotion, a belief or an intention, or some mixture of these.

You will pick it up mainly from the form of words and the tone of voice, aided perhaps by facial and other bodily cues. You express it always as a statement, never as a question, with an opening such as 'It sounds/seems as though you . . .'. You can also use it when a person is not speaking, but full of facial and other bodily cues; then you say 'It looks/seems as though you . . .'.

This intervention often needs a little practice before people get it right. It is a very precise test of empathy. The key to success is only to divine what is actually emerging between the lines. Sometimes you may put back something that goes way down below any lurking content, and this throws the speaker in too deep too soon. Sometimes you may 'divine' your own projected agenda.

Empathic divining overlaps with giving a simple ascription *interpretation* (see Chapter 5, p. 54). But the latter can go beyond empathic divining and penetrate to something that is hidden by the lines, not just showing through them.

Empathic divining can also be used with confronting intent and effect, to raise consciousness in speakers about some emerging attitude in themselves that they are defensively trying not to acknowledge. When applied to distress-charged statements and distress-charged facial and other bodily cues, it may also be used with cathartic effect, bringing the distress further up towards, or even into, discharge.

6.9 Checking for understanding   This intervention, a special case of empathic divination, is only used when clients, groping for words, say something confused or contradictory. You try to divine what they want to say, tidy up their statement to express this clearly, and put it back to them with the preface, 'Let me see, are you saying that . . .'. Then the speaker can either agree; or disagree, clarify what they meant, and get back on a more coherent course; or explore the confusion.

6.10 Paraphrasing   You rephrase in your own words something important which the client has expressed. This manifests solidarity, shows you are really listening and understanding. And it gives speakers a chance to check their formulation against yours, and so find out if they have said what they really wanted to say. This is on a smaller scale than:

6.11 Logical marshalling   Whereas empathic divining deals with what is between the lines, logical marshalling deals with what is in the lines of what clients have said. You organize the explicit content of a whole chapter of their talk, summarize it, perhaps interrelate parts of it, perhaps indicate directions in which it seems to be leading, and put all this back succinctly. This may prompt speakers to reconsider what they have said, and express different perspectives on it; or it may provide a springboard for some new direction.

The last 11 items, from 6.1 to 6.11, can be set out in a simple diagram which represents the basic 'catalytic tool-kit' (Figure 9.6). It is a box made up of four smaller boxes, each of which is divided diagonally into two compartments, for two related interventions of the same basic sort. All the tools can be used for *eliciting*. Empathic divining overlaps with *interpreting*, and can also be used for *confronting* and for moving towards *catharsis*. Questioning can also be used for *confronting*.

Both questioning and divining can focus on facial and other bodily cues, when a person is not speaking, as well as on content and mode of speech. Questioning can be used to follow the client, and to lead off in new directions. Selective echoing, empathic

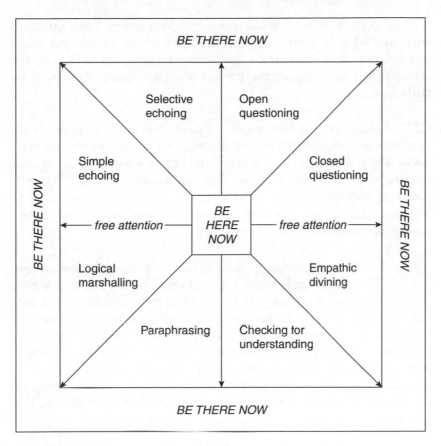

FIGURE 9.6 The catalytic tool-kit

divining and questioning can all be used to get beneath the surface of the presented speech.

6.12 Working with non-verbal cues There are important cues evident in the client's facial expression and body language. There are five basic kinds.

6.12.1 Picking up on pensive cues You ask the open question 'What are you thinking?' when a person has that typical brief reflective expression on his or her face, indicative of an inner thought process. The person may not verbalize these reflections unless asked; but when expressed they often enrich the session. Incidentally, 'What are you thinking?' is an open question rather than a closed one. There is no simple right or wrong answer. The pensive client's presenting thought is usually at the leading edge of a whole cluster of related thoughts.

6.12.2 Picking up on wanting-to-speak cues You put an open question such as 'What is your view?' to a client whose facial and other movements show that he or she wants to say something; or eye contact and bringing in the person with a hand gesture will be sufficient.

6.12.3 Picking up on emotion cues These cues may combine with pensive cues, or wanting-to-speak cues, or may be evident on their own. They show shock, surprise, delight, loving care, irritation, impatience, anxiety and so on. You can use empathic divining, 'It looks as though you . . .'; or open questioning, 'How are you feeling?' Again, the presenting emotion may well have other, sometimes quite different, facets.

6.12.4 Picking up on cathartic cues This is a special case of no. 6.12.3. The eyes, facial expression and other bodily cues show that distress emotion is coming up, moving towards discharge. The fists are clenched (anger); the lips and jaw are trembling (fear); the eyes are brimming over with tears (grief); laughter is about to break out (embarrassment). Empathic divining may bring the distress a little nearer identification, ownership, acceptance and release. So for filling eyes you may say 'It looks as though you're holding on to so much hurt and pain'. For sustained discharge, of course, you will move over into full-blown cathartic interventions.

6.12.5 Picking up on alienation cues The facial expression, and perhaps posture, show that the client is alienated, has mentally and emotionally cut out, and is sunk in his or her own negative internal process. You can use empathic divining and say 'It looks as though you . . .'; or you can gently ask an open question: 'What is going on for you right now?'

6.12.6 Picking up on transpersonal cues See Chapter 8, nos. 17 and 18.

6.13 Following, consulting, proposing or leading When it comes to opening up new territory for clients' self-discovery, there are four options:

6.13.1 They have already started to enter it and you follow.

6.13.2 You consult clients and ask where they would like to go next, with or without reference to some mutually agreed map. If they know where they want to go, then that is where they go.

6.13.3 You propose a new area and seek their assent. If they dissent, then back to preceding or on to the next.

6.13.4 Without consulting or proposing then consulting, you simply ask a question that leads the client into new territory.

The flexible practitioner will be able to use all these four as appropriate. When proposing a shift or leading into it, you do so because you divine it as seeking to emerge; or you see it as appropriate for a balanced programme; or there is a contract to cover it, or it has been left unfinished from an earlier session.

6.14 Bring in, draw out, shut out   In small-group work, you scan the group regularly with your eyes to pick up on non-verbal cues among those who are not talking. Then you can bring in a new speaker, or draw out the current speaker, or shut out the current speaker. You can *bring in* one person by eye contact, hand gesture, questioning, divining. You can *draw out* someone who is already talking by eye contact, hand gesture, echoing, questioning, divining, checking for understanding, paraphrasing, marshalling. You can *shut out* someone who is talking, with a deft gesture from one hand, while simultaneously *bringing in* someone else with your other hand: you can do this without any words, like a *traffic cop*. Or you can also add words – that is, question, divine, check for understanding, paraphrase or marshal what the current speaker has just said, and put this to someone else for comment. Thus, you keep a low profile while effectively managing contribution rates, eliciting self-discovery and interpersonal learning in the group. Figure 9.7 illustrates the possibilities.

In the top box on the left of this diagram, there are those elements of behaviour that underlie the use of the ten further items. 'Being present' means being here now, being there now and giving free attention (6.1, 6.2 and 6.3 above). 'Scanning' means continuously looking round the group to pick up non-verbal cues of the five kinds described earlier. 'Timing' means making interventions deftly and without inappropriate time-lag. 'Choice of words' refers to the diction and the grammatical form of verbal interventions. 'Paralinguistics' refers to your manner of speech and includes: emotional tone of voice; volume and pitch of sound; rhythm and rate of speech; use of inflection and emphasis; use of pauses and silence. 'Body language' covers your use of relative position, touch, posture, facial expression, gesture and eye contact. Relative position is a potent feature of facilitation: where you sit

	BRING IN	DRAW OUT	SHUT OUT
Being present SCANNING Timing Choice of words Paralinguistics Body language			
Eye contact			
Gesture: traffic cop			
Simple echoing			
Selective echoing			
Open questioning			
Closed questioning			
Empathic divining			
Checking for understanding			
Paraphrasing			
Logical marshalling			

FIGURE 9.7   Managing contribution rates

or stand in relation to the whole group or to one person with whom you are working; when and how you move from one position to another (Heron, 1999).

In the list of ten interventions, the first two are non-verbal – eye contact and gesture. These are the two non-verbal behaviours most used in controlling contribution rates and managing inter-action in a group. 'Traffic cop' typically refers to the use of simultaneous hand gestures: one hand is held up to shut out the current speaker, while the other hand is beckoning to bring in someone else.

7 Cultivating the psychological field

The client's psychological field (Figure 9.8) has three interacting areas: understanding, feeling (including emotion) and choosing. *Around* it are the values, norms and imaginative material of the person's culture. *Below* it is the psychodynamic area which includes unprocessed material of his or her childhood: frozen needs, hidden distresses, traumatic memories, that distort some parts of the field. The psychodynamic area also includes all the positive potential of the ground unconscious, the latent gifts of immanent

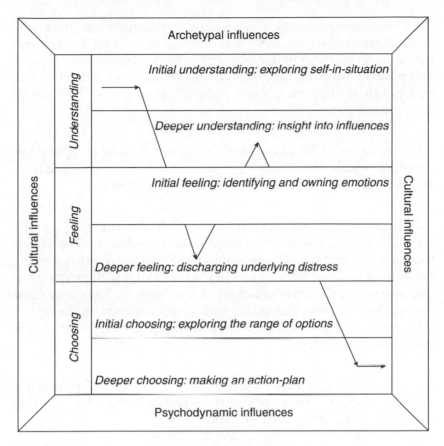

FIGURE 9.8 The client's psychological field

spirit, the entelechy or root self (Houston, 1987; Washburn, 1995). *Above* the field is the imaginal material of the person's mythology or destiny: the primordial imagery of his or her transcendent archetype that has a subtle ordering and transmutative effect on some of the energies of the field. This is rather like the ancient idea of Plotinus that there is a Platonic form for each individual soul.

The six-category practitioner will be using very many of the simple catalytic interventions given in no. 6 above ('Eliciting self-directed learning') to help the client cultivate the field, which has six parts. But the order in which they are presented here is not, as we shall see below, the order in which a person will move through them.

7.1 Initial understanding   Clients explore their self-in-the-situation, getting the lie of the land, clarifying what seems to be going on, what the real issues seem to be.

7.2 Deeper understanding   Clients get deeper insight into their self-in-the-situation, seeing how it is influenced in part by cultural material, or psychodynamic material (which includes both trauma and positive potential) or archetypal material; or in different ways by all of these. There is a major perspectival shift from their initial understanding.

7.3 Initial feeling   Clients are identifying, owning and accepting the emotions which they really have about their self-in-the situation; and they are disowning attitudes that are a pretence.

7.4 Deeper feeling   Clients are busy with the catharsis or the transmutation of distress emotions that are involved in their self-in the-situation, and with the expression of hitherto occluded positive emotion that is pertinent to it. They are working with emotions in one or more of the ways indicated in no. 8 below. They may open to feel their interconnectedness with other persons and beings in this world and in complementary realities; and to their divine potential deep within.

7.5 Initial choosing   Clients are exploring the range of behavioural options open to their self-in-the-situation and the possible outcomes of adopting each of them.

7.6 Deeper choosing   Clients are in touch with their entelechy, their formative potential and with external realities, and are selecting one option, clarifying further its possible outcomes, and making a coherent action plan relevant to self-in-the-situation. For more on deep choice see the section just below.

A classic and comprehensive client route would go from 7.1 to 7.3 to 7.4 to 7.2 to 7.5 to 7.6, as in Figure 9.8. A shorter route would be from 7.1 to 7.3 to 7.2 to 7.5 to 7.6. A still shorter route would be from 7.1 to 7.3 to 7.6. The shortest route, which most people take for relatively superficial issues in life, is to go from 7.1 to 7.6, perhaps spending some time at 7.5. Which route the client takes depends on the subject matter and its importance, the time available, other items on the agenda, their stage of unfoldment and so on.

There is no correct route. None of the routes I have listed provides a therapeutic programme that ought to be followed. The client may go every which way among the six ways, if the practitioner is following as well as leading. Nor does a person deal with issues of choosing, 7.5 and 7.6, in every session. In short, the whole thing has to be handled with great flexibility and variability. Figure 9.8 is to be regarded merely as a source of general orientation, not as a rigid schedule of procedure.

Now of course, when you are helping clients to cultivate their psychological field in these six ways, you are using more than catalytic interventions – you will be using the whole range of the six categories perhaps, including cathartic interventions in 7.4 – but the primary thrust of the enterprise is catalytic, for it is to help clients to do their own cultivation. So the majority of interventions will certainly be catalytic, and many of these will be from the basic tool-kit of no. 6 above.

DEEP CHOICE AND ENTELECHY

Deep choosing, in 7.6 above, appears to be a process of co-creating between human intention and entelechy, by which I mean the immanent formative potential of unique personhood. Carl Rogers made the idea of entelechy a basic tenet of his personality theory. He called it an actualizing tendency. He thought it was inborn in everyone as an 'inherent tendency of the organism to develop all its capacities in ways which serve to maintain or enhance the organism' (Rogers, 1959: 196). 'It is clear that the actualising tendency is selective and directional – a constructive tendency' (Rogers, 1980: 121). It affects both body and mind, and with respect to the latter, it guides people toward increased autonomy, expanded experience and inner growth. Virtually the same idea is found in Maslow, as a self-actualizing need, 'the desire to become more and more what one idiosyncratically is, to become everything one is capable of becoming' (Maslow, 1970: 46). Koestler (1964, 1978) and systems theorists see entelechy as a polarity of autonomous and participatory tendencies; as I do (Chapter 3, p. 25; Heron, 1992).

Jean Houston writes eloquently of entelechy as 'that dynamic purposiveness coded in ourselves, longing for unfoldment and expression. It is the possibility of our next stage of growth and evolution entering into time . . . This Entelechy Self is also the supreme orchestrator and ground of all one's other selves, and serves as the protector and provider of balance and mental health amid the complex and polyphrenic structure of one's inner life. It is the Root Self, the ground of one's being, and the seeded coded essence in you which contains both the patterns and the possibilities of your life' (Houston, 1987: 31).

If there is an archetype of the person in the wider reaches of universal consciousness, then the entelechy is its seeded, embedded representative. It is our capacity for feeling, working as a deep, formative presence within us, the guiding voice of immanent divinity. It emerges into actuality in different states of personhood, the spontaneous, the compulsive, the conventional, the creative, the self-creating and the self-transfiguring; and orchestrates them in an idiosyncratic pattern of development. It is emerging through the wounding and pathology of the compulsive person because, in this epoch at any rate, these are profound sources of the later growth of the self-creating person. It asks only to be both asked and listened to. There have been various techniques for tapping directly into it.

E-Therapy was one (Kitselman, 1953). 'Greatness is in us; how can we let it out? . . . greatness can let itself out; it only needs to be asked.' Kitselman then outlines a simple technique for asking E, the inner voice, which will respond in terms of any one or more of the following: inner ecstatic fire, trembling, body movements, disidentification from personal history, or an impulse toward some strategic action.

The much-researched experiential focusing of Gendlin is another (Gendlin, 1981). This basically consists in making a clear relaxed area in the body-mind so that when a key question – suitably refined and focused – is asked, there is space for the answer to be manifest, in verbal or non-verbal imagery, accompanied by a subtle release of energy. Gendlin describes the whole process as if it were primarily somatic, a description that has always seemed to me to be rather too cautious.

But McMahon and Campbell develop Gendlin's focusing in terms of a bio-spiritual approach. Their bio-spirituality emphasizes 'an experience of grace in the body'. They relate letting go into the body-feeling about an issue, to a movement of the indwelling life-giving presence and power of God (McMahon and Campbell, 1991: 5, 17).

None of these processes is a purely passive receptivity to some guiding internal otherness, although they have a tendency to be described in this way, as I have just done in order to report them in their own terms. But my experience of them, and of related sorts of inner lived inquiry, is that my subjectivity is actively involved at a deep level in selecting and shaping life-processes moving within. The challenge of these methods is not to surrender fully to what comes up from the depths, but to open up that liberated place within where one can be co-creative with immanent spirit. And this with respect to options that shape both the surface and deeper pattern of one's life.

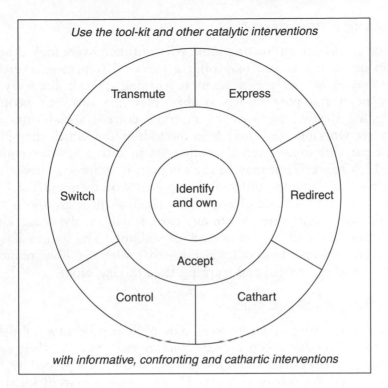

Use the tool-kit and other catalytic interventions

Transmute

Express

Switch

Identify
and own

Redirect

Accept

Control

Cathart

with informative, confronting and cathartic interventions

FIGURE 9.9 Working with emotions

8 Working with emotions

In the first part of the cathartic chapter, I identified eight positive emotional states, awareness of which gives you a comprehensive guide for working with emotions, when you are in the middle of the map of the client's psychological field. First, you help the person to identify and own the emotions, then to accept them as his or her reality, then to manage them, as appropriate, in one of six ways: control, redirection, switching, transmutation, catharsis or expression – as these were defined in Chapter 7 (pp. 85–86). Figure 9.9 portrays the options.

All these emotional states require the client to engage in subtle kinds of internal self-management prior to any outward behaviour. Your facilitation of these falls under catalytic self-help prescription (no. 18 below), preceded perhaps by some informative interventions, and backed up occasionally by some confronting ones. Of course, catharsis will take you back into the cathartic category and to some of the interventions listed in Chapter 7.

9 Offering practical structures

While clients are cultivating some part of their psychological field as in no. 7 above, you may offer a practical structured exercise that may be helpful in eliciting more learning and self-discovery. It may be a role-play in which they play the different people, including themselves, involved in some current social situation they are working on; it may be a monodrama in which they play both parts of some internal conflict (as in cathartic intervention no. 12, Chapter 7); it may be drawing out in graphic symbols the interrelation between different components of their current life-style; it may be a piece of archetypal ritual – there are too many possibilities to list here. But in any case, it will involve some kind of action, as well as, or instead of, talking. The action has a structure, a deeper kind of language – that often can liberate more understanding, insight and learning than talking alone.

10 Offering conceptual structures

When clients are cultivating some part of their psychological field, you can also offer a conceptual structure that may aid their self-learning. Conceptual structures can be to do with procedure, or they can be to do with content. They provide a map of ideas to help clarify the client's experiential journey.

10.1 Problem-solving structures   These are procedural. They analyse problem-solving into a series of steps or stages, which clients can then apply to their own problem. Again, there are many of these. They may offer a scheme for mapping experience, or for gener-ating and evaluating ideas, or for overcoming blocks to creativity, or for goal-setting and role definition, or for life planning, or for decision-making and action planning, or for technical problem-solving and so on.

10.2 General content structures   These are conceptual maps drawn up by you which can be used with any client and which categorize different aspects of the work in hand, as in the maps in nos. 1 and 3 above. Or they cover any bit of theoretical input which you give to someone to illumine their self-exploration: for example, an account of the different states of personhood, or different kinds of resistance, described in Chapter 2 (pp. 25–36).

10.3 Individual content structures   Here you offer an actual map of clients' own experience. You may offer your map of the current state of their psyche; or your version of the factors involved in some situation they are coping with; or your analysis of the range of options, with possible outcomes, with which they are presented in some decision that is to be made. But all this is only to stimulate people to clarify their own perspectives and generate their own decisions.

In these three structures, informative and catalytic interventions overlap. This is also really true of no. 8, offering practical structures. What makes them catalytic is that they are invoked to fit what someone is choosing to deal with and to facilitate their further self-direction.

11 Psi facilitation

Many people are shy about their psi: that is, their out of the body, near death, or extra-sensory experiences and such like. The culture still puts a taboo on talking about, even having, such experiences. But they can be crucial in giving meaning to a person's life, especially in times of crisis. Living-as-learning about psi can be good news to some people, legitimating a whole new two-worlds stance – living in this reality and being in touch with the other reality at the same time (Heron, 1998). This relates to the second kind of passive hierarchy I mentioned in Chapter 9 (p. 124). You can play an important role simply by opening the area up with an open question about a person's psi experiences, and perhaps some self-disclosure (see 13, below) too if it applies.

12 Spiritual facilitation

Psi is to do with subtle perception, subtle energy, subtle worlds. The spiritual is to do with the divine, with a 'presence far more deeply interfused'. Some people, too, are shy about owning the spiritual reality in their lives, their quiet or ecstatic encounters with the numinous – in their souls, in nature, beyond the stars or at the heart of basic human experiences such as loving another, giving birth and so on (Heron, 1998). So you can help legitimate these central experiences, by a well-timed open question about the client's inner, spiritual life.

13 Discreet practitioner self-disclosure

Disclosure begets disclosure. You may feel it appropriate to disclose some of your own experiences and concerns in the area that the person is addressing. This raises the level of intimacy and openness, trust and risk-taking, and it facilitates client disclosure.

As well as being genuine, your disclosure needs to be discreet – not going on too long or getting too deep and involved.

14 Client self-disclosure structure

The catalytic alternative to confronting clients about unaware agendas is to set up a structure which enables them to start to map out the defended, perhaps agitated, territory. You ask a set of very direct, intimate questions in those domains of experience that are typically problematic in the culture. The ground rule is that clients either answer as fully and honestly as possible, or if they choose not to answer, give an honest account of what seems to be at stake in not answering. The questions may look confronting, but technically they are not, since they are not aimed at identified agendas; rather, they provide a test battery for client self-discovery.

15 Self-assessment structure

For learning from past experience, you can guide the client through the following structure. You help with the pacing, with the movement from stage to stage; and prompt and facilitate within each stage; but the assessment is the individual's.

15.1 Identify criteria for assessing learning   Now the client may say, 'But look, I wasn't living my life as learning in those years, it was all a jungle of impulses and old cultural and childhood scripts.' But at any time in a person's life there are guiding ideas on hand that point to the main learning agendas for that time; and the person always has some sense of them, however inchoate. These ideas are that part of the archetypal dimension which I have called personal mythology or destiny. In any case, whether you agree with such a view or not, it is still useful to ask clients, whatever their disavowals, to have a go at identifying how it was open to them to change, grow and learn at that time. What comes up can provide individuals with a liberating perspective on their past.

15.2 Assess, in the light of these criteria, what sort of learning took place   If clients get the criteria pitched at the right level, then they start to get the assessment right, or so is the sense and feel of it. This is not conventional moral, or conventional learning, assessment, but soul assessment. It is in the past experience of pathology, weakness and distress that you first encourage someone to find evidence of growth and learning. Once that kind of assessment is established, the rest will usually follow.

And the rest, of course, is to do with growth and learning that is in the strong, positive and creative side of the personality. But the blooms and branches of the tree of learning are nourished from the roots of learning in the dark earth. Indeed, for clients to draw an archetypal tree of learning for any period of their life may facilitate their whole assessment process.

If you look back at the account of 'resident imagery' in the section on catharsis and transmutation (pp. 104–106), then this assessment work is at the interface between the level of imagination and the level of archetypes. From the perspective of the imaginal and archetypal levels, we pathologize our existence in order to grow. So from this perspective, too, we can see that we were learning something when we were unawarely displacing old distress. But we can only see it from that level. From the perspective of the personal – and cultural – history levels, we were acting out past traumas, in a mess, getting nowhere: at these levels we need catharsis and re-evaluation. Both the imaginal–archetypal and the personal–cultural perspectives are valid and compatible with each other.

15.3 Identify what unfinished learning is left over from the time being assessed, and/or what new learning agendas it generated at the archetypal level The client may find no entries under either of these headings; or there may be entries taken up and dealt with at a later stage; or there may be entries still pertinent to today's living and learning.

There is nothing restricting or oppressive about the archetype of a person's destiny. It is like a time-body of options for growth that a person can only find liberating. The conspiracy of all false religion and all false teaching about the human soul has been to occlude the proper influence of the archetype with moralistic dogmas. Yet paradoxically even these too have been forms of pathologizing in the pursuit of growth. So when cast down, find the growth staring up at you from the floor.

16 Looking forward to the future

What about future experience, the next living-as-learning adventure? Sooner or later this becomes a question for the client – when there is a turning point, when a cycle of one kind of experience ends. The big turning points are when several different sorts of cycle all seem to be ending at the same time: then the whole lifestyle is up for change.

Small turning points, involving only one cycle, raise at least three alternatives: simply do without that kind of experience in the future; have a new and revised version of the same kind of experience, building in learning from the past; open up some brand new kind of experience, launch a cycle of a different kind.

You can facilitate the forward-looking process by inviting the person to take account of some of the following:

16.1 Review of life-style areas   Take the life-style map in no. 1 above: the client gets a sense from it of those parts that call for endings, changes or new beginnings – revising the living-as-learning programme, bearing in mind purposes, resources, constraints. The imaginative use of drawing and graphics may help here: with life lines, life plans, life spirals and so on.

16.2 Review of options and outcomes   Where changes or new beginnings are called for, the client reviews the options and the possible outcomes per option, to get a better sense of the geography of the future. So if the client has decided when doing 16.1 that it is a time for new friends, then the review of options will deal with what sorts of people and what kinds of places to meet them in. Again, the use of drawings may be helpful.

16.3 Archetypal and entelechy review   What vision of challenging ventures, enjoyable learnings radiates from that form of the future which is the transcendent archetype of one's personal destiny? The complementary question is what creative life-impulses emerge from the client's immanent entelechy, his or her unactualized potential in the ground unconscious? If we take a seed metaphor, then this review may throw up three kinds of possibility:

16.3.1 Uncooked seeds   It may no longer be possible to sow and sprout seeds of growth not attended to in the past. But they can be cooked and baked into good form. Parents cannot rerun their early parenting; but they can work to reconstitute the current relationship with their children.

16.3.2 Growing seed   Seeds of growth already sown and sprouting may need some changes in their mode of being cultivated.

16.3.3 New seed   New varieties may need either old and familiar or new and unusual modes of sowing and cultivation.

Archetypal vision and the life-impulse of entelechy may also interrelate with passive hierarchies of the second type mentioned in the preface to this chapter, hierarchies in which decisions made in the tacit universe, the other reality, have implications for the client's future life.

16.4 Decision and action plan   What to do and how and when, and with whom and/or with what.

17 Managing endings

This is a precursor or an ancillary to the above. Just as the culture is not very good at handling death, so with endings generally. Many people overrun cycles of experience: they keep them going when their enjoyment, their usefulness and their learning is done. So living becomes an accumulation of dead husks of once sprouting seeds, of behaving as if one's activities had a point and a purpose which has long since evaporated. You enable clients to identify any such husk, and facilitate, if that is their choice, their management of an ending.

18 Catalytic self-help prescriptions

These are, of course, fully negotiated with motivated clients. You may propose some way of working with emotions, from among the options presented in no. 8 above. You may suggest that they engage in some form of self-help training that empowers them with new skills in being self-directed and co-operative. It may be first person action research training; expression and control, redirection and switching, catharsis and transmutation training; assertiveness and social-skills training; co-counselling training; autogenic training; martial arts training; psi development training; meditation training; relaxation training; how to monitor your own stress level training; creativity training; team development training; and so on. You may do some bits of one or more of these trainings yourself, initiating clients into the appropriate self-help skills, or you may suggest they attend some course or workshop where these things are on offer.

19 Prescriptive—catalytic gradient

Because of its importance, I repeat here in full intervention no. 3 from the prescriptive interventions list (Chapter 4). Classic prescribing to a client is very different from eliciting self-direction

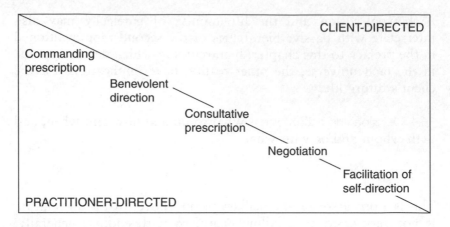

FIGURE 9.10   The prescriptive–catalytic gradient

from a client. There is a gradient from the prescriptive to the catalytic, and some practitioners by the very nature of their particular role need flexibility in moving up and down the gradient.

They may need to be at very different places on the gradient with the same person at different times and in respect of different issues; they may need to be at different places with different people in relation to the same sort of issue; and so on. This is often so for the medical practitioner. Figure 9.10 illustrates the gradient.

19.1 Commanding prescription   You use the full authority of your role and in a commanding manner direct the client to do something, with no consultation before or after the command.

19.2 Benevolent direction   This is a benign and respectful proposal that the client do something, but still with no consultation before or after it. There is a continuum here from mild to strong: you can (a) suggest, (b) propose, (c) advise, (d) persuade.

19.3 Consultative prescription   You propose some behaviour to the client, and consult him or her, eliciting views which you carefully consider. You are responsible for the final prescription, which may or may not take account of these views.

19.4 Negotiation   From the outset you work in a collaborative way with the client on the decision, sharing and comparing views on the issues and the options. Together you work to agree on a final decision.

19.5 Facilitation of self-direction   At this, the fully catalytic end of the gradient, you are concerned only to facilitate clients in making up their mind in their own way in the direction they think best.

20 Catalytic–informative gradient

Similarly, there is a gradient from eliciting information and views from clients, to giving information to them. Several sorts of practitioners, especially those who give tutorials, need flexibility on this gradient. It is shown in Figure 9.11.

The *catalytic* interventions of the tool-kit are included in the second, third and fourth columns in Figure 9.11. To these are added *supportive* interventions on the client-centred side, and *confronting, prescriptive* and *informative* ones on the practitioner-centred side. The items given under each of these further categories are self-explanatory. You could also add, alongside supportive interventions at the group-centred end, *cathartic* interventions, in the form of releasing tension through laughter.

One way for a teacher to use this gradient, in a tutorial where the students are discussing some previously learnt material, is to start off with mainly client-centred interventions to enable students to express what they know and understand. Later on the teacher uses more practitioner-centred interventions to deal with the errors and fill in the gaps in what they have said. This requires a certain flexibility, skill and retentive power.

21 Prescriptive–catalytic gradient in educational decision-making

This prescriptive–catalytic gradient is quite a fundamental one for setting up learning contracts with students in higher education. You consider all the factors involved in putting a contract together: learning objectives, teaching and learning methods, physical learning resources, human resources (staff and other students), topics or subject matter, timetabling, assessment of student performance, evaluation of teaching, evaluation of the contract. There are four basic ways these factors can be decided: by you – as staff member – unilaterally; by you and the students in co-operative decision-making; by you facilitating student self-directed decision-making; by students unilaterally. The gradient shows the seven basic ways in which the contract can distribute the factors over these four sorts of decision-making (Figure 9.12).

No. 1 is purely prescriptive, no. 6 is purely catalytic, no. 7 goes off the intervention map altogether since there are no staff. For 'some factors' you could also read 'some aspects of one factor'. Hence, the numbers of versions of the gradient, when factors or

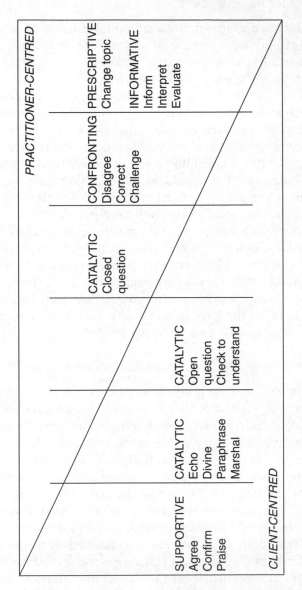

FIGURE 9.11   The catalytic–informative gradient

You alone decide	You and students negotiate	You facilitate self-direction	Students alone decide
1 All factors	None	None	None
2 Some	Some	None	None
3 Some	Some	Some	None
4 Some	Some	Some	Some
5 None	Some	Some	Some
6 None	None	Some	Some
7 None	None	None	All

FIGURE 9.12   The prescriptive–catalytic gradient in educational decision-making

aspects of factors are specified, is very large indeed. In my view, no. 4 is the version that really commends itself.

I have dealt more fully with the application of the six category approach to academic tutoring in my *Behaviour Analysis in Education and Training* (Heron, 1977a), which analyses an extensive range of tutoring interventions under each category; and I refer the reader who is interested in academic applications to that work.

22 Invocations

This is a special class of interventions that can properly be called catalytic. The supposition is that they bring some combination of psi and the spiritual to bear upon the client's whole being in a way that enhances growth and learning and, perhaps, healing.

22.1 Silent invocations   These are life-enhancing thoughts or prayers or visualizations or mantras which you direct mentally and silently to the client, who may be present or absent, but who will not know what is going on unless he or she is unusually sensitive.

22.2 Spoken tacit invocations   These are ordinary greetings and farewells and goodwill statements, but spoken with charismatic awareness and intent to convey an extra dimension of blessing from your heart and mind. 'It's good to see you', 'Have a good day', and so on.

22.3 Spoken explicit invocations   What makes an invocation explicit is its grammatical form. So invocations as a mode of speech are rooted in the traditional usage of the language you speak. Here are two forms of explicit invocation.

22.3.1 Benedictions   typically have the form 'May you be . . .', such as 'May you be whole', 'May you be lifted up in spirit'.

22.3.2 Spiritual commands   issue a benign order such as 'Be whole', or 'Lift up your heart'.

Invocations can be unctuous and sanctimonious when their timing, content and manner of being spoken are distorted by your unowned distress. They are simply embarrassing when they are not really appropriate to the person to whom they are directed, or to the context. When they are truly attuned to the situation, they enrich human encounter.

COACHING

At the outset of this chapter I mentioned the overlap between many of the interventions given above and the practice of coaching. Here is one account, from the International Coach Federation (2000), of the nature and scope of coaching:

- The individual coaching client is someone who wants to reach one or more of the following: a higher level of performance, learning, or satisfaction. The client is not seeking emotional healing or relief from psychological pain.
- The coaching client can take action to move towards a goal with the support of the coach. The successful client is not excessively limited in the ability to take action or overly hesitant to make this kind of progress.
- Coaches and clients arrange the schedule and means of contact (e.g., in person, by phone, or via e-mail) that serve them both. They are not constrained to follow a standardized schedule or means of contact.
- A coach relates to the client as a partner. A coach does not relate to the client from a position of an expert, authority, or healer.
- Coach and client together choose the focus, format and desired outcomes for their work. The client does not relinquish the responsibility for creating and maintaining these nor does the coach take full responsibility for them.
- Coaching is designed to help clients improve their learning and performance, and enhance their quality of life. Coaching does not focus directly on relieving psychological pain or treating cognitive or emotional disorders.

- Coaching concentrates primarily on the present and future. Coaching does not focus on the past or on the past's impact on the present.
- Coaching uses information from the client's past to clarify where the client is today. It does not depend on resolution of the past to move the client forward.
- Coaching assumes the presence of emotional reactions to life events and that clients are capable of expressing and handling their emotions.
- Coaching is not psychotherapy and emotional healing is not the focus of coaching.
- Coaching can be used concurrently with psychotherapeutic work. It is not used as a substitute for psychotherapeutic work.
- Advice, opinions, or suggestions are occasionally offered in coaching. Both parties understand that the client is free to accept or decline what is offered and takes the ultimate responsibility for action. The coach is not discouraged from offering advice, opinions or suggestions on occasion.
- A coach makes a request of the client to promote action toward the client's desired outcome. A coach does not make such requests in order to fix the client's problem or understand the client's past.

CHAPTER 10

SUPPORTIVE INTERVENTIONS

Supportive interventions affirm the worth and value of clients, of their qualities, attitudes of mind, actions, artefacts and creations. They do so in an unqualified manner. They do not collude with client rigidities, defences and negative misidentifications. They are intimate, authentic and caring.

In what follows I deal first with issues of support; secondly, with agendas of support; and thirdly, with a list of supportive interventions.

ISSUES OF SUPPORT

I consider here three main issues: being supportive; definitions of loving; and living as loving.

1 *Being supportive*: This is a wider concept than the concept of a supportive intervention. Being supportive is an attitude of mind that underlies the use of all the other categories of intervention. The combination of 'being here now', 'being there now' and 'giving free attention' (nos. 6.1, 6.2 and 6.3 in Chapter 9) takes us to the heart of this supportive attitude of mind. And it is really a precondition of using any other intervention in any other category. So it gets us to the bedrock of the whole system. This brief paragraph you have just read is, in my view, the most important in the whole book.

Being supportive – being here now, there now and giving free attention – is intensely active but silent and unspoken loving. By contrast, supportive interventions are direct statements of caring, of loving. So it is time to say something about the nature of love.

2 *Definitions of loving*: I have two definitions of loving. One is professional and the other is personal. The professional one runs: 'To love a person is to help to provide the conditions in which that person can, in liberty, identify and realize his or her own true needs and interests – wherever possible in association with other persons similarly engaged.' This definition is basic to all forms of professional helping, to parenting and indeed to

any kind of loving care. The personal definition runs: 'To love a person is to delight in, and take pleasure in enhancing, that person's uniqueness.' Both definitions cover loving oneself as well as other people.

3   *Living-as-loving*: Living-as-learning was a strong theme in the catalytic section. But living-as-loving goes deeper. Nor can living-as-loving be entirely reduced to living as learning how to love.

Of course, there is an art and skill in loving, and so people can learn how to express love and care in all sorts of different ways: sexually, familially, socially, creatively, politically, professionally. But this is the wisdom, even the power, side of loving. The loving side of loving is the simple act of loving, beyond any business of learning how to.

So perhaps there is some kind of hierarchy here. First, there is living-as-the-act-of-loving, which includes but is wider than living as learning how to express love in different ways. And this in turn includes but is wider than living as learning how to do everything else. This means that learning how to do anything is really, when seen in depth, a form of learning how to express love in this, that or the other way, in relation to oneself, others or both.

Always accessible is loving *per se*: and it is clearly an error to be analytic about this. It is a matter of immediate experiential feeling, doing and knowing.

AGENDAS OF SUPPORT

These have already been covered in the definition at the start of this section on supportive interventions. My interventions can be supportive of:

1   persons as such;
2   the qualities of persons;
3   the beliefs, norms and values that persons hold;
4   the actions of persons: both internal, mental actions and external actions;
5   the products, projects, artefacts and creations of persons.

SUPPORTIVE INTERVENTIONS

They are simple, human and small in number. These are the explicitly supportive interventions. All the other types of intervention in this book presuppose a supportive attitude of mind being here now, being there now and giving free attention – as described and defined in Chapter 9 under nos. 6.1, 6.2 and 6.3.

1 Expressing the loving feeling

Simply saying 'I love you', 'I like you', 'I feel great affection for you', 'I'm very fond of you' whatever the nuance or modality of loving feeling is.

2 Expressing care

To say 'I care for you', or 'I care about you', or 'I care about your life', is to direct the love at the other's welfare: it implies a commitment to be watchful, attentive, a readiness to be actively supportive and encouraging at appropriate times. It is future reaching.

3 Expressing concern

'I am concerned about you' carries the love actively over into the other's troubled times. It is both a way of saying that the speaker's help and support is ready and at hand, and a way of exhorting the other to take care of him- or herself.

4 Validation

You celebrate, affirm and appreciate, without detracting or qualifying clauses, the worth and value of clients, their qualities, their attitudes of mind, their actions, or their artefacts and creations.

5 Touching

Loving feeling, care and concern can all be expressed by making physical contact with the client from a fleeting touch with the fingers, to a hand resting on the arm or shoulder, to a full embrace.

Some practitioners avoid touch altogether – except for clinical purposes – for fear of its sexual implications. This is clearly an error and fails to distinguish between nurturance needs and sexual needs. Nurturance needs are for closeness, warmth, caring and emotional support and nourishment, all mediated by physical contact. In nurturant contact the sexual component is invariably absent, marginal or entirely secondary. Of course, nurturance can provide the context for the emergence of explicit sexuality. But practitioner–client contact is normally light-years away from the cross-over. It honours the nurturance needs of both, and is a way of affirming mutuality of respect and warmth.

6 Erotic awareness and energy

In some of your relationships with clients there may be mutual or one-way erotic awareness and energy. It may, of course, be charged with transference and/or counter-transference material – unawarely projected distresses of client and/or practitioner – and then everyone needs to be on the alert that nothing is acted out.

But equally it may not be so charged, and then it can be put to work to subserve and enrich the authentic purposes of the relationship. This means it is noticed, not acted upon, and allowed to nourish what else is going on. Of course, at a more subliminal level, all creative practitioner work will have some tacit and refined component of erotic energy.

7 Doing things and giving things

Loving feelings, care and concern can be expressed by doing and giving, as well as by speaking and touching. So you may lend a book, or get some needed information, or whatever expresses appropriately practical care.

8 Sharing and self-disclosure

You may share your personal experience as a gift, as an expression of solidarity in living and loving, quite independently of whether or not it has a catalytic effect in eliciting self-discloure in the client.

9 Greeting

You affirm the worth of the person, taking pleasure in his or her presence, in the simple act of greeting.

10 Welcoming

You extend the act of greeting into receiving and welcoming the client into your place of work.

11 Apologizing

You care for and respect the client by offering an apology for any lack of consideration, anything hurtful, unjust, forgetful or incompetent in your behaviour.

12 Self-celebration

You encourage clients to love themselves, to celebrate what they know or feel and believe to be their value, their fine qualities, their excellent attitudes of mind, their good ways of doing and being. This is not contradiction (cathartic intervention no. 13, Chapter 7); nor is it imaginal restructuring of self-perception (transmutative intervention no. 5, Chapter 8); for both these are ways of working on the negative self-image.

In self-celebration individuals are encouraged to find their positive self-image, take it off the shelf, blow the dust off it, polish it to make it shine and show it to a friend. This is a worthy intervention with which to end the total list.

There is a paradox about some of these supportive interventions (especially nos. 1, 2, 3 and 4): they may confront the negative self-image of the client who can only find an identity in feeling and believing self-deprecating things. So the person may have difficulty in hearing them or receiving them. They may rapidly disown them or drive them off with a fast compliment in return. If so, this may lead you over into some loving confrontation work, or even into some cathartic work.

CHAPTER 11

BASIC INTERVENTIONS

In this chapter I have included a selection of interventions from each of the six categories. I have picked out the bedrock ones, which also include the all-purpose ones with the widest range of application. I have given only a brief definition of each. For more detail, refer back to the descriptions given in earlier chapters, and read Chapter 2 on preparation for helping. First, a review of the six categories.

- **Prescriptive** interventions seek to direct the behaviour of the client, usually behaviour that is outside the practitioner–client relationship.
- **Informative** interventions seek to impart knowledge, information, meaning to the client.
- **Confronting** interventions seek to raise the client's consciousness about some limiting attitude or behaviour of which he or she is relatively unaware.
- **Cathartic** interventions seek to enable the client to discharge, to abreact painful emotion, primarily grief, fear and anger.
- **Catalytic** interventions seek to elicit self-discovery, self-directed living, learning and problem-solving in the client.
- **Supportive** interventions seek to affirm the worth and value of the client's person, qualities, attitudes or actions.

BASIC PRESCRIPTIVE INTERVENTIONS

1 Prescriptive–catalytic gradient

Prescribing to the client stands over against the catalytic approach of eliciting their self-direction. There is a gradient from the prescriptive to the catalytic (Figure 11.1), and some practitioners need flexibility in moving up and down the gradient.

1.1 Commanding prescription   You use the full authority of your role and in a commanding manner direct the client to do something, with no consultation before or after the command.

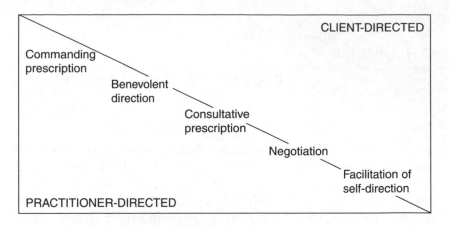

FIGURE 11.1   Prescriptive–catalytic gradient

1.2 Benevolent directive prescription   This is a benign and respectful proposal that the client do something, but still with no consultation before or after it. There is a continuum here from mild to strong: you can (a) suggest, (b) propose, (c) advise, (d) persuade. There are many nuances possible within this one intervention.

1.3 Consultative prescription   You propose some behaviour to the client, and also consult him or her, eliciting his or her views which you carefully consider. But you are responsible for the final prescription, which may or may not take account of these views.

1.4 Negotiation   From the outset you work in a collaborative way with the client on the decision, sharing and comparing views on the issues and the options. Together you work at agreement on a final decision.

1.5 Facilitation of self-direction   At this, the fully catalytic end of the gradient, you are concerned only to facilitate clients in making up their minds in their own way in the direction they think best.

BASIC INFORMATIVE INTERVENTIONS

1 Personal interpretation

You interpret – that is, give a meaning to – the client's behaviour, or experience, or situation.

1.1 Simple ascription   You ascribe a simple motive, intention or emotional state to what the person says or does.

1.2 Psychodynamic   The meaning which you give to what the client says or does derives from some properly formulated psychodynamic theory.

1.3 Psychosomatic   This is the interpretation in which a physical symptom is attributed to some unowned emotional and mental state. The psyche is displaced into the soma.

1.4 Sociodynamic   Here the interpretation rests more on theories to do with group processes, with social and cultural phenomena.

1.5 Transcendental   The interpretation invokes concepts to do with altered states of consciousness, other realities, psi and extrasensory states, and the mystical and religious domain.

2 Presenting relevant information

Apart from interpretation, you may give information that is relevant to the client: illuminating background knowledge – factual, technical, theoretical. Certain simple principles apply:

2.1 Attunement   Empathize with the presence and attitude of mind of the listener, so that everything you say is shaped for him or her, related to his or her learning needs, existing knowledge and beliefs.

2.2 Overview   Give a brief advance account of the main areas you are going to cover.

2.3 Throw the basics into relief   Make only a small number of key points, which stand out clearly. Use non-technical language where possible.

2.4 Illumination   Illustrate each main point with examples and instances that are of relevance and interest to the listener.

2.5 Command of manner   Use tone and volume of voice, rate of speech, pauses and silences, inflection and emphasis, to enhance the content, and rivet the listener's attention.

2.6 Recapitulation   Before closing, summarize the main points again, underlining any that are especially relevant.

2.7 Check for comprehension   Engage with the listener about the content of what you have said, to see if he or she has understood, if there are queries, doubts, confirmations from his or her own experience, and so on.

3 Feedback

You give clients informative, non-evaluative feedback on their performance in, for example, a role-play or skills training exercise. Or it may be feedback and comment on homework they have undertaken between sessions and have just produced or reported on. It is particularly useful to identify what has been unnoticed by them.

BASIC CONFRONTING INTERVENTIONS

1 Raising consciousness about a confrontation agenda

This is the first, simple and obvious and quite basic kind of intervention. Easy to state, often difficult to do, because it has to be done in a clear and uncompromising but non-punitive and non-moralistic way. It involves five stages:

1.1 Identify the agenda   State what sort of issues it is you want to raise.

1.2 Explain how it is you see the client falling foul of this agenda   This will involve negative feedback (as defined below) or educative feedback (see below).

1.3 Explain why you think it is relevant and appropriate to raise this matter with the client in this way at this time   This is optional: sometimes it is obvious and so it is silly to state it; at other times your apparent presumption needs full and adequate justification.

1.4 Give the client plenty of space to react to what you have said   You now give the person time to accommodate to the shock. Do not overtalk them. You may ask how they are feeling. You respectfully but firmly interrupt any defensive reactions. Hold your ground and be ready for anything: you may need to be supportive, cathartic, catalytic, informative or yet again confronting, and in any order –

to help clients come to terms with the confrontation, both in their emotions and in their understanding.

1.5 Follow through   You seek to help the person to identify the source of the unaware behaviour or attitude of mind, to find a way of dealing with this source and to work towards a better way of being.

2 Negative feedback

You feed back to clients impressions about what they are saying or how they are saying it, where these are impressions of conventional or compulsive states and resistances: some social ignorance and inertia, something restrictive, maladaptive, unaware, denied, defensive. The impressions may refer to past unaware behaviour. The feedback is non-punitive, non-moralistic. It is owned for what it is – your subjective impressions. It is not put forward as heavy-handed 'objective' criticism or appraisal. And it is uncompromising.

3 Educative feedback

You confront clients' unawareness of their lack of education or training in some area, their reluctance to accept this lack, to discover its degree, and to realize that there is quite a task of learning ahead.

4 Direct question

You ask a direct question aimed at what it is you sense clients are concealing, denying, avoiding, unaware of.

5 Rattle and shake

You challenge clients' disavowals and denials, by statements and questions about the evidence or contrary evidence for their view, its incoherence or inconsistencies, its implausibility or dubious assumptions, and so on.

6 Correcting and disagreeing

You correct clients' factually incorrect statements, and disagree with their opinions and views; and in a way that seeks to raise their consciousness, without invalidating their feeling.

BASIC CATHARTIC INTERVENTIONS

WORKING WITH CONTENT

This means working with what the person is saying, with his or her stated difficulty, with meaning, story-line and imagery.

1 Present-tense description

Interrupt analytic talking about a problem, and ask the person to describe – in the present tense as if it were happening now – a specific, traumatic incident, evoking it in literal detail by recall of sights and sounds and smells, of what people said and did.

2 Psychodrama

As the distress comes to the fore through no. 1, invite the person to re-enact the incident as a piece of living theatre, imagining he or she is in the scene and speaking within it as if it were happening now. Ask the person to express fully what was left unsaid at the time, and to say it directly to the central other protagonist in the scene.

3 Shifting level

When a person is making a charged statement to the central other protagonist in a psychodrama about an incident later in life, you quickly and deftly ask 'Who are you really saying that to?' The person may then very rapidly shift level to a much earlier situation and become, for example, the hurt child speaking to its parent; and the catharsis intensifies.

4 Earliest available memory

Simply ask a person for his or her earliest available memory of an incident typical of a current difficulty, and work on that with literal description and psychodrama. Depending on how it goes and how early it is, you may get the client to shift level inside that psychodrama too.

5 Scanning

When a person identifies a current problem, ask him or her to scan along the chain of incidents, all of which are linked by the same sort of difficulty and distress. The person evokes each scene, then moves on to the next, without going into any one event deeply. This loosens up the whole chain.

6 Slips of the tongue

When a word or phrase slips out that the person didn't intend to say, ask them to repeat it a few times, and to work with the associations and/or process cues. This invariably points the way to some unfinished business.

7 Contradiction

Ask the person to use words, tone of voice, facial expression, gesture, posture that contradicts, without qualification, his or her self-deprecating statements and manner. This interrupts the external invalidation the child within has internalized to keep its distress suppressed, and rapidly opens up into laughter, followed, if you are quick on the cues, by deeper forms of catharsis.

8 Validation

As the distress comes up, gently and clearly affirm clients, their deep worth, the validity of their pain, their need for release, how much they deserve this time, support and care.

9 Free attention

If clients are sunk in their distress, ask them to recount some recent pleasant experiences. This will generate some free attention, without which catharsis cannot occur. Go on to the other techniques.

10 Association

Work with a person's spontaneous, unbidden associations. These include 'what's on top' at the start of a session; the sudden surfacing of an earlier memory while working on a later one; the extra bits of recall that come up to illumine a remembered event. Especially important are the thoughts, insights, reappraisals, that arise during a pause in catharsis, and as it subsides: this restructuring of awareness is the real fruit, not just the release itself.

11 Integration of learning

After a major piece of cathartic work that has generated a good deal of insight and re-evaluation, prompt clients to formulate clearly all they have learnt, and to affirm its application to new attitudes of mind, new goals and new behaviours in their lives now. At this point cathartic work finds its true *raison d'être*.

WORKING WITH PROCESS

This means working with how the client is talking and being – that is, with emotional tone and charge and volume of voice, breathing, use of eyes, facial expression, gesture, posture, movement.

12 Repeating distress-charged words

Ask the person to repeat such words and phrases, several times, and louder, and perhaps much louder. This will start to discharge the underlying distress, or bring it nearer the surface. It is particularly potent at the heart of a psychodrama, when someone is expressing the hitherto unexpressed to some central other protagonist from the past.

13 Exaggerating distress-charged movements

Ask the person to repeat and exaggerate small involuntary agitated movements until they become large and vigorous, then to add the sounds and words that go with them. This too will start to discharge the underlying distress, or bring it nearer the surface.

14 Amplifying deepening of the breath

Ask the person who suddenly and unawarely breathes in deeply to continue deep and rapid breathing (hyperventilation – see next item), making a crescendo of sound on the outbreath. This may release deep sobbing, or screaming and trembling, or a discharge of anger.

15 Hyperventilation

This is a rapid breathing which becomes defensive if it is excessively fast or too slow. There is a frequency which opens up the emotionality of the whole psychophysical system, if it is sustained long enough. It can be used to lead the client into discharge from scratch, by working on basic character armour.

To prevent tetany and excessive dizziness, get the client to do it in many cycles, with pauses in between. When carried on for a sufficient period of time, this is a very direct and powerful route to primal and perinatal experiences.

16 Mobilizing distress-locked rigidities

Ask the person to become aware of some bodily rigidity, exaggerate it to let the distress energy pile up in the lock, then to throw the energy out in vigorous movement, finding appropriate sounds and words. Thus, a tight fist and rigid arm are first exaggerated into even greater tension, then converted into rapid thumping on a pillow. You will need to encourage the client not to throttle back the sound, and behind that the long-repressed words.

17 Acting into

When a person is already feeling the distress, wants to discharge it, but is held back by conditioned muscular tension, you suggest that he or she act into the emotion – that is, create a muscular pathway for it, by vigorous pounding and sound for anger, or trembling for fear. If the client produces the movements and sound artificially, then very often real catharsis will take over.

18 Physical pressure

When a person is just struggling to get discharge going, or has just started it, or is in the middle of it, you can facilitate release by applying appropriate degrees of pressure to various parts of the body: pressure on the abdomen, midriff or thorax, timed with the outbreath; pressure on the masseter muscle, some of the intercostals, the trapezius, the infraspinatus; pressure on the upper and mid-dorsal vertebrae timed with the outbreath to deepen the release in sobs; pressure against the soles of the feet and up the legs to precipitate kicking – extending the spine over the practitioner's knee, timed with the outbreath, to deepen the release of primal grief and screaming; and so on. The pressure is firm and deep, but very sensitively timed to fit and facilitate the cathartic process. Anything ham-fisted and ill-attuned is destructively intrusive.

19 Physical extension

As the person is moving in and out of the discharge process, you can facilitate the release by gently extending the fingers, if they curl up defensively; or by gently extending the arms; or by drawing the arms out and away from the sides of the body; or by extending an arm while pressing the shoulder back; or by gently raising the head, or uncurling the trunk; and so on. All these extensions are gentle and gradual, so that the client can choose to yield to them and go with them.

20 Relaxation and light massage

This is an alternative mode of working on physical rigidity. You relax the person and give gentle, caressing massage to rigid areas. Catharsis and/or memory recall may occur as muscle groups give way to the massage. Gentle and light oscillation, or rocking, applied to various areas will have the same effect.

21 Physical holding

You reach out lightly to hold and embrace the person at the start, or just before the start, of letting go of grief in tears. This intensifies the release. It can be combined with touch on the upper spine on each outbreath. Holding hands at certain points may facilitate discharge. When discharging fear, the person can stand within your embrace: your fingertips apply light pressure to either side of his or her spine.

22 Pursuing the eyes

By avoiding eye contact with you, clients are often also at the same time avoiding the distress emotions. You gently pursue their eyes by peering up from under their lowered head. Re-establishing eye contact may precipitate or continue catharsis.

23 Regression positions

When process cues suggest birth or prenatal material, you can invite the person to assume prenatal or birth postures, start hyperventilation and wait for the primal experiences to rerun themselves. This may open up deep and sustained cathartic work in the primal mode. If so, you need to keep leading the person to identify the context, to verbalize insights and at the end to integrate the learning into his or her current attitudes and lifestyle. Regression positions may also be less ambitious, like lying in the cot, sucking a thumb and so on.

24 Seeking the context

When clients are deeply immersed in process work and in catharsis, you may judge it fitting to lead them into the associated cognitive mode, asking them to identify and describe the event and its context, to verbalize insights, to make connections with present-time situations and attitudes.

25 Ending a session

At the end of a cathartic session, it is necessary for you to bring clients back up out of their cathartic regression into present time, by chronological progression at intervals of five or ten years, by affirming positive directions for current living, by describing the immediate environment, by reciting simple lists, by looking forward to the next few days and so on.

BASIC CATALYTIC INTERVENTIONS

1 Making a life-style map

You sit down with the client and together draw up a map which shows all the major aspects of living, including those in which the person both is and is not active, whether the person is satisfied or dissatisfied with the activity or inactivity, and whether or not the person wants to change any of these four possible states. This map can then be a basis for a systematic review of current experience, learning from past experience and planning future experience. The map will, of course, be used over several sessions.

2 Using the experiential learning cycle

Whether clients are considering current, past or future experience, you can enhance their self-discovery by inviting them, through questions and other catalytic interventions, to think in terms of the experiential learning cycle. In this cycle, shown in Figure 11.2, the individual moves between experience and reflection, to and fro, with a two-way influence.

After living a certain kind of experience, a person takes time out to uncover the emotions and attitudes involved in it, to reflect on it and get some insight into it, and to prepare to take this awareness back into life. Each session with the practitioner is itself a reflection phase, a processing of current or past experience, with preparation for future experience.

3 The catalytic tool-kit

The purpose of the following interventions is to elicit clients' self-directed learning about living, or more specific topics, and to do so with the minimal behaviour from you. They enable you to be highly effective and to maintain a low profile; and to balance following clients with leading them deeper into their own territory.

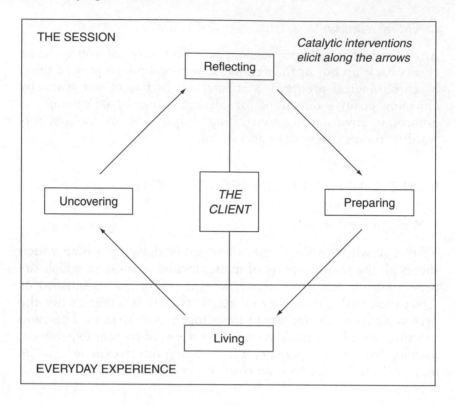

FIGURE 11.2　The experiential learning cycle

3.1 Be here now　You are centred, present, with your awareness unencumbered, in the moment that is now.

3.2 Be there now　To be here now is very much also to be there now. When you are attuned to your own centre, you are already very open to the reality of the other. Within the 'I' is found the divine reality of the unifying relation with the 'Thou' (Buber, 1937).

3.3 Giving free attention　A subtle, intense activity of consciousness mediated by gaze, posture, facial expression, sometimes touch. It has the quality of being supportive of a person's essential being and worth.

3.4 Simple echoing　You echo back to the client the last word, or the last few words, they said before pausing.

3.5 Selective echoing　You echo back something not at the end but from the middle of the client's talk, some word or phrase that carries an emotional charge or stands out as significant in its context.

3.6 Open questions/3.7 Closed questions   The open question does not have one right answer, but gives plenty of space for the client to come up with several possible answers – for example, 'What do you remember about your first school?' The closed question only permits of one answer, the correct one – for example, 'What was the name of your first school?'

3.8 Empathic divining   When a client says something that has an implicit emotion, thought or intention which is lurking between the lines and which is not fully expressed, you divine this and put it back as a statement, not a question, of the form 'It seems as though you'. This can be applied to the client's non-verbal manner too.

3.9 Checking for understanding   When clients, groping for words, say something confused or contradictory, you try to divine what they want to say, tidy up their statement to express it clearly, and put it back with the preface, 'Let me see, are you saying that . . .'.

3.10 Paraphrasing   You rephrase in your own words something important which the client has expressed.

3.11 Logical marshalling   You organize the explicit content of a whole chapter of the client's talk, summarize it, perhaps interrelate parts of it, perhaps indicate directions in which it seems to be leading, and put all this back as a succinct recapitulation. Figure 11.3 portrays all the items from 3.1 to 3.11 together.

4 Working with non-verbal cues

There are important cues evident in the client's facial expression and body language. There are six basic kinds which you can identify.

4.1 Picking up on pensive cues   You ask the open question 'What are you thinking?' when the client has that typical brief reflective expression on his or her face, indicative of an inner thought process.

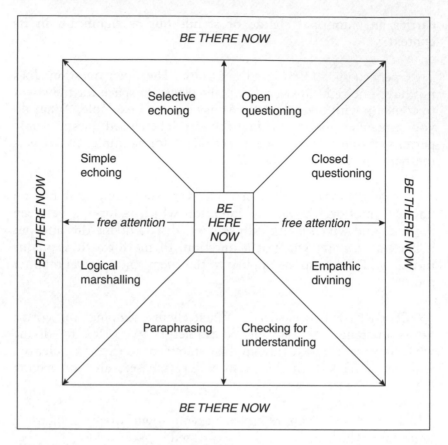

FIGURE 11.3   The catalytic tool-kit

4.2 Picking up on wanting-to-speak cues   You put an open question such as 'What is your view?' to a client whose facial or other movements show that he or she wants to say something.

4.3 Picking up on emotion cues   These cues include shock, surprise, delight, loving care, irritation, impatience, anxiety and so on. You can use empathic divining, 'It looks as though you . . .'; or open questioning, 'How are you feeling?'

4.4 Picking up on cathartic cues   This is a special case of 4.3. The eyes, facial expression, other bodily cues, show that distress emotion is coming up, moving towards discharge. The fists are clenched (anger); the lips and jaw are trembling (fear); the eyes are filling with tears (grief); laughter is about to break out (embarrassment). Empathic divining may bring the distress a little nearer identification, ownership, acceptance and release. For sustained discharge, of course, you will move over into full-blown cathartic interventions.

4.5 Picking up on alienation cues   The facial expression, and perhaps posture, show that the client is alienated, has mentally and emotionally cut out, and is sunk in his or her own negative internal process. You can use empathic divining and say 'It looks as though you . . .'; or you can gently ask an open question: 'What is going on for you right now?'

4.6 Picking up on transpersonal cues   See Chapter 8, nos. 17 and 18.

5 Following, consulting, proposing or leading

When it comes to opening up new territory for clients' self-discovery, there are four options:

5.1 They have already started to enter it and you follow.

5.2 You consult them and ask them where they would like to go next, with or without reference to some mutually agreed map. If they know where they want to go, then that is where they go.

5.3 You propose a new area and seek assent. If they dissent, then go back to 5.2 or on to 5.4.

5.4 Without consulting or proposing then consulting, you simply ask a question that leads the client into new territory. The flexible practitioner will be able to use all these four options as appropriate.

6 Bring in, draw out, shut out

In small-group work, you scan the group regularly with your eyes to pick up on non-verbal cues among those who are not talking. You can *bring in* one person by eye contact, hand gesture, questioning, divining. You can *draw out* someone who is already talking by eye contact, hand gesture, echoing, questioning, divining, checking for understanding, paraphrasing, marshalling. You can *shut out* someone who is talking, with a deft gesture from one hand, while simultaneously *bringing in* someone else with your other hand: you can do this without any words, like a traffic cop. Or you can also add words – and question, divine, check for understanding, paraphrase or marshal what the current speaker has just said, and put this to someone else for comment. Thus, you keep a low profile while effectively managing contribution rates,

	BRING IN	DRAW OUT	SHUT OUT
Being present SCANNING Timing Choice of words Paralinguistics Body language			
Eye contact			
Gesture: traffic cop			
Simple echoing			
Selective echoing			
Open questioning			
Closed questioning			
Empathic divining			
Checking for understanding			
Paraphrasing			
Logical marshalling			

FIGURE 11.4   Managing contribution rates

eliciting self-discovery and interpersonal learning in the group. Figure 11.4 shows the options.

7 Working with emotions

In the cathartic interventions chapter (Chapter 7, pp. 85–86), I identified eight positive emotional states, awareness of which gives you a comprehensive guide for working with a person's emotions. First, you enable clients to identify and own their emotions, then to accept them as their reality, then to manage them, as appropriate, in one of six ways: control, redirection, switching, transmutation, catharsis or expression. This is portrayed in Figure 11.5.

8 Offering practical structures

You may offer a practical structured exercise that may be helpful in eliciting more learning and self-discovery; for example, a role-play in which a person plays the different people, including self, involved in some current social situation he or she is working on. The action has a structure, a deeper kind of language – that can often liberate more understanding, insight and learning than talking alone.

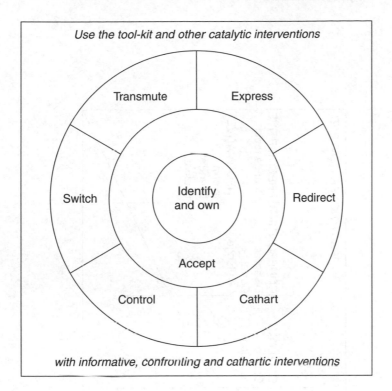

FIGURE 11.5 Working with emotions

9 Offering conceptual structures

You can also offer conceptual structures that may aid the client's
self-learning: they may be life-style or life-planning maps, steps in
problem-solving and so on. Conceptual structures can be to do
with procedure, or they can be to do with content, or both
together.

10 Discreet practitioner self-disclosure

Disclosing some of your own experiences and concerns in the area
that the other person is addressing raises the level of trust and
facilitates his or her disclosure.

11 Catalytic–informative gradient

There is a gradient from eliciting information and views from
clients, to giving information to them. Several sorts of practitioners, especially those who give tutorials, need flexibility on this
gradient, which is shown in Figure 11.6.

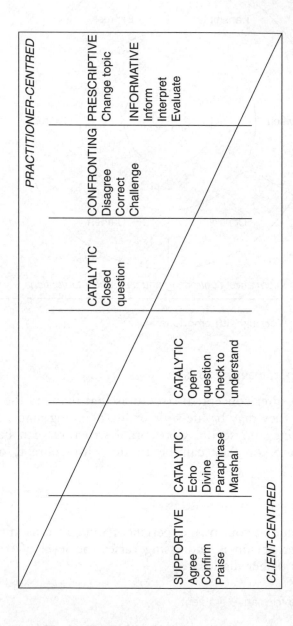

FIGURE 11.6   Catalytic–informative gradient

The *catalytic* interventions of the tool-kit are included in the second, third and fourth columns in the figure. To these are added *supportive* interventions on the client-centred side, and *confronting*, *prescriptive* and *informative* ones on the practitioner-centred side. The items given under each of these further categories are self-explanatory. You could also add, at the far client-centred end, *cathartic* interventions, in the form of releasing tension through laughter.

BASIC SUPPORTIVE INTERVENTIONS

1 Validation

You celebrate and affirm the worth and value of clients, their qualities, attitudes and actions, or their artefacts.

2 Touching

Loving feeling, care and concern can all be expressed by making physical contact with the client, from a fleeting touch with the fingers, to a hand resting on the arm or shoulder, to a full embrace.

3 Doing things and giving things

Loving feelings, care and concern can be expressed by doing and giving, as well as by speaking and touching. So you do whatever expresses appropriately practical care.

4 Greeting

You affirm the worth of the person, take pleasure in his or her presence, in the simple act of greeting.

5 Welcoming

You extend the act of greeting into receiving and welcoming the client into your place of work.

6 Self-celebration

You encourage clients to love their self, to celebrate what they know or feel and believe to be their value, their fine qualities, their excellent attitudes of mind, their good ways of being.

FIGURE 11.7   The six categories in their total context

The six categories, culminating in support, are manifest in their total world. They are a set of basic skills which each practitioner can apply within the self; which are used with others in face-to-face, one-to-one encounters; and which are exercised within the contexts of organizational life, spiritual reality and the planetary environment. This is shown in Figure 11.7.

In one-to-one relations, the main focus of their application, they seek to serve the interests of the 'client's psychological field', a map which I reproduce again in Figure 11.8. It shows the client's capacities for feeling, understanding and choosing, set in the context of archetypal influences, cultural and psychodynamic influences.

This figure, from no. 7 in Chapter 9, is a reminder of the kind of journey the client may take. A classic and comprehensive client route would be as shown by the arrows on the figure. But which route the client takes depends on the subject matter and its importance, the time available, other items on the agenda, the client's stage of unfoldment and so on.

There is no correct route. The route I have drawn on the figure does not provide a therapeutic programme that ought to be followed. The client may go every which way to and fro among

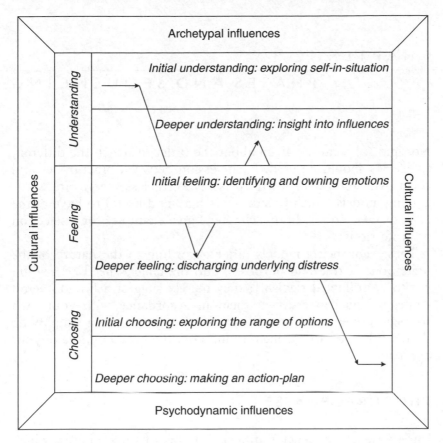

FIGURE 11.8   The client's psychological field

the six layers, if the practitioner is following as well as leading. Nor does a person deal with issues of choosing, in every session. In short, the whole thing has to be handled with great flexibility and variability.

CHAPTER 12

PHASES AND SEQUENCING

No rigid rules can be given about the order in which the different categories should be used. Each session between practitioner and client will follow its own rules. Nevertheless, there are some guiding models which practitioners may find useful to have at the back of their minds. In this chapter I give examples for a selection of professions.

These sequencing models differ according to the nature of the practitioner's role and purposes, and the client's needs. They are not to be followed slavishly; they merely suggest a broad overall strategy. You can redesign them in accordance with your own strategic preferences. For this the six categories are a simplifying shorthand: you can use them to map out the broad outline of your approach.

THE THREE PHASES

I present each sequencing model in terms of three phases, which constitute the natural rhythm or cycle of any well-rounded session for any kind of practitioner–client relationship.

1 *The first phase* is one of *exploration*, survey and reconnaissance, in which the practitioner is largely catalytic, and the client is unfolding his or her reality.
2 *The second phase* is one of *consummation* and fulfilment, in which the practitioner's interventions are brought most closely to bear upon the client's self-disclosure, and the client revisions his or her reality.
3 *The third phase* is one of *assimilation* and follow-through, in which the practitioner is assisting the client to integrate the learning in his or her understanding and life.

In the first phase, catalytic interventions are paramount, with some back-up from informative interventions. In the second phase, the primary interventions will be confronting, informative, cathartic, catalytic, depending on the sort of practitioner–client relationship, and the purposes of the session. In the third phase, again it will be mainly catalytic interventions, but with some use of prescriptive interventions, depending again upon the practitioner's role. Supportive interventions can occur in all phases as appropriate.

These three phases, of course, exactly mirror the client's three within-session stages of the experiential learning cycle, discussed in Chapter 9 (pp. 119–120). They were: *uncovering* some experience in full, *reflecting* on and getting insight into it, and *preparing* to take this learning back into living.

SEQUENCING MODELS

1 Academic tutoring

This sequence is for the tutor working with a student in the cognitive mode, facilitating learning of some subject matter the student has previously studied.

1.1 First phase   Many catalytic interventions enable students to rehearse their learning: to explore their understanding of the subject matter, articulate their perspective on it and begin to exercise some critical judgement about it. Mixed in with these, occasional supportive interventions agree with students, confirm their understanding and validate their critical grasp.

1.2 Second phase   As this exploration brings into relief the extent of students' knowledge of the subject matter, and depth of critical grasp, confronting questions throw this knowledge and grasp more sharply into relief. More confronting interventions disagree with and correct students' misunderstandings and misjudgements, followed by catalytic interventions to draw them into dialogue about the issues raised, and to prompt them to revise their understanding and grasp of the subject matter. In and among, very light cathartic interventions relieve tension in laughter. Then informative interventions fill in the gaps in the students' knowledge and critical awareness.

1.3 Third phase   Catalytic interventions invite students to rehearse their revised understanding, to raise issues that are still obscure, and to make their own decisions about fruitful directions for future study. Supportive interventions affirm their new understanding and their new direction. Prescriptive interventions may add the tutor's guidance about future study.

2 Collaborative assessment

This sequence is for the trainer who is doing collaborative assessment with a trainee on the latter's performance on a course. More widely it can be applied as collaborative appraisal of performance on the job. It is a significantly person-centred approach to assessment and appraisal.

2.1 First phase   Mixed informative, prescriptive and catalytic interventions negotiate a set of criteria for assessing performance: these criteria are mutually agreed, not imposed. The trainee makes a fully self-directed commitment to them.

2.2 Second phase   Catalytic interventions elicit the trainee's self-assessment of his or her strengths and weaknesses of performance in the light of each criterion. Some confronting questions may be needed to help the student identify weaknesses. Informative interventions give the trainer's assessment of the trainee's strengths and weaknesses using the agreed criteria. During this, supportive interventions affirm strengths the trainee played down or ignored; confronting interventions identify weaknesses the trainee glossed over or omitted.

2.3 Third phase   Catalytic and informative interventions negotiate an agreed final assessment, with space for dissenting minority reports of either party. Catalytic interventions elicit from the trainee his or her own plans for using the assessment, especially identified weaknesses, to direct future study and practice. Prescriptive interventions add the trainer's suggestions for the trainee's further study and practice. Supportive interventions validate the trainee's developing skills in self-assessment.

3 The medical consultation

This sequence is for the doctor, general practitioner or consultant – who is seeing a patient presenting with some symptoms for the first time. It brings out the patient-centred, holistic approach to patient care; and the distinction between the patient's experience of illness, and the doctor's diagnosis of disease.

3.1 First phase   Supportive and catalytic interventions help the patient relax and settle in. Catalytic interventions elicit the patient's full account of the presenting symptoms and of their possible causes. These interventions are sustained long enough for the patient to uncover any relevant psychosocial factors and to give personal meaning to the illness – some confronting interventions may help this process too. Cathartic and supportive interventions may be appropriate if emotional distress breaks through. Informative interventions state simply and clearly the point and purpose of any physical examination to be used.

3.2 Second phase   Informative interventions explain clearly in ordinary language the diagnosis and the prognosis of any disease present; or the possible diagnoses and further tests needed. (Where the information is shocking to the patient, the intervention will be confronting, needs to be handled as such, and may also need to be followed by cathartic attention.) Catalytic and informative interventions create dialogue: give space for the patient to ask questions and clarify the diagnosis and prognosis and their implications; and to relate all this to his or her own unfolding perspective on the illness. Supportive interventions give all possible reassurance to the patient.

3.3 Third phase   Prescriptive interventions state what treatment the doctor proposes to help get the patient better from the disease, with catalytic interventions to clarify the patient's understanding of these, and acceptance of them. Catalytic interventions elicit the patient's own ideas for self-help in getting better from his or her illness. The doctor may add some prescriptive suggestions about patient self-help. Supportive interventions affirm the patient's self-direction in managing the illness, and re-affirm continuous medical back-up in treating the disease. Prescriptive interventions propose a follow-up visit.

4 The bank manager's interview

This sequence is for the bank manager who is interviewing a customer in order to decide whether to meet the customer's request for a loan.

4.1 First phase   Supportive and catalytic interventions help to relax and settle the customer. Catalytic interventions elicit the customer's precise requirements, the reasons for them, their social and financial context. Confronting interventions may be appropriate to uncover issues being avoided or distorted. Cathartic attention will be needed if any emotional distress breaks through, followed by supportive reassurance.

4.2 Second phase   Informative interventions state what the bank can or cannot offer, and the reasons for this. The addition of catalytic interventions elicits dialogue, so that the customer can clarify his or her understanding of the bank's position and reflect fully on the issues.

4.3 Third phase   Prescriptive interventions state what the customer should do to take advantage of the bank's offer, or they propose alternative solutions if the bank can make no offer. Catalytic and informative interventions create dialogue, seek mutual understanding and agreement. Supportive interventions affirm continued service.

5 The office supervisor's disciplinary interview

This sequence is for the manager of staff, who is having a private interview with an employee about some behaviour that is in breach of contract and/or is causing upset among other employees in the office.

5.1 First phase   Supportive and catalytic interventions help the employee relax and settle in. Catalytic interventions elicit employee self-assessment about performance at work and behaviour in the office, and about any relevant background factors. This may or may not lead openly into the next phase.

5.2 Second phase   Confronting interventions give direct, unequivocal feedback about the unacceptable behaviour, with informative evidence and reasons. This is sustained until the employee ceases to be defensive and starts to come to terms with the feedback. Catalytic interventions invite the employee to share his or her reactions, thought and emotions, and perspective. Supportive interventions value the person. Cathartic attention may be needed if emotional distress breaks through.

5.3 Third phase   Catalytic, informative and prescriptive interventions seek to negotiate a solution and elicit employee commitment to change of behaviour. Failing this, prescriptive interventions impose a solution, with catalytic interventions to ensure that it is understood.

6 Personal development counselling

This sequence is for counsellors and psychotherapists who include regression and catharsis as a basic part of their approach.

6.1 First phase   Many catalytic interventions are used to elicit client self-discovery, with occasional informative ones – personal interpretations, and brief conceptual inputs to illumine the growth process and methods.

6.2 Second phase   As self-discovery starts to uncover deeper atti-tudes, confronting interventions highlight defensive states, and cathartic interventions discharge the underlying distress, and give space for spontaneous insights and re-evaluation. Supportive interventions uphold the client in this work.

6.3 Third phase   Catalytic interventions draw out the client to consolidate and integrate the learning into current attitudes, and to consider future options and action plans if relevant. Supportive interventions affirm the client's self-direction and self-creating.

7 Transpersonal therapy

This sequence is for the therapist who is working with clients at transpersonal (spiritual) levels. It can, of course, be interwoven with the preceding sequence (no. 6).

7.1 First phase   Many catalytic interventions to elicit client self-discovery in the psychic and spiritual domains of experience, with occasional informative ones – personal interpretations, and brief conceptual inputs to illumine transpersonal processes and methods.

7.2 Second phase   As self-discovery starts to uncover more subtle attitudes, confronting interventions highlight contracted states of awareness, and catalytic interventions invite the client to use transmutative methods, report on the states entered and to verbal-ize insights. Cathartic attention may be needed for incidental release of distress. Supportive interventions uphold the client in this work.

7.3 Third phase   After the use of transmutative methods, catalytic interventions draw out the client to integrate the learning into current attitudes, and to consider future options and action plans. Supportive interventions affirm the client's self-discovery and self-transfiguration.

CHAPTER 13

DEGENERATE AND PERVERTED
INTERVENTIONS

There are four basic kinds of degenerate intervention that can afflict any and every category. They run across the board. To say that an intervention is degenerate, in the sense intended here, is not to say that it is deliberately malicious or perverted (I deal with this type later); but rather that it is misguided, rooted in lack of awareness, lack of experience, of insight, of personal growth or simply of training. The four kinds are: unsolicited; manipulative; compulsive; and unskilled.

UNSOLICITED INTERVENTIONS

The grossest kind of unsolicited intervention is when there is no formal practitioner–client relationship at all, and one person simply appoints him- or herself as 'practitioner' to another, and without being asked, starts to inform, advise, interpret, confront or elicit in ways that are interfering and disrespectful of the autonomy and good sense of the other. These occur all too frequently in ordinary social relations.

Where there is some formal practitioner–client role relationship, such as counsellor and client, doctor and patient, bank manager and customer, then the practitioner's role roughly defines the sorts of interventions the client is expecting. It also roughly defines what sorts of interventions would be unsolicited and intrusive. So customers may find marital advice from their bank manager improper and unsolicited, but financial advice entirely proper and solicited.

There are grey areas, however, and when in doubt the practitioner can always seek a contract for the use of certain types of intervention. What is degenerate within a formal practitioner–client relationship is when practitioners insensitively blunder over into unsolicited territory, without any contract with the client, interfering and intruding in the mistaken supposition that they are doing their job.

There is, however, a more subtle and slightly more insidious kind of unsolicited intervention. This is when the practitioner is doing his or her proper and solicited intervention, but in a manner that is intrusive, disrespectful, curt, brusque, aggressive or unloving. This kind of professional sadism has been a besetting sin in the helping business. The vulnerable client receives two messages, and is put in a very painful double-bind, needing the technical skill, but appalled at the human invasion. So all interventions need to have a manner that is basically respectful of client autonomy and responsibility, that honours the client's fundamental worth. The practitioner puts them forward in a way that accepts the client's right to think, be, do, say, feel something different; and is not compulsively attached to their importance or to the importance of the client's compliance with them.

A special case, as we have seen, arises with respect to confronting interventions. They are by their nature unsolicited, since they point to what the client is not aware of. Practitioners can, of course, set up a contract with the client that legitimates their being confronting. But even so, this or that particular confrontation will still be unsolicited in terms of its own peculiar content. And whether there is a confronting contract or not, there is always a question of how far to go in raising consciousness, and even more simply when to do so.

Another special case is where the role relation requires the practitioner to engage in unsolicited interventions: the parent, the schoolteacher, the policeman, the probation officer and many others. Where possible, when the client's attendance is involuntary, the practitioner can try to set up some kind of voluntary contract within the statutory or other constraints.

MANIPULATIVE INTERVENTIONS

These are interventions in which practitioners are motivated by self-interest regardless of the interests of the client. They are therefore manipulating the client to make sure that they get what they want out of the interaction, irrespective of whether the client gets anything worthwhile or not. Classic examples are when practitioners manipulate the client in order to get sex, money or the satisfactions of power play. A less obvious but equally insidious example is when they manoeuvre the client into saying and doing things only in a form that fits the therapeutic, educational or professional belief system to which they are wedded: that is, they always lead, and never follow, the client.

Manipulative interventions can be more or less deliberate. In the less deliberate form, the practitioner slips over into manipulation through some combination of stress, lack of awareness and control. Where manipulation is quite calculated and intentional, then we are veering towards the perverted kind of degeneration (see below).

If manipulation is defined as the practitioner being motivated by self-interest regardless of the interests of the client, then facilitation can be defined as the practitioner being motivated by a real concern for the interests of the client. The distinction is both clear and fundamental. Nevertheless, some clients insist for a period on seeing all true facilitation as manipulation. This is because in critical past situations that were supposed to be caring they have only ever encountered manipulation. It takes them some time to believe and see that they have encountered an authentic concern for their interests.

Some practitioners sometimes 'facipulate'; perhaps all practitioners sometimes 'facipulate'. 'Facipulation' is a mixture of facilitation and manipulation, such as following the client in a way such that the client ends up where the practitioner wants him or her to be – for the client's own good, of course. If the client does not seem to be able to determine what his or her own interests are, when given the opportunity, and the practitioner has a good idea of what the client's interests are, then the practitioner manoeuvres the client's self-direction so that it 'finds' these interests.

At its best, 'facipulation' is much, much better than outright manipulation; at its worst, it is just a way of saving the face of a client-centred approach.

The client who is most vulnerable to outright manipulation is the client who is in great need of the expertise of the practitioner; is totally ignorant in the area of expertise; and who has a strong unconscious projection directed on to the practitioner.

COMPULSIVE INTERVENTIONS

These degenerate interventions are rooted in unresolved and unacknowledged psychological material – the frozen needs and occluded distresses of earlier years – which practitioners have not worked through and which they are projecting quite unawarely into their interactions with the client. They tend to be very widespread in our culture in which training in the helping professions does not include any training of practitioners in their own emotional competence (see Chapter 2, p. 15) that is, in the emotional skills of expression, control, catharsis and transmutation.

The professional role is used both as a defence against, and as an outlet for displacing, distress. These degenerations are typically manifest in the compulsive helper, the practitioner who is unawarely still acting out the conformist 'good boy', 'good girl' survival strategy of earlier years, within which lurks a good deal of occluded anger. The compulsive helper usually has a limited range of interventions, which are frequently misapplied, partly because they are limited and so do not always fit the situation, and partly because even when they fit they are mismanaged.

The compulsive helper also works too hard, sees too many people, takes on unrealistic levels of responsibility for their welfare, and suffers bouts of guilt and therapeutic impotence – bouts that drive the afflicted helper more relentlessly around the treadmill. This onerous life serves, pathologically, to displace a good deal of the occluded anger, both through mismanaged interventions on clients, and through self-punishment on the treadmill.

Compulsively mismanaged interventions have a thousand forms, but there are three basic sorts: (a) those that punish, attack, abuse, invade the client; (b) those that coddle and collude with the client; (c) those that avoid, evade, miss, overlook the client. The third sort is either the non-intervention (the omission), or the irrelevant one that misses the mark.

Typical medical examples of these may be, but not necessarily in all cases are: (a) treatments with unpleasant side-effects; (b) repeat prescriptions of psychotropics; (c) overlooking the psychosocial aspect of the complaint. Typical academic examples are: (a) giving non-stop lectures for too long, without any breaks, with too much information and too many visual aids; (b) making too many educational decisions for students about what they should learn, how they should learn it, when they should learn it and whether they have learnt it; (c) ignoring emotional and interpersonal aspects of education.

There appears to be one golden rule for all would-be practitioners: never become a helper until you have worked on how angry you feel at your parents' and teachers' mismanagement of you in the interests of making you 'good': hence the importance of preparation and training in emotional competence, as discussed at the end of Chapter 2 (p. 15).

UNSKILLED INTERVENTIONS

There is clearly a class of degenerate or mismanaged interventions which are not unsolicited, nor manipulative, nor compulsive. They are simply incompetent; because the practitioner has never had any interactive-skills training, has no grasp of a wide-ranging repertoire, and is stuck with an *ad hoc* array of interventions that is too limited in its scope and too variable in its quality or suitability.

Unskilled practitioners need the following, as do practitioners suffering from the other three kinds of degeneration (although they also need a little more).

1 *To learn* a comprehensive repertoire of interventions, so that they can identify them when others are producing them, and, more importantly, produce them at will in their own behaviour.

2 *To assess*, with the help of feedback from others, their own strengths and weaknesses across the total repertoire (their weaknesses including those interventions they omit altogether and those they make a mess of).

3 *To practise*, with the help of feedback from others, interventions in which they are weak, until they are good or better at them.

4 *To have some model* of what it is to do the interventions well, whether the modelling is through verbal descriptions, or through live or video demonstrations.

Six Category Workshops are designed to meet these four training needs with a strong emphasis on practice and feedback.

The most degenerate interventions are those that are simultaneously unskilled, compulsive, manipulative and unsolicited . . . unless, perhaps, they are those that are simultaneously skilled, compulsive, manipulative and unsolicited.

ANALYSING DEGENERATE INTERVENTIONS

There is a simple analytic framework for identifying degenerate interventions in terms of behaviour analysis, so that we can get a grip on them for training purposes, and for self-monitoring and self-assessment. This framework uses just five dimensions:

1 *Category of intervention*: for example, whether catalytic, say, or prescriptive.

2 *Particular intervention within the category*: for example, whether an open question, say, or a closed question within the catalytic category.

3 *Content of the particular intervention*: for example, whether the open question is about this, or about that.

4 *Manner of delivering the content*: for example, whether the open question is asked with, say, an appropriate tone, and with appropriate inflection, or not.
5 *Timing*: for example, is the question asked too soon, too late or at the right time. Timing not only deals with when the intervention is used, but also with how long it is used for – whether run on too long, cut off too soon, or sustained for just the right period.

In assessing any intervention, therefore, we can ask: (a) Was it the correct category for what was going on in interaction with the client? (b) And if the category was right, was it the right intervention within that category? And if so, was (c) the content appropriate, (d) the manner appropriate, and (e) the timing good?

However, a technical, analytic account of degenerations does not reach the imagination as well as a colloquial and everyday account. So I now run through a whole range of degenerative interventions under each category, but free of any detailed analysis. It is a familiar list, full of baleful error. In Six Category Workshops we sometimes invite trainees to do intentional negative practice on their own selection.

PRESCRIPTIVE DEGENERATIONS

1 Interfering take-over

Giving advice to a client who does not need it and does not want it, and whose self-direction needs honouring. Close to:

2 Insulting take-over

The practitioner gives the client advice, the content of which implies the client is an idiot.

3 Benevolent take-over

Creating dependency by giving advice to an insecure client who would be better encouraged to be self-directing.

4 Misdirection

The practitioner proposes behaviour to the client which points him or her in quite the wrong direction.

5 Moralistic oppression

Imposing on the uncertain client authoritarian 'shoulds' and 'oughts' and 'musts' so that they become alienated from a sense of their true needs and interests.

6 Weak authority

The practitioner goes flabby in manner when an authoritative prescription is called for, and the client becomes more insecure.

7 Incompetent authority

The practitioner gives advice, the content of which is feeble and inadequate, even when the advice is aimed roughly in the right direction.

8 Catalytic compulsion

The practitioner is trying to elicit self-direction when proposing behaviour to the client would be more appropriate: the improper avoidance of prescription.

9 Collusive authority

The practitioner gives advice which the practitioner knows the client wants to hear for defensive or malingering reasons.

10 Sadistic authority

The practitioner advises the client to do something which will involve unnecessary pain and discomfort.

11 Manipulative authority

The practitioner proposes behaviour to the client that will gratify the practitioner's desires and interests, regardless of any benefit or harm to the client.

12 Unsolicited territory

The practitioner blunders into giving advice in an area of the client's life that is quite outside the tacit or explicit remit of the practitioner's role.

13 Consultative error

Either the practitioner is directive when he or she needs to be consultative, or is consultative when he or she needs to be directive.

14 Loss of charismatic nerve

The practitioner is weakened by diffidence and doubt, fails to give a charismatic command and loses hold of his or her personal power.

15 Oppressive authority

The practitioner dominates the client tyrannically.

INFORMATIVE DEGENERATIONS

1 Seductive overteach

The practitioner goes on for too long in fascinating the client with interesting information, so that the client is seduced into excessive passivity and away from self-directed learning.

2 Oppressive overteach

The practitioner goes on for too long giving out information, even though the client clearly needs to contribute, or is distracted and alienated or gives evidence of fatigue. The client is held back from self-directed learning.

3 Incompetent content

The practitioner gives out information that is inaccurate, or behind the times, or disorganized, or incoherent, or biased, or pitched too high, or pitched too low or too jargon laden and so on.

4 Incompetent delivery

The practitioner's voice is too low, or too fast, or his or her speech has too many redundancies; or posture is wooden, gestures too few or too many, and so on.

5 Inaccurate diagnosis

The practitioner misses the real trouble and identifies the wrong complaint; or answers a question which he or she can answer but which the client did not actually ask.

6 Web spinning

The practitioner wraps the client up in a web of interpretations in which the client's capacity for self-generated insight is permanently cocooned and trapped. It may be seductive or oppressive.

7 Pushy perspective

The practitioner imposes on the client's experience the practitioner's favourite way of interpreting such things.

8 No explanation

Practitioners never say what they are doing or why they are doing it. Clients may be mystified and miss the relevance of what is going on.

9 Dogmatic prognosis

The practitioner predicts an outcome that ignores the client's untapped potential for intentional self-healing, or personal growth, or autonomous risk-taking and decision-making.

10 Talking over

The practitioner interrupts the client's contribution and buries it under a load of more information.

11 Compulsive teaching

The practitioner thinks it is primarily his or her responsibility to make the client learn things by putting over more and more information – not having grasped that it is primarily the client's responsibility to learn things, and that the practitioner's information-giving responsibility is entirely secondary.

12 Compulsive eliciting

The practitioner compulsively never teaches, and inappropriately tries to elicit from a client what should be taught.

13 Faltering delivery

The practitioner does not believe what he or she is saying and so disconcerts the client.

14 Manipulative content

The practitioner gives out information or an interpretation whose content is designed to influence the client to say or do something that is in the practitioner's interests, irrespective of whether it is in the client's interests.

Then there is unsolicited content, insulting content, interfering content, and so on, and so on.

CONFRONTING DEGENERATIONS

1 Going round the mulberry bush

The practitioner tries to confront the client, but talks round and round the issue, too anxious to bring it up directly. The client is baffled or quietly triumphant.

2 Avoidance

The practitioner is too anxious to raise the issue at all with the client. The confrontation agenda is never faced.

3 Sledgehammer

The practitioner raises the issue aggressively and punitively, displacing his or her anxiety into improperly attacking the client. This is the bully who picks on the weak client to deal with the day's distress.

4 Swinging

The practitioner goes around the mulberry bush, then sledgehammers, swings back again guiltily trying to clean up the mess.

5 Authoritarian parent

The practitioner is scolding parent seeing the client as naughty child – another version of no. 3.

6 Giving away power

The practitioner raises the issue, but apologetically or pleadingly or defensively or uneasily, or in some other way gives away power so that the client is dominating the discussion – a relative of no. 1 above.

7 The smiler

The practitioner becomes 'The smiler with the knife under his cloak' (Chaucer). He or she raises the issue by cutting into the client under the guise of a smile – another version of no. 3 above.

8 Projected agenda

The practitioner raises what for him or her would be a confronting agenda, only to find that it is not so for the client, who may find it non-problematic, interesting or even liberating.

9 Misplaced agenda

It is not projected, and it is still wrong.

10 Moralistic criticism

The practitioner raises the issue in a way that makes a critical, moralistic judgement about the client – a version of no. 3 above.

11 Pseudo-objective appraisal

The practitioner raises the issue as if writing an objective appraisal report on the client – a version of no. 3.

12 Shock overtalk

The practitioner has got the confrontation right, but overtalks the client's need to have space to assimilate the news and the shock.

13 Win–lose

The practitioner falls from grace. Instead of engaging in aware and supportive consciousness-raising, he or she has degenerated into win–lose combat with the client. This is a possible consequence of no. 3 and its variants.

14 Manipulative confrontation

The practitioner raises the client's consciousness about an agenda, but only so that the practitioner can get something out of it, irrespective of whether the client does.

15 Unsolicited confrontation

As we have seen, every confrontation is in a sense by its nature unsolicited. But what I mean here is the confrontation that really goes over the top: it is uncalled for, inappropriate, the timing is wrong, the context does not legitimate it, it goes too deep too soon, and so on.

16 Nit picking

The practitioner confronts the client with a trivial, irrelevant, inconsequential agenda.

CATHARTIC DEGENERATIONS

These are all rather more technical. We do not meet many of them in the ordinary cut and thrust of life like we do so many in the previous three sets of degenerations. However, the first six in the following list are familiar ways the culture has of keeping distress suppressed.

1 Not giving permission

The practitioner fails to give the client – who is embarrassed at the overflow of distress emotions – verbal permission and encouragement to unload them.

2 Not reaching out

The practitioner fails to reach out to give appropriate physical support, when the client is on the brink of tears.

3 Suppressive embrace

The practitioner goes over to hold the client who is just entering catharsis, usually of grief in tears, but the embrace is a bear-hug which is unawarely trying to stop the distress coming up.

4 'There there'

The practitioner is unawarely sympathizing with words and in a tone that cuts the client off from the release of the distress.

5 Suppressive overtalk

The practitioner talks over and ignores the body cues which show that the client needs to be cathartic.

6 Analytic misdirection

The practitioner gets the client to talk about, to analyse, the distress emotions which are rising to the surface for catharsis. The analysis suppresses the emotions.

7 Picking up on expressive cues

Instead of on distress-charged cues.

8 Time lag

The practitioner picks up on a process cue (i.e. body cue) too long after it has occurred, and misses the 'time window' within which the pick-up is effective.

9 'Why?'

The practitioner short-circuits imminent catharsis by asking the client why he or she has produced this or that body cue, instead of having the client amplify and energize the cue so that it can tell its own story in and with the catharsis. The 'Why?' question prematurely throws the client into a suppressive, analytic mode.

10 Cue hopping

The practitioner hops aimlessly from process cue to process cue without any guiding hypothesis about the client's dynamic, and goes round in circles with the client.

11 Rigid hypothesis

The practitioner holds the client to the content of the practitioner's hypothesis, when the process cues are urgently pointing elsewhere.

12 Hammering a process cue

The practitioner goes on and on having the client repeat and amplify a process cue that has lost its charge and is cut off from any emotion.

13 Lack of confluence

The practitioner pursues the client's content and understanding at the expense of catharsis; or facilitates the client's catharsis at the expense of content. Content here means understanding the context through self-generated insight.

14 Too deep too soon

The practitioner makes too steep an intervention into deeply buried distress which the client is not yet ready to handle, resulting, perhaps, in unaware and uncontrolled dramatization.

15 Coming out too soon

The practitioner unawarely cuts off the client's catharsis prematurely, often just when it is about to deepen and intensify towards its climax. The practitioner's own defended material is usually the problem here.

16 Total avoidance

The practitioner unawarely passes over both content and process cues which would take the client into sorts of catharsis the practitioner cannot handle in him- or herself.

17 Improper ending

The practitioner fails properly to bring the post-cathartic client back into present time, disattending from distress.

18 Colluding with dramatization

The practitioner ignorantly mistakes dramatization for catharsis and goes on encouraging a hysterical show.

19 Feeble integration

The practitioner does not give enough time and encouragement for the client to marshal his or her post-cathartic insight and to integrate it into his or her current way of being, doing and thinking.

20 Slow shift

The practitioner colludes with client resistance and is unable to, or slow to, shift the client from analytic talk to literal description, or from the latter into a psychodrama, or from the heart of a later psychodrama to the heart of an earlier one.

21 Heavy hook

The practitioner gets painfully hooked by the client's heaviness, and so loses the light touch for deft interventions of all kinds. Contradiction in particular needs a light, deft touch.

22 Lumbering about

The practitioner is heavy-handed and insensitive in trying to use physical pressures and extensions on the client's body during catharsis.

23 Heavy-duty catharsis

The practitioner forgets the emotional point of catharsis, that it is to give space for joy, elegance, grace, delight in being, the concomitants of liberated insight. So the whole process becomes too earnest, duty laden.

24 Mismanaging attention

The practitioner fails to help the client generate enough free attention before catharsis; or fails to help the client regain his or her balance of attention when it gets lost during cathartic work.

25 Wrong-category damage

The practitioner advises, interprets, informs, confronts, with a damaging timing that interrupts active catharsis or suppresses incipient catharsis.

26 Cathartic compulsion

The practitioner suffers from the belief that all the client's distress emotions are to be catharted and so does not point the way, when appropriate, to the transmutative power of imaginal and archetypal work.

CATALYTIC DEGENERATIONS

1 Too many closed questions

The practitioner harries the client and keeps him or her to the narrow field of right (or, worse, wrong) answers.

2 The compulsive search for order

The practitioner unawarely deals with his or her own anxiety by prematurely trying to bring some meaning and order into the client's talk. The catalytic interventions are centred on the practitioner's, not the client's, search for meaning.

3 Prescription and information in catalytic clothing

A gross version of no. 2 in which the practitioner prescribes and informs in the guise of 'catalytic' questions, for example 'Don't you think it would be a good idea for you to . . .?', or 'Would you like to . . .?', or 'Don't you think that . . .?'

4 Curiosity

Another practitioner-centred degeneration, in which the practitioner draws out from the client material to satisfy the practitioner's curiosity rather than enable the client to talk in ways that are meaningful to him or her, the client.

5 Blind alley

The practitioner elicits a lot of client exploration in quite unproductive territory.

6 Scraping the bowl

The client's exploration has been productive, but the practitioner goes on trying to enable the client to find more to talk about in the same area, when it would be better to go on to something else. The client may try to rescue the practitioner with pseudo-work to help the practitioner allay anxiety about professional effectiveness.

7 Interview rape

The practitioner over-elicits too skilfully and intrusively so that clients are left feeling they have said more than they wanted to, or were ready to, or feel safe in disclosing. Feelings of over-exposure may lead the client to stay away and not come back.

8 Poking at junk

The practitioner unawarely colludes with the client by eliciting more and more maladaptive moaning, complaining, scapegoating, self-deprecation and so on. This usually leaves the practitioner exhausted under a pile of the client's junk, after both have poked it round for an hour.

9 Dull antennae

The practitioner misses those critical or sensitive periods in a session when the client is ripe for a shift of perspective, a restructuring of an attitude, a movement to the level of learning from experience, a decision to make an ending or make a beginning or make a modification.

10 Ground floor only

The practitioner elicits talk only at the level of living, about (for example) being in a relationship, and never at the level of living as learning, about how to be in a relationship; or at the level of learning, rather than at the level of learning how to learn.

11 Feeding the map

The practitioner elicits the client's exploration in order to fill out and feed some life-style map, for example. Feeding the map with client experience becomes more important than client self-discovery and learning.

12 Absent awareness

The practitioner is not here now, and not there now, but distracted.

13 Bad echo

In using selective echoing, the practitioner reflects the wrong bit; or puts an evaluative inflection on some word in the echoed phrase, or gives it an evaluative and an interrogative twist.

14 Missing the brick line

In using empathic building, the practitioner goes beyond the meaning lurking in the client's lines to a deep-level interpretation which is clearly not just about to emerge; or simply gets the lurking meaning wrong.

15 Stuck on the gradient

The practitioner cannot shift flexibly and appropriately when trying to use a prescriptive–catalytic gradient, or a catalytic–informative gradient.

16 Misworking with emotions

The practitioner facilitates the wrong way of working with the client's emotions, encouraging control when it should be expression, redirection when it should be switching, transmutation when it should be catharsis, and so on.

SUPPORTIVE DEGENERATIONS

Many of these arise because the practitioner is unawarely displacing fear of true intimacy, caring and sharing – into some inauthentic and distorted attempt at support.

1 Moral patronage

The practitioner climbs into a pulpit in order to congratulate the client on his or her self-improvement. The client, of course, feels subtly insulted and put down.

2 Experiential patronage

The practitioner pats the client on the head for having so effectively gone along the same road that the practitioner covered a long time ago.

3 Qualified support

The practitioner appreciates the client, but adds a negative qualification: 'You are a loving person, but it's just a pity that you . . .'. The practitioner's own self-deprecating agenda is projected into the qualification.

4 Overdone support

The practitioner appreciates the client in a eulogy that becomes inauthentic through excess – false compliments.

5 Misplaced sympathy

The practitioner colludes with clients' distortions by sympathizing with their rehearsal and displacement of pain rather than with their need to work through it.

6 Inappropriate inhibition

The practitioner inappropriately holds back a human impulse to touch; to express love, care, concern, appreciation; to share and be self-disclosing.

7 Sexual collusion

The practitioner and client act out a mutual sexual attraction that is the displacement of old frozen needs and distress. During positive transference this becomes psychological incest.

This review of different sorts of degenerate interventions under each of the six categories does not claim to be exhaustive, only reasonably comprehensive.

PERVERTED INTERVENTIONS

Degenerate interventions are rooted in lack of awareness, in lack of experience, lack of personal growth, lack of training. Perverted interventions are something rather darker: they are quite deliberately malicious; they *intend* harm to the client, they seek to do clients down and leave them in some way disabled, disadvantaged and in distress. Their purpose is to damage people.

The difference between a manipulative intervention and a perverted intervention is that the former for self-interested reasons simply disregards the real interests of the client, whereas the latter intentionally seeks the detriment of the real interests of the client.

Any systematic analysis here would be an excursion into what might be called the black intervention arts: the domain of the spy, the secret policeman, the political *agent provocateur*, the interrogator, the torturer, the brainwasher, the propagandist, the professional criminal. Their interventions are always unsolicited, frequently immoral by any human standard, and their 'clients' either constrained against their will, or unwitting of the conspiracy that is being hatched around them, until it is too late.

One view of perverted practitioners is that they have been so emotionally hurt and scarred in early life that they can only misguidedly get caught in the vicious circle of seeking to alleviate their deeply buried pain by reproducing pain in other people. Their accountability and responsibility are low because they are so inveterately compulsive.

Another view is that while they have been heavily scarred, there has been for them a point of choice between living with their hidden pain in a relatively harmless way, and compounding it with a policy of deliberate malignity. They are thus accountable and responsible to some significant degree.

A third view is that their accountability has nothing to do with the psychodynamics of the matter. If they have the intelligence and the intention to be malign in a sustained and systematic way, then they are fully accountable and responsible, however much emotional trauma was present or absent in their early life. I favour this view.

Throughout human history perverted interventions have been the stock-in-trade of those who move in the darkest areas of human interaction. Witness the following list:

1 Perverted prescription

The deliberate use of force, threat, pain, compulsion in constraining a person to act against that person's needs and interests.

2 Perverted information

The deliberate use of misrepresentation, lies, calumny, slander to harm the person about whom they are put forth, or to whom they are addressed.

3 Perverted confrontation

Deliberate, punitive psychological attack on a person to wound and incapacitate him or her emotionally. Torturing a person to tell the truth, or to 'confess' to things never said or done.

4 Perverted catharsis

Deliberately producing cathartic collapse and disintegration through subjecting a person to extreme mental and physical stress and pain. The disintegrated person may then be reintegrated in terms of imposed suggestion and indoctrination.

5 Perverted catalysis

Deliberate and malicious seduction, both in the sexual and in the wider sense; intentionally leading a person on to his or her own undoing by eliciting self-indulgent and self-destructive tendencies.

6 Perverted support

Affirming, supporting and encouraging the weak, distorted and corrupted behaviour of a person.

Such perversions, of course, are nothing to do with normal practitioner–client interactions, which usually suffer only the relatively unaware degenerations analysed earlier. However, they

FIGURE 13.1 The six categories in their total context

are still widely in use in various parts of our planet, and we need to get the measure of them, not least to help their victims (those who survive) deal with the after-effects.

For this purpose and for all other positive endeavour in reaching out one-to-one to other people, the six categories, manifest in their total context, as shown in Figure 13.1, can be of assistance.

CHAPTER 14

SIX CATEGORY TRAINING

This chapter throws more light on the whole system for the general reader. But it is primarily addressed to trainers and facilitators who have an interest in the principles and practice of six category training. So the person referred to as 'you' throughout these chapters is the interpersonal skills trainer putting on a six category workshop. For a full account of group facilitation, see Heron (1999).

In Chapter 2, I distinguished between seven kinds of helping:

- Giving informal support to friends, neighbours, relatives, colleagues in times of change or crisis.
- Offering the service of special technical expertise through a professional role such as that of lawyer, bank manager, accountant, architect, engineer.
- Offering physical, social and cultural services through the helping professions of medicine and complementary therapies, nursing, social work, education, policing and many others.
- Offering organizational service through skilled communication and interaction in the workplace;
- Offering psychological services for personal growth and development, through both short- and long-term counselling and psychotherapy.
- Offering spiritual services through the roles of transpersonal practitioner, priest, shaman, seer, spiritual healer.
- Offering mutual support in organized peer self-help groups for life-management and personal development, such as co-counselling, mentioned just above.

Helpers in all of these categories will benefit from the kind of training that I discuss in this chapter. It covers the use of intensive short workshops, up to five days long, in which the six category model is adapted and used selectively to meet the needs of participants.

All the points made in the 12 sections that follow are ones that can be made to trainees at the outset of or during the workshop. They provide conceptual orientation for the training: they give it a context, provide a rationale and outline its structure. If you can get them all in, succinctly, with appropriate amounts of discussion, and in a way that engages everybody, so much the better.

You can be selective about the three sections after the first one below, depending on what sort of trainees you have.

TRAINING AND EDUCATION

It is a good idea to tell trainees that their training needs a context of education. While interpersonal training deals with learning specific skills, interpersonal education deals with acquiring background knowledge about personal development, interpersonal processes, group dynamics, organizational development and current trends in social change.

You can weave some of this educational content into the presentation of the skills. This sets them in the broader context of a perspective on social change, including the educational, organizational and professional revolutions described in the next three sections.

There is an important sense in which the person who changes his or her range of interpersonal behaviour is part of a much wider cultural transformation. It can be liberating for trainees to see what people are doing in this way.

THE EDUCATIONAL REVOLUTION

In the past 40 years there has been a dramatic shift from the idea of teaching as imparting knowledge to students, to the idea of *teaching as the facilitation of learning* by students. Learning is acknowledged as being fundamentally a self-directed activity, hence the student is involved in educational decision-making through learning contracts and participative assessment (Boud, 1988).

Parallel with this is the idea of learning by the whole person (Boud and Miller, 1996; Heron,1999). The old model of education, going back to classical times, dealt only with the education of the intellect, theoretical and applied. The new model integrates this with emotional, interpersonal and political competence. Nowadays we have people who are learning by thinking, feeling and doing – bringing all these to bear on the acquisition of new knowledge and skills. There is also an increasing concern to ground all this in a new kind of spiritual opening.

Interpersonal skills training is a good example of this new holistic learning. It means learning by doing, by practising the various skills. You need to think about what is involved in the skill before doing it, after doing it, and on your feet while doing it. Your emotions radically affect how you do it, and are the basis for being attuned to the state of the other people and to their reaction to you. Your capacity for spiritual openness – for being here now, being there now and having abundant attention (nos. 6.1, 6.2, 6.3 in Chapter 9) – is a foundation for all other skills.

Flexibility and range of interpersonal skill are needed by the new teachers, the facilitators of learning, in negotiating learning contracts and course design, in collaborating in assessments, in both eliciting self-direction and confronting oversights in students.

In covering all of this, therefore, you are providing your trainees with an educational context for the training they are about to receive; and you are giving the teachers and tutors among the trainees a professional rationale for doing the training.

THE ORGANIZATIONAL REVOLUTION

There is also an organizational revolution afoot. What is at stake is the inexorable march forward of doctrines of human rights, advancing from the political to the economic arena. All human beings have a right to participate in decisions that affect their needs, interests and activities in the work place, to have an increasing measure of self-determination in the production of goods or services. These moral claims are enhanced by the spread of educational and psychological claims for personal fulfilment and expression.

At the same time there is a pronounced tendency in the modern world towards large organizations. If these become monolithic, hierarchical bureaucracies, then three interrelated problems set in: unmanageable complexity, relative inefficiency and human alienation among staff. So the organizational revolution stems from the need for manageable complexity and for efficiency; as well as from needs for self-determination and self-realization for persons at work.

Alongside this moral, educational and structural shift, and supporting it, is a revolution in the technologies of information, communication and artificial intelligence. As a result, a new era dawns for organizational forms: learning companies, organizations of consent and of contract, industrial democracies, co-operatives, project teams, autonomous work groups, networks, flexible work patterns, intrapreneurship, decentralization and federalism (Handy, 1985).

The key to management, in newly emerging ways of structuring the world of work, is great flexibility of style in handling power. The effective manager in the organizational revolution that is currently afoot is one who can move swiftly and elegantly, as the context requires, between exercising power over people, sharing power with people and handing power to people (Heron, 1999). And this, of course, means great flexibility and range of interpersonal skill.

Here you have a rationale for six category training for all leaders, managers and supervisors in organizational settings.

THE PROFESSIONAL REVOLUTION

From psychiatry to law, the helping and service professions have been under attack, from the writings of George Bernard Shaw to those of Ivan Illich and beyond, for oppressing the laity with improper claims to expert power. The professional revolution, also currently afoot, acknowledges the point without surrendering to it. The movement forward is towards a degree of deprofessionalization. This in turn means a shift from telling the client or patient what to do in the light of the professional's expert knowledge, to co-operating with the client or patient as a self-determining person who gives his or her own significant meaning to the issues. The two parties collaborate in devising the outcome of the consultation.

Sometimes the professional may shift right over to facilitate the person's entire self-direction. At other times, the traditional, totally authoritative and directive approach may be appropriate. So here again great flexibility and range of interpersonal skill is required to manage the spectrum from direction, through negotiation, to facilitated delegation. Doctors and other professional helpers among the trainees can benefit from this rationale for six category training.

MARGINS FOR BEHAVIOUR CHANGE

If people need interpersonal skills training, this presupposes that their current range of behaviour is limited. Some of this restriction is simply due to ignorance: people have had no prior training, are unaware of the repertoire of possible behaviours and are just stuck within a narrow, conventional band. Some of the restriction may also be due to rigidities of attitude held in place by repressed distress from early hurtful experiences.

So there are two wider margins to which the current limited range can be extended. The first, which involves a big increase of new behaviours, can be achieved simply by skills training: seeing a repertoire, identifying the parts of it you never use, and then learning them. Reaching this margin is only a matter of dealing with prior ignorance.

The second margin, more extended and yielding a further range of behaviours, may require deeper psychological work: unpicking repressions, discharging the underlying distress, restructuring rigid attitudes of mind into more flexible forms, and acquiring a good measure of emotional competence as defined in Chapter 2 (p. 15).

Short-term six category training, such as a 5-day workshop, is primarily about reaching the first margin, and since this margin is a long way out from most people's conventional and unreflective starting place, there is plenty to do. But it is unwise totally to separate interpersonal skills training from personal development work and the acquisition of emotional competence, so some of the exercises on a 5-day workshop relate to it. This is to honour the principle and affirm a connection, even though any extensive in-depth work on the second margin is not on the 5-day agenda.

The most relevant way to do this is in exercises on the cathartic category: trainees in the client role can be real clients, their practitioners helping them – gently and to an appropriate degree – to dismantle repressions and discharge distress. What is important here is that trainees are encouraged to acknowledge in principle that professional skills should never be divorced from personal growth, and to deal with this in practice by becoming real clients for each other. It is also important to encourage those who have gone through this discharge process for the first time to follow it up, and to give them details of workshops and centres where this can be done. Basic co-counselling training, and association in a co-counselling network, can meet this need for follow-up very well.

BEHAVIOUR-ANALYSIS HIERARCHY

In order to create a repertoire for interpersonal skills training we have first of all to analyse behaviour into manageable parts – the basic elements of the repertoire. But behaviour falls into a hierarchy of levels, and we have to choose at which level to pitch the analysis. The first level is that of mere movements, which are defined only in kinetic and geometric terms, such as 'the eyes rotate up and to their left as the head and neck drop slightly forward'.

The second level is that of simple actions, where the analysis is in terms such as 'walks', 'points', 'talks', and where the social purpose of the simple action is not stated. A term at this level may include many species: thus, 'talks' includes 'describes', 'asks' and so on.

The third level is that of intentions, where the analysis is in terms of the social purpose of behaviour, such as 'greeting a friend', 'paying the bill', 'suggesting a route'. So we have a three-level hierarchy, in which intentions include actions, and actions include movements. A higher level adds an extra dimension to the lower levels which it includes.

Now the six categories themselves are on the third level of behaviour analysis. They are simple and basic intentions set strategically in the mid-range of all intentions: 'recommends behaviour to', 'gives new information to', 'challenges the restrictive attitudes of', 'releases tension in' and so on.

When the behaviour analysis is applied within a single category, it is also at the level of intentions. But occasionally, a single intention within a category is further analysed into the second level, that of actions. Thus no. 6 in the catalytic category (Chapter 9) is 'eliciting self-directed learning' (intention level), and this includes items such as 'asking an open question' (action level).

It is important for the trainee to grasp that the categories, and the interventions within each of them, are basic intentions. They have an interpersonal purpose built into them. This gives them their practical power and adaptability. Once a person has grasped the purpose of an intervention, then they can give expression to it in many different verbal and behavioural forms, choosing one that is precisely suited to the context of its use.

OVERARCHING VALUES

Intentions have their own hierarchy. Thus, my intention in pointing is to show you where George lives; and my intention in showing you where he lives is to influence you to visit him; and so on. At the apex of this hierarchy there are, whether I am aware of it or not, some very general values (or disvalues), which I am seeking to realize by my immediate intention.

If we trace the basic six categories, through their hierarchy of intentions, back to their overarching and guiding values, then in my view they all ultimately seek to enhance the self-determination of the client in the expression and fulfilment of his or her person in relations with others. The supreme values of the hierarchy are those of autonomous persons in co-operative relations with other autonomous persons (cf. pp. 122–123). We are concerned with the person as autonomy-in-connectedness, intrinsically immersed in communion, not as the isolated and alienated Cartesian ego (Spretnak, 1995).

Chapter 3 develops the idea of three degrees of autonomy: the creative, the self-creating and the self-transfiguring degrees. But there is a third value, as well as those of autonomy and co-operation. It is implicit in the practitioner's role, and in what the practitioner on occasion says and does. It is the value of 'hierarchy', of unilaterally doing things for the client, as when the practitioner is prescriptive, informative and confronting.

The value of hierarchy is subordinate to the values of autonomy and co-operation: the two latter provide a rationale for the former. For the creative hierarch is someone who does something for the other in the longer term interests of enhancing that person's capacity for autonomy and co-operation.

Until trainees have got a feel for the basic human values that guide the immediate use of the six categories, they will be thrashing about in the dark. For the values tell us what it is we are really seeking to achieve in our work with our clients.

THE FOUR PILLARS OF INTERPERSONAL SKILLS TRAINING

Once we have done the behaviour analysis and designed the six category repertoire, then we can facilitate the training – which has four parts. (For full details see Chapter 15.)

1 *Discrimination.* Trainees learn the repertoire, so that they can identify, in their own and other people's behaviour, basic interventions within each of the six categories. They also learn to identify what their particular strengths and weaknesses are within the repertoire.
2 *Modelling.* Trainees are given an account, or a demonstration or a video, of what it is to do the interventions within each category well, as a model for learning how to do them.
3 *Practice.* Trainees practise building up skill in those parts of the repertoire in which they are weak or absent.
4 *Feedback.* They get information from other trainees and the trainer about how far their practice is on or off track.

Presenting these four pillars to the trainees at the outset orientates them within the design and rationale of the training. It sets the scene for the immediate use of discrimination training exercises.

THE GYMNASTIC PRINCIPLE

Many exercises, especially during discrimination training, when trainees are learning the repertoire, are effective because they are highly artificial: trainees are restricted to one or two behaviours, or are stretched over a large number, or given an arbitrary sequence, or play a behavioural card game, and so on.

It helps trainees to drop their resistance, accept the artificiality and get its benefits, if you explain before using these exercises that they are based on the gymnastic principle. They pick out certain behaviours to be done in a manner that does not occur in real life, in the same way that in a gymnasium selected groups of muscles are exercised with movements never used in daily life. But just as artificial physical exercises in a gym build up muscle for real physical work, so artificial behavioural exercises in a workshop build up psychological 'muscle' for real-life encounters with other people.

Of course, not all the exercises are based on this gymnastic principle. When the training moves on from learning the repertoire to practising in areas of weakness, then the exercises move towards simulations of real situations, and beyond this to real practitioner–client interactions between trainees.

THE STRETCH EFFECT

You need to be aware that when the trainees do a lot of artificial exercises, however pleasant and light-hearted the learning may be, there is something else going on. All these odd, unusual ways of behaving are loosening up the soul. It is being aroused from its conventional slumber. It is being stretched.

As the stress of embarrassment is being discharged in intermittent bursts of laughter, deeper layers of repressed pain will be given space to move nearer the surface. And all this quite unnoticed, as everyone enjoys their learning in the behavioural gym.

This means that unwittingly the trainees are all coming a little closer to the role of the cathartic client. You need to be sensitive to this current in the group, and to be ready to put it to work when moving into the cathartic category later on in the workshop. You can also alert trainees to this process, in a relaxed way, as the exercises are going on. They will not take a lot of conscious notice, but their souls will register the point, and will respond later to the implicit permission-giving of your statement.

THE VOLUNTARY PRINCIPLE

It is essential that the trainees should attend the workshop on a voluntary basis. Authentic change of behaviour can only be based on the free and informed choice of a person. If people attend the training because they have been told to do so, then their new skills will be based on survival and expediency, and the way they are used is likely to be disturbed by their hidden resentment.

Sometimes the motivation to attend the training is ambiguous: people are free to choose, yet choose to come because they think it would be impolitic in the eyes of the organization not to. These are organization people, wedded to its competitive, manipulative norms and values – which will corrupt the way the new skills are applied. So it is important for you to confront this situation, and challenge people to be there in their own right, as persons with their own values, who can choose to act as change agents within the organization, and transform their previous puppet status. This relates to the earlier section in this chapter on the organizational revolution.

EXPERIENTIAL INQUIRY

The six category system is presented not as a dogma, but as a practical working hypothesis to be tested through experience of the training. Six category training is not a formal, full-blown co-operative inquiry, but it is a close relative: an experiential inquiry into the system by the participants individually and together, guided by the trainer. After the training, participants can explore the application of the six category model to daily professional and personal life, using first-person action research, in which the practitioner develops practical knowledge through self-directed inquiry into his or her own behaviour. For more on this, see self-monitoring (Heron, 1977a), reflection-in-action (Schon, 1983), experiential research (Cunningham, 1988), action inquiry (Torbert, 1991, 2000), radical practice (Heron, 1996). The model can also be adopted by a group of practitioners meeting at regular intervals as a full-blown co-operative inquiry team to review and revise the use of the categories in their ongoing professional work with clients. For details and examples of this type of inquiry, see Heron (1996), Heron and Reason (2000), Reason (1988, 1994). For an overview of participative forms of research in general, see Reason and Bradbury (2000).

DESIGN FOR A 5-DAY SIX CATEGORY BASIC TRAINING

The purpose of this section is to give a comprehensive outline of a design for a six category basic training which covers five consecutive days. It is offered as a good model, but not the only model, not even the best model. It presents the main sequence of events, and what is done at each stage. It does not give the detailed structure of exercises, just the basic sorts of exercise. There is a timetable towards the end.

This model starts the workshop with a lot of intellectual activity – presentation of basic ideas with plenty of discussion around them – before launching into sustained action. This is a matter of choice and style. Remember that you can do it a different way. For example, after introductions and culture setting, you can briefly present the six categories, then go straight for the action with a lot of discrimination training, and bring in the basic ideas as they relate to the trainees' feedback and review on the different exercises. Then close down the discrimination training with an intellectual session that reviews the basic ideas so far covered and adds those not yet touched upon.

INTRODUCTIONS

Introductions in the whole group start the workshop: they break the ice, give everyone a chance to speak and so bring everyone in from the very beginning. They let everyone learn a little bit about everyone else. They establish the principle of equal contributions in the large group. They give you useful information about the level at which to pitch the training, about who can make a special contribution to it, who may need special attention, and so on. They establish your presence and your benign and attentive authority. You are light, easy, informal, relaxed and friendly.

Exercises Everyone is seated in a large closed circle, including yourself. You invite people to share the following: their name, where they live, their age, their present occupation and for how long, their previous experience of interpersonal skills training, their previous experience of personal growth work of any kind, their feelings here and now about being in the workshop, their reasons for coming to the workshop. You ask someone to start, and then go round the circle from person to person. Ask people to make only a brief statement on each item.

You can either ask each person to cover all these points in the one turn, in which case it is best if you have the points on a flip-chart, otherwise people will forget them. Alternatively, you can have a series of rounds, each person covering only one or two points on each round. Gently interrupt those whose anxiety makes them go on too long; gently draw out someone who is reticent. Remind someone if they have overlooked a point.

You can follow all this with a getting-to-know-you exercise in which people informally mill around to learn more about people in whom they are interested from the introductory rounds.

CULTURE SETTING

This is where you set the scene and create the climate for the whole workshop. The main part of it is where you make a contract on the value and ground-rules for the training.

1 Administration

You establish clearly times for starting and finishing, for mid-morning and mid-afternoon breaks, and for lunch. Make clear where toilets, food and refreshment can be found. Seek agreement on a no-smoking rule in the workshop room, and on a smoking area (outside if all else fails). Deal with any outstanding details about payment of workshop fees. Invite people to say if they have to miss any part of the training for whatever reason. I sometimes deal with these administrative matters before the introductions that were discussed in the previous section.

2 Description of workshop

You give a brief overview of what kind of workshop people have come to. It is for skills building using cycles of exposition, structured exercise, feedback and review. Practical exercises for skills building are the main focus: some of them are 'gymnastic', some use role-play, and in some of them people work as real clients. 'Learning by doing' is the keynote.

3 Values and ground-rules

This is the heart of culture setting. You affirm and recommend some core values for the group culture:

- This is a place of loving care and support.
- This is a place where each person's right to be self-determining is deeply respected.

You look round the group and seek general assent to these values. You then go on to affirm and recommend some basic ground-rules to guide behaviour throughout the training. And with each of these, you also look round the group and seek general assent. The ground-rules include the following.

- You, the trainee, participate in the workshop as a whole and in individual exercises because you freely choose to do so and for no other reason – it is your right and privilege to choose not to participate; but if you choose not to participate, at least ask yourself why you so choose.
- You abandon all professional defensiveness and posturing, and allow yourself to be honest with yourself and others about your ignorance and lack of skill.
- You are open and willing to take risks in trying out new behaviours.
- You allow yourself to be vulnerable in the real client role.
- You respect confidentiality about personal disclosures.
- You will be honestly and supportively confronting, and not shirk giving negative feedback on other people's practice.
- You will keep to time discipline about starting, finishing, breaks, lunch, returning to the large group after small-group exercises.

Seeking assent to each of these from each participant, by a word or a nod, is important. It means there is then a contract for how people are going to learn, a contract to which you can appeal and by which you can rally people when they become defensive or resistant. You may want to put all the values and ground-rules up on a background flip-chart.

Exercise   Display the values and ground-rules prominently so that everyone can see them. Invite people to form into small groups of four or five and discuss informally how they feel about these values and ground-rules. After a few minutes, with people still seated in their groups, gather in feedback and comment from all the groups.

---

4 Facilitator style

Here you state briefly how you will run the workshop in terms of your decision mode. You say you will be directive about the programme of training in the early and middle stages; and you will negotiate it in the later stages, especially when application to the trainees' professional roles comes to the fore. All practice will be autonomous in small groups, with you (and your assistant or co-trainer) dropping in on them from time to time to intervene in the practice and the feedback. You recommend a participants' 'initiative clause', which invites anyone at any time to propose and seek general assent to a shift in the direction which the training is taking. Seek general assent to all this.

BACKGROUND PRINCIPLES FOR TRAINING

Now you start to present ideas that define the training as such, and that set it in its educational context. The most complete account would be to cover all the sections at the start of this chapter, but four of these (behaviour-analysis hierarchy, overarching values, gymnastic principle, stretch effect) are covered in later parts of the training. The voluntary principle has already been covered in the first ground-rule above. And you can be selective about the first four sections.

I think there are four basic items to cover here:

- Say something about the educational revolution to set the wider context.
- Present the two 'margins for behavioural change', with a look at the relationship between skills training and personal development.
- Describe the four pillars of interpersonal skills training.
- Offer the model of experiential inquiry for the workshop.

Give space for discussion around these topics.

EXPOSITION OF BASIC TERMS

Here you describe the behaviour-analysis hierarchy (see above) of movements, actions and intentions. You stress that the concept of 'intention' is central to the model: the six categories are six basic kinds of intention. And they are described in terms of verbal behaviour: you can say that this can be presented in three ways – by a verbatim account, by a linguistic description, in terms of intention – and that it is mainly the last that is used in six category training. This gives the system its flexibility and power and makes sure that an intervention is not identified with just one form of words. (See Chapter 1 (pp. 3–4) for a discussion of this important issue.)

> *Exercise*   Invite people to form into pairs. For a few minutes they do the following: one person states an action, such as 'points', the other raises it into an intention, such as 'indicates where George lives'; they keep alternating these roles. Feedback in pairs, then follow with review and discussion in the whole group.

You give definitions of 'practitioner', 'client', and say how these can be extended informally. You define 'intervention', and talk about the 'enabling relationship' that is central in the model. All these matters are covered in Chapter 1 (pp. 1–4).

> *Exercise*   Invite people to form into different pairs. They take it in turns to share how currently in their lives they have been both formal and informal practitioners, and formal and informal clients, and what it has felt like in these various roles. Feedback in pairs, then follow with review and discussion in the whole group.

OVERVIEW OF THE SIX CATEGORIES

Now, with a flip-chart on display, you give an outline account of each of the six categories, with examples, questions, discussion and clarifications. Stress again that these are six basic helping 'intentions'.

> *Exercise*   Invite people to form into new pairs. Each person takes it in turn to do the following: they take any one of their present formal or informal practitioner roles (as bank manager, doctor, parent, or whatever), and give examples of how they would use each of the six categories within that role. With each example, the listener can intervene and challenge the speaker if the example does not fit the category being illustrated. Feedback in pairs, followed by review and discussion in the whole group. If this exercise goes well, repeat it again with a change of pairs, and each person choosing a different kind of practitioner role. Note that before people get into this exercise you will need to illustrate some basic sorts of cathartic interventions, which people can then adapt to the role with which they are dealing. They will intuitively find their way into examples of the other categories.

After this, you can present the 'overarching values' discussed above (pp. 212–213): enhancing autonomy and co-operation in the client's life. And there are many points you can bring in from Chapter 1 (pp. 5–9): the authoritative–facilitative distinction; the six categories' claim to be exhaustive and mutually exclusive; sub-categories not exhaustive; category overlaps; of equal value in principle, in practice value depends on the context; mainly for one-to-one work; relatively theory-free; catalytic functionally important, supportive morally important. Throughout all this, encourage plenty of discussion and mental testing.

DISCRIMINATION TRAINING

So far there has been a great deal of talk and discussion. Now you need to prepare people for a dramatic switch into sustained action learning for the rest of the workshop. Explain that 'discrimination training' is to help people learn the repertoire: to familiarize them with the six categories, to start to get an intuitive feel for using them, and to be able to identify which ones are being used by others or by themselves. It uses a lot of artificial exercises. So explain the 'gymnastic principle', as described earlier (p. 214). Encourage trainees not to waste time by being defensive about the artificiality of the exercises. In and among the training here you may want gently to alert people to the 'stretch effect', also described above (p. 214).

Exercises There are a very large number of possible exercises for discrimination training: categorizing transcripts/videos/live demos, restriction exercises, stretch exercises, suffixing, prefixing, sequencing, any order, self-scoring, card games, intentional degenerations. All these are explained in the next chapter. You will need to make a selection, and within the time available for this part of the training, get a good mix and balance. So you need some restriction exercises, and some stretch exercises; some sequencing and some any-order exercises; some exercises entirely within one category, and some covering several categories. With regard to exercises within one category, always include here exercises on the catalytic tool-kit (no. 6 in Chapter 9). The tool-kit interventions are absolutely fundamental for every practitioner of any kind.

These various exercises will be done in pairs or small groups of three or more. They need to be carefully and fully explained, with who does what and when and for how long. You need to model the interventions that are to be used – that is, describe and show what it is to do them well. After each exercise, have feedback and reflection in the pair or small group, followed by a review and discussion in the whole workshop.

Your own role during the exercises is twofold. Make it clear you are there to be called in to sort out any kind of confusion about the exercise or dispute about categorizing interventions. But also seek permission to visit any small group at any time to observe and help get the exercise back on track if it has become derailed.

The golden rule here is: if trainees have done it wrong, give them corrective feedback, and have them rerun the behaviour until they get it right. This immediate, over-the-shoulder corrective feedback, with instant reruns, is at the very core of your effectiveness as a trainer.

OVERVIEW OF DEGENERATIONS

You now introduce how the six categories can be used degenerately, first in general terms across all categories. Give an outline account of unsolicited, manipulative, compulsive and unskilled degenerations, as described in Chapter 13 (pp. 186–190), with questions, discussion and clarification.

The main thing to focus on here is 'compulsive helping', the besetting sin of the helping professions. Make it clear you are committed to deprofessionalization, in the sense of dismantling the use of the professional role as a defence against the practitioner's own repressed emotional pain.

Exercise   Invite people to form into new pairs. All in turn take a few minutes to explore what it is, if anything, they are busy not attending to in their own personal development by being a professional helper. How, if at all, are they using the role compulsively and defensively? The listener prompts with a probing question or two, but does not take over with his or her own agenda: the listener waits for his or her turn. Feedback in pairs, then review and discussion in the whole group.

After this you can present examples of particular degenerations within each category, from the extensive list in Chapter 13. Then the trainees can do some discrimination training in the form of 'intentional negative practice'.

Exercise   Invite people to form into new pairs. One person is the real client, with respect to some very *trivial* actual issue in his or her life, for example, what colour to paint the living-room walls. The other person is the practitioner, using a negative-stretch exercise. This means the person uses at least one degenerate intervention from each of the six categories. Reverse roles and repeat. Feedback in pairs, followed by review and discussion in the whole group.

The rationale of intentional negative practice is that to make a degenerate intervention quite deliberately tends to undermine the tendency to do it unawarely. It is important that the real client only talks about something entirely trivial, for there is then a lot of learning in and among the laughter. But you do not want to have really sensitive issues trampled on by deliberate blundering.

The above exercise is only one example. You can use the full range of discrimination-training exercises for intentional negative practice.

SELF-ASSESSMENT AND FORWARD PLANNING

This is the final stage of discrimination training. Having got a working grasp of the six categories and of how they can degenerate, the trainees now assess what their individual strengths and weaknesses are.

> *Exercise* Invite people to form into pairs and take it in turn to identify their two strongest and two weakest from among the basic six categories. Weakest categories include both categories people never use or tend to avoid, and categories they make a mess of. It is important that this assessment is made regardless of whether people consider that certain categories are not relevant to their practitioner roles. Listeners can pace speakers to make sure they cover all six in the time available, and can confront them in defensive or deluded areas. All people write down their two strongest and two weakest on a piece of paper, without their names on it. You collect all the papers.

Time the above exercise so there is a break immediately after it. During the break, you collate all the self-assessments, and make a flip-chart display with a strongest column and a weakest column running through the six categories. Enter the total scores as appropriate in each of the twelve boxes. Circle the top two scores in the strongest column and the top two scores in the weakest column.

Present the flip-chart display of the collated data on the self-assessments to the whole group. Get a good discussion going on the implications of the data. Then move into some negotiated planning. You propose that the highest scores in the weakest column should determine what is done in the next major phase of the training, which is practice in areas of weakness. Do not impose this idea; consult, discuss, negotiate until you reach agreement with the group on a provisional plan for practice in areas of weakness: what to do first and for how long, what to do next and for how long.

Make sure plenty of time is left in the total programme for practice in other categories and for special applications.

PRACTICE IN AREAS OF WEAKNESS

This is the main part of the course. It has just been planned with the trainees on the basis of their self-assessments. The training exercises focus on the two categories self-assessed as weakest by most people in the workshop. Very frequently these are the confronting and cathartic categories, which over and over again come out with almost equal scores at the top of the weakest list. When this is so, it is much the better plan to do the confronting practice before the cathartic practice.

At this stage of the workshop, you move on from the artificial, gymnastic exercises of discrimination training, to the use of role-plays in which the categories are applied in the way they would be in the real world; and to the use of real client exercises, in which the trainee in the client role deals with something of significance, and the practitioner applies the categories with serious intent.

Exercises   For the practice of confronting or prescriptive interventions, it is best, to begin with, to use role-plays with purely imaginary scenarios, rather than role-play incidents from the practitioner's real life. These highlight the skill, without the practitioner getting bogged down in real-life issues.

For the practice of cathartic or catalytic interventions, real client exercises are best: role-played simulations do not have the subtlety and reality of content that is needed to build up skills in these areas.

The exercises can be done in small groups of four: practitioner, client and two observers, who have six category score sheets on which they number the practitioner's interventions in sequence. Feedback to each practitioner is immediately after his or her turn, in this order: from self, from client, from observers. Negative feedback on practice can immediately be converted into brief reruns of the critical bit of behaviour until the practitioner gets it on track. Everybody takes a turn in the practitioner role. Review and discussion in the small groups, followed by the same in the large group.

A practice exercise will focus on one category, but it will use other categories. So there are two training issues: first, the skill with which the focal category is used; and secondly, the skill with which the whole sequence of categories is put together. Before the exercise, therefore, you will need to model the focal category by describing or showing what it is to do it well; and to give some guidelines about an effective and appropriate sequence. And you will need to remind the practice groups to consider both these issues in their feedback to the practitioner.

Seek the trainees' agreement that you can drop in on the practice groups at will, doing more modelling, and contributing to feedback, reruns or reflection.

It is in these practice exercises that the experiential learning cycle is most fully used. To summarize the cycle again: you say or show what it is to perform the skill well (modelling); you explain the content, procedures and timing of the exercise; trainees take turns to practise the skill in small groups; after practice each person gives feedback to self followed by feedback from peers; negative feedback is converted directly into reruns of practice, to go for immediate improvement in skill; after all have taken a turn with practice, feedback and reruns, then the small group reflects on the issues arising; finally the small groups come together in the large group to share reflections and review the skill model with each other and the trainer.

For cathartic practice, with other trainees as real clients, you can suggest for the clients a topic such as a separation experience, through death or parting. To make this more intimate for the clients, you can do the exercise in pairs, without observers, although it will work perfectly well with observers. A supportive and caring climate is essential.

If clients get in deep, then their attention must be brought back into present time at the close of their session. Feedback and reruns need to be handled off the client (facing an empty chair) – that is, in a way that does not take the client back into the content of his or her session.

PLANNING AND FURTHER PRACTICE

Having spent some time working to build up skills in the area of the trainees' two weakest categories, you now negotiate with the group a plan for further practice. Different small groups may do different things. The three main options are as follows:

1 *Other categories*: practice in categories not judged to be weak, especially the middle two in the self-assessment (neither weak nor strong).
2 *Sequencing*: practice focuses on the sequence of interventions, on what a good sequence is in a given context. This can also include work on gradients and phases (see Chapters 11 and 12).

3   *Special applications*: practice focuses on the trainees' own on-the-job applications of the model, in tutoring, in medicine, in nursing, in counselling, in banking, in business, in law; in community and political commitments; in personal and domestic relationships; and in any other professional and social role that any trainee wants to explore.

The last of these, special applications, is really the most important. It brings the whole training to bear upon the trainees' own professional roles. It will include sequencing and other categories. It builds a bridge to the real world beyond the workshop.

Exercises For trainees' own on-the-job applications of the six categories, use role-plays of past real-life critical situations in which the trainee got into difficulty; or future real-life critical situations about which they feel anxious and insecure. The practitioner briefs another trainee as to how to play the client. There are two observers scoring the sequence of categories. Before the role-play practitioners can say what they feel the focal category will be, and then model it, that is, say how they feel it should be done. They can also outline an appropriate sequence of interventions. Then practice, feedback, reruns, reflection – and review of the practitioner's starting ideas about focal category, modelling and sequencing. (You can be busy going round the practice groups, intervening to improve what is going on at any point in all this.)

For practising sequencing in terms of a catalytic–informative gradient, using the three phases, use the moderator exercise. The moderator chooses a topic, such as a specialist hobby, in which he or she is knowledgeable, and the other four or five trainees in the small practice group are not so.

For phase one, the moderator uses largely catalytic interventions to elicit the buried and lurking bits of knowledge about the topic which the others do have somewhere in their minds.

In phase two, confronting interventions throw their ignorance into relief, correct their errors; and informative interventions give them the basic knowledge which it is now clear they do not have.

In phase three, catalytic interventions enable them to rehearse their new knowledge, raise issues that are still obscure (dealt with by some final informative interventions) and elicit directions they might take for further study. Supportive interventions affirm their new understanding and their new direction. For this and other examples of sequencing and phasing, see Chapter 12.

TRANSFER, REVIEW AND FAREWELL

You now draw the workshop to a close with three activities, one on transfer, one a review and, finally, the farewells.

Exercises Trainees, in pairs or small groups, consider how they will transfer their learning to appropriate areas of their professional and, perhaps, personal lives; they may, or may not, wish to make a commitment to a modest action plan. If there is to be a follow-up meeting, they may wish to firm up the action plan with the intent to report, at the follow-up, on the implementation of it. Follow with some sharing in the whole group about these plans for transfer.

Invite the trainees together to review the training, especially in the positive mode, with each person identifying his or her learning benefits. Create a focal seat to which each person in turn goes in order to share whatever he or she can now identify as useful learning from the workshop. This generates mutual reinforcement of positive gains before departure.

In a closing circle, making physical contact, people affirm and celebrate each other – say what they have enjoyed and valued in each other and in the time together – and say goodbye.

TIMETABLE FOR A 5-DAY TRAINING WORKSHOP

Each day is divided into four sessions of 90 minutes each: two in the morning with a break between them; and two in the afternoon with a break between them. The entries below refer to the different subsections of this chapter, and include the exercises given in each of them. The balance between discrimination training, practice in areas of weakness and further practice varies with each workshop.

Day 1 1 Introductions. Culture setting. Background principles.
       2 Exposition of basic terms. Overview of the six categories.
       3 Discrimination training.
       4 Discrimination training.

Day 2 1 Discrimination training.
       2 Discrimination training.
       3 Discrimination training.
       4 Degenerations. Self-assessment.

Day 3 1 Presentation of self-assessments and planning.
       2 Practice in areas of weakness.
       3 Practice in areas of weakness.
       4 Practice in areas of weakness.

Day 4 1 Practice in areas of weakness.
2 Practice in areas of weakness.
3 Further practice: other categories and sequencing.
4 Further practice: other categories and sequencing.

Day 5 1 Further practice: special applications.
2 Further practice: special applications.
3 Further practice: special applications. Transfer.
4 Review. Farewells.

For 4-, 3- and 2-day workshops, everything has to be scaled down proportionately, and you have to be more and more selective in choosing exercises.

CHAPTER 15

TEACHING INTERPERSONAL SKILLS

For teaching interpersonal skills based on behaviour analysis, there are four basic ingredients of the learning process, four elements the trainer has to provide: discrimination, modelling, practice and feedback (Cross, 1976) – and they all overlap and interact with each other. In all active exercises involving these four elements, the trainee is busy applying *self-monitoring* and raising it to the level of *first person action research* (see the final section of this chapter). Action research is thus the hub of the whole process.

DISCRIMINATION

The trainee is given the opportunity to learn to distinguish between the different behaviour categories, to identify them in others' behaviour and in his or her own. A variety of passive and active exercises aid this process. In the first three exercises below the trainee is a passive witness, discriminating someone else's behaviour, using a six category score sheet to number the sequence of interventions under the appropriate categories.

1 Live demo

The trainee witnesses a live practitioner–client interaction, for real or role-played, and categorizes practitioner interventions.

2 Audio/visual

The trainee sees and/or hears a recording of a practitioner–client interaction and categorizes practitioner interventions.

3 Transcript

The trainee is given a written account of the verbal interaction between practitioner and client and categorizes the practitioner's interventions.

In what follows the trainee is active, discriminating his or her own behaviour. In so doing, he or she is also building up self-monitoring skills. As well as being discrimination exercises, the active exercises also provide an opportunity for practice and feedback. What distinguishes them from primary practice exercises (see no. 3 Practice, below) is their artificial and contrived nature – by virtue of which, however, they aid discrimination (cf. Rackham and Morgan, 1977). They use the gymnastic principle (see Chapter 14, p. 214).

The trainees in the next exercises are in threes, unless otherwise stated. Each takes a turn as practitioner, client and observer. The observer provides corrective feedback to the trainee–practitioner after his or her turn. The role-play situations can incline to the bizarre to keep the whole thing light and humorous.

4 Restriction exercises

The trainee role-plays the practitioner in some practitioner–client situation, and is restricted to the use of certain behaviour categories only. In terms of six category intervention analysis, the restriction may be to a small number of interventions that are all within one of the six major categories, or it may be to one or two of the six.

5 Prefixing exercises

In a practitioner–client role-play the trainee as practitioner verbally identifies in advance each intervention, that is, he or she labels it before making it.

6 Suffixing exercises

The trainee verbally labels each intervention after he or she has made it, again as practitioner in a practitioner–client role-play.

7 Self-scoring exercises

The trainee numbers each intervention, on a six category score sheet, as he or she makes the intervention as practitioner in a practitioner–client role play. The score sheet also serves as a self-monitoring reminder diagram of what interventions can be made.

8 Card game exercises

Four trainees are players in a card game, using a 24-card pack with four cards for each of the six categories. The cards are shuffled and each player is dealt six cards. When he or she plays a card, that is, puts it down face-up, that player has to produce verbal behaviour corresponding to the named behaviour on the card, spoken to an imaginary client who is talking about his relationship with the telephone. Various systems of rules, with challenges and penalties, can be devised.

9 Stretch exercises

The trainee as practitioner in a practitioner–client role play has to cover a wide range of behaviours, for example all six categories, twice over, within a specified time limit.

10 Slow role-play

With restriction and/or suffixing/prefixing. Plenty of time is taken to deliberate on, comment on, analyse each practitioner (trainee) behaviour as it is made.

11 Sequencing exercises

The trainee, as practitioner in a practitioner–client role-play, applies a sequence of interventions. The sequence may be devised by the trainer, or by the trainee, in advance of the role-play (in relation to intended client outcomes). The trainee may then prefix or suffix each intervention as he or she goes through the sequence.

12 Degeneration exercises

The trainee, as practitioner in a practitioner–client role-play, caricatures specific degenerative interventions (see Chapter 13). This is a particular type of restriction exercise, where the restriction is to degenerations only. Prefixing or suffixing can be added.

The above discrimination exercises should familiarize the trainee with some of the main types of intervention within each of the six categories. The trainee is then ready to go on to a very important kind of discrimination exercise – which is about him- or herself.

13 Self- and peer assessment exercise

The trainees are in pairs, and each takes a turn as client and counsellor. The primary role here is that of the client trainees who are invited to assess their main strengths and main weaknesses among the six categories. They pick out the two at which they consider they are most effective in their professional and private roles, and the two at which they are least effective – either because they do them badly, or because they avoid them altogether, or because they are convinced there is no need for them. The counsellor's job here is to help the client gain a fair and comprehensive self-assessment, by a variety of supportive, confronting and catalytic interventions. The self-assessment results for each client are recorded.

The results from this last exercise can be used to influence the design of the variety of practice exercises (see under Practice, below) to ensure that as far as possible these exercises enable trainees to meet individualized skills-learning goals, that is, to make good their identified areas of weakness.

Finally, there is something fundamental involved throughout all discrimination training – and that is clear trainer *exposition*. This is conceptual modelling, which leads us into the next section.

MODELLING

This has two aspects: the trainer provides the trainee with a model; and the trainee actively models on it. The presented model can show how to do well a particular type of intervention or a particular sequence of interventions – in relation to client states and reactions, and to intended client outcomes. The model exemplifies the trainer's evaluation of good practitioner performance in relation to desirable client effects. The model is put forward as a recommended working hypothesis, in principle open from the very outset to evaluative revision by the trainee.

If the model seems initially plausible, the trainee uses it to build up skills, while testing it out experientially all the while. Modelling of this sort simply provides a chrysalis within which the trainee's own notion of what constitutes good performance can mature. When this maturation has occurred, the original presented models will have been assimilated and transformed into a personal style, and bits of the model that have proved in personal practice to be extraneous will have been discarded.

1 Exposition

The trainer gives a clear conceptual account of the category system, the rationale of its formulation, the practical principles involved in its application – presenting all this not as a dogma, but as a working hypothesis for trainees to test first of all intellectually and then experientially in and through the various training exercises and subsequently in professional work. As the course unfolds, the trainer describes high quality practitioner performance for each behaviour within each category, analysing its elements and its defining norms. He can then illustrate with items from nos. 2, 3 and 4 below to bring the analysis to life.

2 Live modelling

The trainer can himself or herself be a live model of high-quality practitioner performance in front of the trainee group in five ways:

- By what he or she does for real in facilitating the trainees throughout the course. In other words, by his or her ongoing trainer behaviour that is not part of any formal demonstration. This is undoubtedly the most important sort of live modelling.
- The trainer offers the elements of model practitioner behaviour in terms of corrective feedback given to a trainee during the trainee's practice sessions. *How* the trainer does this falls under the previous item.
- By being the practitioner in an imaginary role-played practitioner–client situation, with a volunteer trainee as unrehearsed client, or with a colleague as rehearsed client.
- By being the practitioner for a volunteer trainee on a real issue.
- By being the practitioner for a real client who volunteers to come in from outside the group.

3 Audio/video modelling

The trainee hears/sees a recording of a practitioner–client interaction (real or role-played) with high-quality practitioner performance.

4 Transcript modelling

The trainee reads from a transcript of a practitioner–client interaction (real or role-played) with high-quality practitioner performance.

The above three items were also listed under discrimination training. There they are used simply to identify interventions, to learn the repertoire. Here they are used to identify *good* interventions, to learn how to apply the repertoire well.

The above four procedures are all ways in which the trainer can present a model to the trainees. What follows are ways in which the trainees can themselves model on the presented model. The first two below are based on live or recorded demonstrations.

5 Direct copying

Trainees aim for a literal copy of the modelled behaviour, in a matching role-play exercise, with corrective feedback from trainer and/or peers and replay until they get it right. They aim to get their verbal and non-verbal behaviour more or less identical with that of the model.

6 Analogy

Trainees seek not a literal copy of the presented model but a correspondence of style and quality. Their behaviour shows equivalent intention, but the verbal and non-verbal behaviour may differ. The practice role-play need not be a precise match of the original, only analogous. There will also be corrective feedback from trainer and/or peers and replay until trainees get it right.

7 Reconstruction from exposition only

This avoids the other-directed impact of live or recorded demonstrations on trainees. They are just given the analytic exposition as in point 1 above, then invited to reconstruct this into effective high-quality behaviour. They only have their own imagination to go on, their own notion of what the exposition means when translated into action. Corrective feedback from trainer and/or peers will help them to refine both their internal imaginative model and their external performance.

Everyone models on someone at some time. This is a truism of training in any field. It is better to acknowledge it and raise it into a positive practice rather than let it lurk about only tacitly acknowledged. Once the process is made fully explicit and overtly incorporated into training, then the trainee can get on with the business of divining his own internal model, his idiosyncratic archetype of high-quality performance, the personal exemplar within.

PRACTICE

The active discrimination and active modelling exercises all provide sorts of practice, but real practice sessions take off beyond these two types of exercise, giving the trainee more creative scope to build up a mature body of skills. In the following exercises, the trainee is not acquiring the ability to discriminate within an artificial structure, nor following a model, but, with discrimination and modelling established, is engaging in the conscious and creative exercise of his or her humanity in some human situation. This is where *self-monitoring* starts to turn into *first person action research* (see the section on this below).

1 Imaginary situations

The trainee is invited to role-play the practitioner in an entirely imaginary practitioner–client situation which is characterized in advance in enough detail to present the trainee with a challenging human predicament. Such imaginary predicaments challenge the exercise of trainee skills, with plenty of scope for feedback, revision of strategy and replay. In such an exercise it is entirely up to the trainees to determine the type and sequence of interventions they use, although they may well modify this in subsequent replays, in the light of feedback received. Imaginary situations can be:

1.1 Extreme or bizarre: possible, but outside the everyday range of experience.

1.2 Typical: situations that are representative of different parts of the normal range of experience.

1.3 Job-related: situations falling within the trainee's current or future professional role.

1.4 Off-the-job: situations to do with personal or domestic life, or citizenship roles, or with some profession or job that has nothing to do with the trainee.

Thus there are four basic types of imaginary situation: extreme job-related, typical job-related, extreme off-the-job, typical off-the-job. The extreme types have a big immediate training pay-off, in my experience.

2 Real past situations

The trainee is invited to role-play some situation from the past. It may have been:

2.1 Typical and usual.

2.2 Rare and unusual.

2.3 Non-problematic.

2.4 Problematic and critical.

2.5 The trainee's past experience.

2.6 Someone else's past experience.

2.7 Job-related.

2.8 Off-the-job.

It probably makes most sense to take a typical, problematic, trainee's own, job-related past situation, since this presumably identifies a major area of skills weakness. To say the situation is problematic means here that the trainee had difficulty in dealing with it effectively, or avoided dealing with it at all. The trainee may be invited to re-enact it more or less as he or she originally mishandled it, then replay it trying out alternative more effective sequences of interventions, with feedback.

3 Real present situations

These are practice exercises which are neither imaginary nor to do with past events, but concern the real situation in present time.

3.1 Trainee two-way   The co-counselling model. Two trainees take it in turn to be practitioner and client. The one who is the client is a real client, that is, he or she talks about real issues. With feedback to practitioner, after the interaction, from the client, and from any observers present.

3.2 Real visiting client   A volunteer from outside the group is recruited to come in and to be a real client for a trainee practitioner. With feedback as above.

3.3 Any interaction in the group   Any interaction a trainee has in the training group, whether in or out of session, whether a formal training exercise or informal impromptu exchange, can be used by that trainee as an opportunity to practise his or her intervention skills.

In the first two of these, the trainee practitioner after feedback can use replay with revised interventions, but this requires sensitive handling, since the client is dealing with a real issue. But if the real issue is relatively trivial (where to go on holiday this year), then replay is non-problematic. The client is still dealing with his or her experience wherever they are on the gradient from the light and trivial to the searching and profound. So it sometimes makes sense for the trainer to ask clients to choose real but trivial issues, so that the trainee practitioner feels free to try things out, explore the repertoire and replay interventions that were off the mark.

3.4 Anticipated future situations   Trainees can role-play the practitioner in some future problematic situation with which they know they are going to be faced. The situation may involve other persons with whom they are familiar and whose attitudes and responses they can also anticipate; or it may involve persons unknown. The other group members in the role-play, plus the observers and the trainer, can give feedback, followed by replay if needed.

4 Parameters of practice

In all these practice exercises what the trainee who is the practitioner, and those who give feedback, have to bear in mind are the following:

4.1   All the *observable client verbal and non-verbal behaviours*, with their implications.

4.2   The *appropriate intervention now*, and the appropriate sequence of interventions, in response to current client behaviours, and in the light of intended outcomes for the client.

4.3   The *full range of possible valid interventions*.

4.4   The different ways in which *interventions can degenerate* (both in general and in particular).

FEEDBACK

Feedback means information given about trainee behaviour in a just-completed training exercise, or in some part of such an exercise. So it is retrospective. Its purpose is to raise trainee awareness about strengths, weaknesses and omissions in his or her recent behaviour. In a practice exercise, it is a good idea to follow feedback with a rerun of the exercise or a part of it, so that the trainee can have a go at correcting weaknesses and omissions, and build on strengths.

1 Focus

Feedback is about what is going on in one, or any combination, of the following:

1.1   In the practitioner.

1.2   In the practitioner to client transaction.

1.3   In the client.

1.4   In the client to practitioner transaction.

And in each of these cases it is about one or both of the following:

1.5 Verbal behaviour: the content of speech, the meaning of what is said; the intention of what is said; the choice of words and construction of statements; also the paralinguistic aspects of speech such as tone of voice, volume, pitch, speed of delivery, inflection, redundancies, pauses and silences.

1.6 Nonverbal behaviour: eye contact and use of eyes; touch; facial expression; posture; gait; gestures of arms/hands/legs/head and neck; relative position (near, far, beside, opposite, behind, above, below); breathing.

Feedback about the client is only used and is only relevant to clarify and elaborate feedback given to the practitioner. In a trainer-training context, it is irrelevant, as well as offensive and intrusive to give feedback about client competency.

2 Awareness

Feedback distinguishes between behaviour that the trainee apparently intended and was aware of, and behaviour that was apparently unintended and unaware.

3 Source

Feedback can come from four different sources. To maximize learning it is best if it is given in the following sequence:

3.1 Practitioner to self: the trainee gives him- or herself feedback aloud before the group on their immediately past performance as practitioner.

3.2 Client to practitioner: the trainee who role-played or was the real client gives feedback to the trainee who was his practitioner.

3.3 Observers or scorers to practitioner: trainees who watched or scored the role-play give feedback to the trainee who was the practitioner.

3.4 Trainer to practitioner: the trainer gives feedback to the trainee who was the practitioner; also perhaps to the other trainees present about their feedback to the trainee-practitioner.

4 Corrective

This sort of feedback corrects an obvious error, blunder or omission.

5 General

This sort is an expression of opinion about the appropriateness of this or that intervention, timing, interpretation of client response, sequencing, alternative strategies, and so on.

6 Subjectivized

Feedback is given as a subjective impression (right or wrong, for what it's worth, as it seems to me over here), disavowing any claim to be a well-supported objective judgement. This may or may not be followed by a statement of the subjective emotional reaction evoked by that impression. Subjectivized feedback allows the recipient to appropriate any useful information it contains without having to battle with the feeling of being judged. It also allows the speaker to offer it honourably even though there may be an element of unidentified projection in it.

7 Objectivized

This is given as an objective judgement which the speaker is prepared to back up with supporting reasons. It is offered as a statement of what, on good grounds, he believes or knows to be the case about the behaviour of the person to whom he is addressing it. This is a stronger or tougher form of feedback than subjectivized feedback, although not necessarily more effective. It is much more open to abuse and potentially damaging, since the speaker's unidentified projections can be masked by pseudo-objective judgements. But sometimes the training situation clearly warrants its use.

8 Descriptive

The feedback merely describes a movement, a posture, in terms such as 'eyes moved to the left', or 'fist clenched on the knee'; or it describes a minimal observable action in terms such as 'talks', 'points', 'weeps'.

9 Attributive

The feedback attributes meaning to verbal or non-verbal behaviour in terms of basic psychological concepts such as motive, intention, wish, desire, emotion: for example, 'It seems to me from your facial expression and the look in your eye that you wanted to attack him'; 'What you said gave me the impression you were very angry'. This the primary kind of feedback used in six category training, where trainee behaviour is construed in terms of the various interventions, their degenerations and their sequencing.

10 Psychodynamic

The feedback interprets what has been said or done by relating it to hypothesized internal defences or external distortions of behaviour that are due to past conditioning, interference and distress.

11 Sociodynamic

The feedback interprets what has been said or done more in terms of prevailing social determinants of behaviour: for example, in terms of tacit cultural norms and social stereotypes, of role-identity crisis, of authority and leadership issues, and so on.

12 Transcendental

The feedback interprets what is said and done by relating it to transcendental concepts such as archetypes, unseen presences, the movement of the spirit, and so on.

In all that has been said here, feedback is seen as retrospective and static. It is about recent past behaviour, and it can be given by self, by peers and by the trainer. It is in static form, in statements that have no immediate effect on behaviour, but can only be applied to modify future behaviour. For convenience, this retrospective and static feedback can be regarded as a kind of assessment.

There is a prior and more fundamental sort of feedback which is concurrent and dynamic. It is the feedback one gives to oneself about one's own behaviour while it is going on, and which one can use to influence and modify such ongoing behaviour. It can only be self-managed (although other people can influence that self-management by signs or statements). Concurrent and dynamic feedback to oneself can be called self-monitoring to distinguish it from retrospective self-assessment.

Self-monitoring, as explained in detail below, is creative intelligence in action in the situation; it is purposive, flexible, adaptive, forward-looking and above all directly change- and action-oriented. Self-assessment is past action recollected and evaluated in tranquillity; and its impact on action may be less because of the gap in time that separates it from future relevant action.

FIRST PERSON ACTION RESEARCH

This is the hub of the whole training process and is entirely a matter of trainee intentionality and self-direction. First person action research is an enhancement of self-monitoring.

1 Self-monitoring

This means attending to and modifying one's own actions while one is acting. Everybody uses minimal self-monitoring in managing any bit of ongoing behaviour. You notice what you are doing, how you are doing it, when you are doing it, what effect it is having, how you need to change it to manifest your strategy and achieve your goal, and then you notice how you change it – and so on round the feedback loop, sustaining or modifying or stopping your behaviour as the relation between your goal, your strategy, your action and its effects, and your situation require. This process is habitually used to maintain the *ad hoc* status quo of everyday life.

When self-monitoring is used in a training context it becomes a richer enterprise, since it is concerned with developing the excellence, and extending the range, of behaviours. It is pervasive: it is involved in all the active training exercises, especially those to do with full-blown *practice*. It has started to turn into the following.

2 First person action research

This is self-monitoring used with full creative intent and awareness so that it is raised up from being a routine form of self-maintenance to being a vehicle for the radical transformation of one's way of life (cf. Torbert, 2000). Human action has an intrinsic logic, an innate conceptual structure, which brings it to the forefront of all forms of psychological and sociological inquiry. There is an *agent* with a certain *goal* and a *strategy* to realize it, expressed in an *action*, with certain *effects* in a *situation*. The agent is governed by *values* with respect to the goal, *norms* with respect to the strategy and the current action, and *beliefs* about the situation. These components are embedded within an envelope of: *self contracts*, *social contracts*, *planetary contracts* and *cosmic contracts*. By 'contracts' in these four phrases I mean tacit or explicit understandings about, respectively: how to care for oneself; how to relate from within one's various social roles to other people and organizations; how to care for the planet; and how to relate to the wider, multidimensional cosmos.

Overarching all this is a *vision* of possibilities for human flourishing on this planet in this cosmos; and within it all is an indwelling *ground* of human motivation, which, I believe, is the aspiration to participate in ever wider unities of being as a distinct, autonomous creative entity. In the world of action, this ground is a dynamic potential within the human being, generating impulses and options for liberating behaviour in diverse situations.

The research is about how, in and through action, to create worthwhile forms of human flourishing by reshaping all the above dynamic components to bring them into a mutually enhancing relation with each other.

CHAPTER 16

CO-COUNSELLING

I commended co-counselling in Chapter 2 as a peer self-help approach to developing the kind of emotional competence and house-cleaning needed for effective helping. It is a method of personal development through mutual support for persons of all ages and both sexes including, with suitable modifications, children. It is not for those who are too emotionally distressed to give attention to a fellow human on a reciprocal basis. It is a tool for living for those who are already managing their lives acceptably by conventional standards, but wish significantly to enhance their sense of personal identity and personal effectiveness. It is part of a continuing education for living which affirms the peer principle, and thus avoids some of the psychodynamic hazards of institutionalized and professionalized one-way helping (Heron, 1997; House and Totton, 1997). It is also a vital form of first person action research, as defined at the end of the last chapter: it involves alert and dynamic self-monitoring, and all interventions are primarily for the client to use on him- or herself.

THEORY

My formulation of the theory on which the practice of co-counselling rests is as follows. All persons are differentially stressed by virtue of their immersion in the human condition which has at least the following sources of stress: the separation trauma of birth and death; the tension between physical survival and personal development; the relative inscrutability or apparent meaninglessness of many phenomena; the intractability of matter; the inherent instability of unprogrammed and probably unlimited human potential; the presence of other stressed humans; amnesia about one's inherent participation in the whole, one's cosmic citizenship.

On the one hand such stressors can be enabling, providing the shock of awakening that promotes personal development and cultural achievement. On the other hand they can be over-whelming and disabling, so that personal and interpersonal behaviour become distorted and persons interfere with each other, either unawarely or deliberately and maliciously. There are thus two sources of distress: the primary source in the human condition, the secondary and derivative source in the interference of other people. The latter is what co-counselling is most immediately concerned with.

Human infants have remarkable though undeveloped capacities for love, understanding and choice but lack the experience, information and skill with which to actualize them. They await wise and loving education, but are also highly vulnerable to interference by others – the blocking, frustration, rejection or neglect of their deep human potential. The result of such interference is a line of distress in the mind-body, the emotional pain of grief, fear, anger, shame or embarrassment, together with correlated physical, often muscular tension. The effect of such distress is to suspend the effective response of human capacities – of love, understanding and choice – so that the child is left with an undiscriminating recording of the traumatic interfering interaction, including the child's own desperate response. These distress recordings can become ingrained and extensive through cumulative repetition of interference from parental and other sources. There is invariably a double interference, first with the deep human potential, and secondly with the child's attempt to find a way of releasing and healing the pain of this through tears, tantrums and trembling – none of which are tolerated. Hence repression and the double-negative message: 'Your human capacities are no good, and the pain you feel at their suppression is no good.'

In our emotionally repressive society, distress recordings acquire a dynamic functional autonomy, often unidentified and unacknowledged. They are the source of unaware, compulsive, maladaptive and rigid behaviour *patterns*. Some of these patterns are periodic, triggered by particular types of situation that significantly resemble the early interference situations: for example, when rational behaviour breaks down in the presence of someone seen as an authority figure. Others are endemic or chronic, a persistent distorted way of feeling and thinking and doing that infects behaviour in a wide range of situations: for example, a chronic self-deprecatory attitude. Here the trigger is being in the world at all – which has become associated with a deeply ingrained distress recording.

When triggered in later life, the distress recording unawarely plays itself out, either the child's end or the parent's end of the recording being reproduced in behaviour and attitude, depending upon the situation. Or both may be reproduced at the same time, as in a chronic internal pattern of self-condemnation. Typical recordings, which can combine and interact in various ways, are those of:

- *The victim*: the compulsion to be trampled on and abused, to give power away, to feel worthless.
- *The oppressor*: the compulsion to dominate, to control, to manipulate, to denigrate and despise.
- *The rebel*: the compulsion to oppose authority figures, to resist and fight the established system.
- *The rescuer*: the compulsion to be responsible for, to solve others' problems for them, to take on their burdens.

Such patterns may be acted out, in interactions with other people; or they may be acted in, in internal transactions within the self. In either case they are, for the adult, maladaptive. For the child they have some survival value – the trauma and pain become encoded as a ritual distortion that at least enables the person to continue on without total breakdown and disruption. But they restrict and constrain a mature, flexible and innovative response to changing circumstances in the adult.

Co-counselling theory also holds that catharsis is a way of releasing distress from the mind-body. Keeping some attention in the place of the aware adult in present time, the client in co-counselling reaches down into the hidden place of the hurt child, honours and experiences the pain, and releases it through:

- *Grief* in tears and sobbing.
- *Fear* in trembling.
- *Anger* in loud sound and storming movement.
- *Primal pain* in screaming.
- *Embarrassment* and socially imposed shame in laughter.

This is a healing of the hidden painful memories, a reintegration of the occluded past. The effects of sustained catharsis are:

- *Spontaneous insight*: the traumatic past is seen in a new light, re-evaluated, perceived with a truly discriminating awareness for the first time. Its connection with current distortions is understood in a way that illuminates.
- *The break-up of compulsive, rigid, distorted behaviour and attitude*: the tension of contained distress that sustains them has been released.
- *The liberation of frozen needs and capacities*: love is freed from its distorted childhood fixation, intelligence can function

flexibly instead of in a stereotypic and dogmatic way, choice is released from the grip of powerlessness.

The person can thus live more creatively and awarely in response to what is going on now.

The way of regression, catharsis and reintegration of the distressed past is complemented by the way of celebration – the affirmation of felt strengths, of experiences and projects that are worthwhile, enjoyable and creatively rewarding. Other basic aspects of the client's work include goal-setting and action planning, creative thinking and problem-solving. Transforming all these, there is spiritual expression and transfiguration, for dealing with the primary sources of stress in the human condition, and unfurling the divine potential of the human being.

PRACTICE

Co-counselling is a two-way process among peers, each taking a turn as client and counsellor (or worker and helper). It typically involves a two-hour session with each person taking an hour in each role. Client and counsellor exercise appropriate skills, acquired on a basic training course of at least 40 hours, with on-going groups, intensive workshops and advanced workshops for systematic follow-up.

Co-counselling is not simply client-centred, it is client-directed. The client is the person who is taking his or her turn, working initially on the way of regression and catharsis, and the way of celebration and affirmation. The basic techniques are primarily for the client to work with on him- or herself, with the aware supportive attention of the counsellor. This is particularly important in the early stages so that the client does not become strongly dependent on counsellor interventions.

The counsellor does not interpret, analyse, criticize or advise on problems, but only acts within a contract chosen by the client. This contract may ask for non-verbal attention only; for occasional interventions when it seems to the counsellor that the client is missing his or her own cues, is getting lost in his or her own defences; or, at a later stage when the counsellor has acquired the requisite skill, for interventions that work intensively with client cues and that focus in on areas of primary material. The counsellor's interventions are always in the form of a practical suggestion about what the client may say or do. The rationale of the suggestion is not verbalized; and the client is in principle free to reject the intervention.

On the way of regression and catharsis, the client is trained to take charge of the cathartic process by always keeping a focus of attention in the place of the aware, mature adult outside the distress of the child within, and to work with accessible and available distress, with what is on top. This ensures that the healing of the memories occurs in a relatively undisruptive way, in a sequence and at a pace which the client can readily handle. The client works not only upon childhood experiences but also on more recent and present relationships, both personal and professional, and also on future expectations and on political and institutional tensions. Some of the introductory techniques the client uses, and which the counsellor recommends when he or she intervenes, are:

- *Literal, evocative description* of early events, rather than analytic talk about them.
- *Repetition of words and phrases* that carry an emotional charge or loading.
- *Association*: catching emergent thoughts, images, memories, insights that occur spontaneously.
- *Psychodrama*: becoming oneself in the early scene and expressing directly the negative or positive emotions that were suppressed at the time.
- *Contradiction*: verbally and non-verbally putting energy in the opposite direction to the constraints of the negative self-image.

Many other techniques are used, and co-counselling at its various stages of development can accommodate the four primary ways of managing catharsis: active imagination, passive imagination, active body work and passive body work (see p. 80). Trans-personal co-counselling (see Spiritual expression, below) is an important development for working on the repression of, and for transforming one's being by, the sublime and archetypal, and by the movement of indwelling spirit. It addresses some of the primary sources of tension in the human condition, mentioned in the theory section above. Fundamental throughout is the vali-dation, affirmation and celebration of the inalienable worth of humans and their capacities.

HISTORY AND ORGANIZATION

Co-counselling was developed out of other sources by Harvey Jackins in Seattle, USA in the 1950s and 1960s (Jackins, 1978).

Under his auspices it spread through the USA and Europe in the late 1960s and early 1970s, and thereafter to other parts of the world. Networks of co-counsellors were organized under the title of Re-evaluation Counselling Communities. This organization early on became theoretically rigid and internally authoritarian. In 1974 Co-counselling International (CCI) was formed as an alternative network, which I support. It federates entirely independent communities of co-counsellors in several countries, working in a spirit of inquiry. These communities develop their own decision-making procedures consonant with the peer principle, and their own approach to the training, assessment and accreditation of teachers of the method. International workshops are held regularly in the USA, Europe and New Zealand.

Co-counselling as a practice primarily occurs in people's own homes on the basis of one-to-one informal arrangements. The purpose of a network or community is to provide up-to-date address lists of trained co-counsellors, and to provide a continuous programme of groups and workshops for follow-up, group support, intensive co-counselling, refresher course, advanced training, teacher training and social change activity.

BASIC PRINCIPLES OF METHOD

Each partner (from now on referred to as 'she') takes a turn as both counsellor and client.

1 Role of client

The client is in charge, is self-directed, decides what to work on, how to work on it, how long to work on it. It is her time. The basic working techniques described later on are first and foremost for the client to use in working on herself. She also chooses what kind of a contract to have with her counsellor (see below). She is free to accept or reject the counsellor's suggestions. She is concerned with the liberation of her own potential. Her working options include, among others:

1.1 Discharge of past distress followed by spontaneous insight.

1.2 Affirmation and celebration of strengths.

1.3 Creative thinking and problem-solving.

1.4 Goal-setting and action planning.

1.5 Extending the reach of awareness: spiritual expression and trans-figuration.

She deals with what's on top, with what she can handle and needs to work on at the time, with whatever combination of methods seems to her appropriate.

2 Role of counsellor

2.1 The counsellor gives supportive, expectant free attention; she is present for the client.

2.2 She does not interpret, analyse, criticize, give advice, etc.

2.3 She has a contract to intervene when the client appears to have lost her way, to be blocking, to be 'in pattern', to be missing her own cues. This is the normal contract (see below).

2.4 Her interventions are in the form of suggestions about what the client may say or do, based on verbal and non-verbal cues and a tentative mental guess about what is going on in the client. In six category terms, these interventions are a mixture of the cathartic, the catalytic and the supportive.

3 Free attention

This is all available attention that is not distracted by events in the environment, and that is not sucked into, and swamped by, internal distress. Free attention is the facilitating energy of awareness. Giving free attention is an intense activity, a fundamental validation of the person to whom it is given.

4 Contracts

The client needs to make it clear at the start of a session what kind of contract she wants. She is free to change the contract at any time during her session.

4.1 Free attention contract   The counsellor gives free attention only – no interventions. The client is self-directed: she is picking up on her own cues and intervening in her own process.

4.2 Normal contract   The counsellor intervenes when the client appears to have lost her way, to be blocking, to be 'in pattern', to be missing her own cues. There is a co-operative balance between client self-direction and counsellor suggestions. Occasional interventions.

4.3 Intensive contract   The counsellor works intensively with client cues, making as many interventions as seem necessary to enable her to deepen and sustain her process. This may include leading a client in working areas being omitted or avoided. Frequent interventions.

5 Discharge

Facility in discharge of past distress is one of the early goals of the client. Discharge sooner or later elicits spontaneous insight, fresh recall, a reappraisal of the area being worked on. It is to be distinguished from dramatization or pseudo-discharge, which is to act out distress without discharging it (e.g. pseudo-grief or pseudo-anger).

6 Balance of attention

The client can only discharge when she has enough free attention outside the distress and when her attention is balanced between the distress material within and what her free attention is engaged with outside it, such as the supportive presence of the counsellor, or the content of the technique she is currently using to release free attention.

PRESENT TIME TECHNIQUES

These techniques are for you as client (a) to get your attention out, to release your free attention, at the start of a session, so that you may have attention available for maintaining a balance of attention when working; (b) to restore your free attention if you get shut down in the middle of your session; (c) to bring you back fully into present time after working on past events.

1 Good news

Relate your current good news, what is going well in your life at present, what agreeable events have occurred.

2 Present description

Describe the immediate environment, give a literal account of what you can see and hear and touch around you. Describe your counsellor, give a literal description of the appearance of your counsellor.

3 Future promise

Relate what you are looking forward to doing over the next few days.

4 Simple pleasures

Relate any simple pleasures of your life that come to mind; or your favourite colours, smells, tastes, sounds, textures, etc.

5 Micro upsets

Describe very trivial little upsets you have had recently.

6 Reverse calculation

Say the eight times table backwards: 8×12 is . . . 8×11 is . . . etc.

7 Movement

Move around slowly in the environment, noticing changes of view and perspective. Or move in an agile way, leaping, jumping, dancing, etc.

8 Change the environment

Rearrange items on the table, on a shelf, in the room.

9 There and now

Describe in imagination the scene beyond your visual field. Then expand this to describe more and more of the planet. Describe what you imagine is going on in a particular place you know well.

10 Out of the body view

Describe yourself now from a position outside yourself.

CONTROL LOOSENING TECHNIQUES

To loosen up embarrassment and the denial and repression barriers:

1 Facial expression

Describe in detail your last meal, exercising all the muscles on the face in every possible direction.

2 Gesture

Describe a house and garden of your childhood, with elaborate gestures at shoulder height and above.

3 Tone of voice

Express your present state of mind and feeling in glossolalia (jabbertalk), or have a conversation with your counsellor in glossolalia.

4 Act into laughter

Sustain a loud, very vigorous artificial laugh.

5 Act into fear

Stand, press your finger-tips lightly but firmly into your counsellor's back and tremble all over (hands, arms, shoulder, head, neck, jaw and knees), hyperventilate, let some sound out.

6 Act into anger

Kneel in front of your counsellor, pound the air with your fists beside her head, and yell 'No' very loud into her eyes. Or the same on a cushion on the floor.

7 Mad dog

Shake an imagined mad dog vigorously off your left leg and yell. Repeat with your right leg.

8 Body shake

Shake each limb, then head and trunk.

9 Rapid breath

Breathe in and out very quickly saying 'Oh' on the out breath.

BASIC WORKING TECHNIQUES

These are for you as client to use in a self-directed way to dislodge control patterns and to facilitate discharge of stored distress and tension, and subsequent release of insight.

1 Literal description

Describe and evoke, in the present tense, the sensory texture of a traumatic event, the sights, sounds, smells, behaviours, the exact dialogue used. Don't analyse the event, but be literal and detailed; and repeat the description.

2 Repetition

Repeat several times words and phrases that contain a hint of distress, some charge of emotion. Try repeating them louder, exaggerating the posture or gesture that accompanies them.

3 Amplification

Exaggerate and repeat any sudden distress-charged movements of hands, arms, feet, legs, pelvis, head and neck. Find the sound that goes with the amplified movement, then the words. Who are you saying them to, and about what? For tight, rigid body postures, exaggerate them extremely, find the sound that goes with this, then the words, then develop the psychodrama. Or use body-rigidity contradiction (see below).

4 Psychodrama

Play yourself in an early traumatic scene. Let the counsellor be the other person in that scene. Say, and repeat to her several times, things that you never said at the time, but which express and help discharge the distressful emotions. Combine with acting into.

5 Acting into

Act into fear or anger, when appropriate, during repetition and when saying things in a psychodrama. This means simulating vigorously, and purely physically, the movements and sounds of fear or anger discharge. It often helps the real discharge come through, and sometimes this may be different from the acted emotion.

6 Free association

Let deeper levels of your mind work spontaneously through unbidden associations.

7 Catch the thought

Verbalize any idea or image that suddenly presents itself during literal description, repetition, role-play, acting into, etc., and work with it, using any of the basic working techniques, as appropriate.

8 Re-evaluation

Verbalize any insights, new connections, thoughts or images that present themselves after discharge. Give them voice or work with them.

9 Move around the pile

Follow associations from event to event around the pile of distress to find an emotionally charged memory, the working area for your session.

10 Start with what's on top

Relax, take up the attention of your counsellor and wait until what is on top presents itself whether thought, feeling, memory or whatever. Then work on it, or move around the pile.

11 Silent free association

Relax, take up the attention of your counsellor in silence and allow the stream of consciousness to flow freely without control or interference, notice the whirlpool patterns, compulsive flows, restrictions and blockages in it.

12 Spoken free association

Relax, take up the attention of your counsellor and start talking quickly, loudly and non-stop, without control or censorship.

13 Conscious dreaming

Relax, take up your counsellor's attention, close your eyes, imagine a meadow of free attention and describe it. Then imagine a house of patterns on the edge of meadow. Invite a pattern out into the meadow, describe it, ask it what its message is, use this as a basis for a direction for working.

14 Phantasize occluded material

For operations under general anaesthetic, buried traumatic memories, imagine/phantasize what happened and work on the content of phantasy as if it were a memory.

15 Phantasize on recall

Let your imagination go on actual events you can remember and work on the content of the phantasy interwoven with reality.

16 Contradiction

Outwit your control patterns of self-deprecation by saying and doing things that contradict the pattern, by putting energy or attention in the opposite direction. This releases discharge of the underlying distress. This is the art of the light direction. You use this when you feel put down, or when you find yourself putting yourself down in some major or minor way.

16.1 Full self-appreciation   You affirm yourself in every way, con-tradicting any hint of self-invalidation in:

- What you say.
- Your tone of voice.
- Your facial expression.
- Your gesture and posture.

16.2 Partial contradiction   What you say is self-deprecating, but your tone of voice, facial expression, gesture and posture are entirely positive.

16.3 Double negative   You strongly exaggerate, in a theatrical way, the negativity in every way: in what you say, in your tone of voice, in your facial expression, and in your gesture and posture.

17 Body-rigidity contradiction

For shallow, restricted, taut breathing, use hyperventilation, with increasing sound on the outbreath. For rigid gestures and body postures, contradict them with wide open, freeing-up gestures and postures. Find the sound that goes with these, then the words, and thence into a psychodrama.

18 Contradiction about the other

You can use positive, affirmative statements that contradict the negative emotions and thoughts about someone you are referring to. This will often release discharge of the emotional distress associated with that person.

19 Direction-holding

A direction is a well-aimed statement or word that releases discharge on a chronic pattern. To hold a direction is to work by repeating the statement or word, in order to release discharge. The repetition of the direction levers off the pattern and lets the discharge out. This is for the more experienced client, but beginners need to start building up the skill. Direction-holding deals with a great chunk of congealed history and distress. It is complementary to working on particular memories.

20 Scanning

You choose one major category of distress experience, and one by one scan the memories that come to mind within that category. You briefly sketch in each memory and move on to the next. The idea is to loosen up a whole chain of linked experience, and thereby any primary underlying traumatic events that hold it in place. Here are some options:

- Scan forwards in time from the earliest available memory.
- Scan backwards in time from the present.
- Choose a very general category, such as food, sex, money, religion or relationship, and scan the painful memories that arise within it.
- Choose a specific negative category, such as times you have been rejected, missed opportunities, etc.

21 Identification check

You do this when co-counselling for the first time with anyone, in order to find out whether there are any unconscious projections at work. There are four steps:

1 Co.: Who do I remind you of?
   Cl.:   Mr. X
2 Co.: How am I like Mr. X?
   Cl.:   [*replies*]
3 Co.: What is left unsaid from you to Mr. X?
   Cl.:   [*speaks to Mr. X in a psychodrama*]
4 Co.: How am I not like Mr. X?
   Cl.:   [*replies*]

You can also use this whenever any irrational irritation or negative emotion arises between co-counsellors. Thus A is irritated by B's habit of doing Z, so B says to A: 'Who does my doing Z remind you of?' Then B takes A through the last two steps.

22 Counsel on blocks in counselling

Always counsel on blocks in a session, that is, when you are stuck as client. Work on being stuck, for example, with contradiction.

23 Calling up fear

You may need to yell, shout, scream, call out and hyperventilate to pull up fear and start the fear discharge. You need to relax immediately after the shout, to let the fear roll off. Try the finger-tip grip: dig the tips of your fingers firmly but lightly into the small of the counsellor's back to help the fear discharge.

24 Night-dreams

Work on night-dreams exactly as you do on real-life events, that is, use literal description, repetition, psychodrama, acting into, etc. Or try monodrama, which means you speak as each of the different key images in the dream, creating a discussion between them.

25 Playing the other end of the distress recording

The client may sometimes find it helpful to start work on a distressful incident by role-playing the behaviour of the person who hurt her.

GETTING INTO A REGRESSION SESSION

What follows is for a session that is on the way of regression and catharsis. As client, make clear to your counsellor the kind of contract you want. Then your working options, among many others, include:

- Present-time techniques.
- Control-loosening techniques.
- Identification check (with a new partner).
- Choosing what past distress you will work on before starting the work:
  - Unfinished business from a previous session.
  - Scanning incidents of a certain type.
  - Working on a particular traumatic incident by a combination of: literal description; repetition; amplification; association; psychodrama; acting into; contradiction.
  - Direction-holding.
- Choosing to let past distress come up, without knowing what it will be before starting to work:
  - Work with what's now on top, then work by association down the pile of memories to find the charged working area for that session.
  - Recount recent good experiences until work comes relentlessly into relief.
  - Enter reverie, relaxation, meditation, or a symbolic day-dream: see what emerges, let work float up.
  - Active body work: hyperventilate, vocalize, shake/loosen/thrash, do self-massage heavy or light. See what is released.
  - Passive body work: have counsellor use pressure points, work on tense muscle, use light or heavy massage. See what is released.
- Finishing the session: this means you are coming back into present time. Options include:
  - End the work by summarizing the insights you have gained.
  - Affirm a positive direction for future living.
  - Use any of the present-time techniques.
- Reminder: remember that regression is not the only way of working. A session may include any one or more of the following, with or without regression time:
  - Celebrate yourself, your capacities and powers.
  - Spiritual expression (see below).
  - Do some creative thinking or problem-solving.
  - Do some goal-setting and action planning.
- Basic polarities in the client's work:
  - Going the way of way of regression and catharsis, or some other way (celebration, etc.).

- If going the way of regression and catharsis then choosing to work on a known X or choosing to let an unknown X, whatever it may be, come up.
- Working on a particular incident or on a pattern (that is, a whole lump of distress).
- Working in a light way with light discharge to get attention up and out, or work in a deeper way for heavier discharge, when there is ample attention to sustain it.
- Going by the route of imagery (memory, imagination) or by body work. There are four routes to catharsis: active imagination, passive imagination, active body work, passive body work (see p. 80).

COUNSELLOR'S TOOL-KIT

For the person whose turn it is to be counsellor. The interventions here and in the next section are for the way of regression and catharsis.

1 Free attention

Give supportive, sustained, expectant, totally aware and alert free attention, always wider and deeper than the content of your client's speech.

2 Remember

The distinction between the person and the distress pattern: it is the basic rationale of giving free attention.

3 Clarify the contract

If your client forgets to specify the contract, prompt her to state clearly what kind of a contract she wants.

4 Identification check

Remember to remind a new client about this.

5 Interventions

On a normal or intensive contract, make practical prompts, based on client cues, about what your client may say or do to facilitate discharge.

All the following items presuppose there is a normal or intensive contract:

6 Client cues

Work with both process and content cues (see pp. 80–81) your client provides: slips of the tongue, sudden phrases that show a hint of discharge, distress-charged body cues, negative statements that need contradiction, and so on.

7 Accept your client's rejection of your suggestion

Don't be attached to your interventions.

8 Always interrupt a pattern

Always intervene with a suggestion when your client is talking or behaving compulsively, in the grip of a distress pattern.

9 Interrupt premature closure

Clients often tend to avoid further discharge in some area by coming out too soon. With a normal or intensive contract, encourage your client to open up the area again with more description, repetition, psychodrama, acting-into, etc.

10 Help gear change

Be alert to cues that suggest your client's need to change from literal description to a psychodrama, from one psychodrama to another at a deeper level, from the discharge of anger to the discharge of fear, from grief to anger, etc., and intervene to help the change.

11 Validation of your client

Affirm your client, when appropriate, during discharge (thus you may say 'You really are loved' while she is discharging on rejection); by touching/holding/supporting during discharge; by verbal encouragements; at the end of the session.

12 Interrupt withdrawal from fear

A client unaccustomed to fear discharge may curl up, withdraw, run away; so reach out and hold her supportively, encourage her to stay in touch with it.

13 Light techniques to switch levels

Be a master of light directions to help the client switch to a lighter level of discharge when her attention gets sunk, swamped by too much distress.

14 Mirror

Mirror the client's control pattern in facial expression, tone of voice, gesture, posture, in what she says. This is a very effective tool if it is used while giving totally supportive free attention.

15 Counterpartal psychodrama

Play negative figures that the client is discharging on, and use triggering phrases, facial expression, tone of voice, gesture.

16 Look for bodily rigidities

Encourage your client to contradict them.

17 Watch for dramatization

Allow for some dramatization since it may lead into discharge, but interrupt persistent dramatization by suggesting a phrase or an action that gets authentic discharge going.

18 Help your client back

Remember to bring the client to insight-gathering, positive directions, and to present time at the end of the session.

SOME MORE TECHNIQUES

These are for you as client to use when you have a good grasp of basic working techniques and can discharge freely.

1 Take charge now

You assume you are distress-free now and give a non-stop account of how you will take charge of your life in all respects and transform it. This may lead to copious discharge.

2 Non-verbal

Work for a whole session or part of a session using non-verbal directions: sounds, gesture, posture, gaze, moving to and from your counsellor. No speech is used. Contradict the control patterns built into your normal use of speech by working without speech.

3 Body contact

Work standing or kneeling in your counsellor's arms or kneeling with head and shoulders lowered on her lap.

4 Bad parent–good parent

When you are in touch with deep infantile rage, discharge about the bad parent (attack a cushion, etc.) with blows and cries while your counsellor acts out the parent with cries and moans, falling about, etc. When the bad parent is finished off, the counsellor becomes the good (ideal) parent, holding you, giving love and support, while you express positive emotions to the good parent.

5 Regression positions

Assume infantile positions, for example, lie on your back, knees in the air (as if in your cot); suck your thumb; play peek-a-boo with your counsellor; suck your counsellor's elbow as if your mother's breast); act into infantile screaming and rage (lie on your back, kicking and screaming). And so on.

6 Primal

When well into early material, hyperventilate, act into screaming (for example, cry out for Mummy/Daddy), let full autonomic discharge occur with fine trembling, 'streaming', primal cries; let it continue until it works itself out; give space for the flow of insight afterwards.

7 Birth work

When in touch with perinatal material, as for example in a foetal position feeling pressures or tensions in your head, neck, shoulders, buttocks, etc., invite your counsellor to externalize these pressures with cushions, then allow the emotions behind the tensions to surface and discharge. Allow plenty of space for rest, and hyper-ventilation to contradict controls on deeply occluded material. Training in client and counsellor skills is recommended and available in workshops on birth re-enactment.

CELEBRATION AND EMPOWERMENT

These are techniques for celebrating and exercising your personal strengths and powers. They affirm and manifest the real you, the empowered person, in charge of self-creation, social change and ministry to the planet. They consummate and go beyond discharge techniques – they manifest the potential released by healing the memories. They also go beyond the healing, affirming strengths you have had for years, and potentials never blocked yet still uncovered. They can be used in part of, or for the whole of, a session. It is quite a good idea to use them for the last part of a discharge session as a way of coming back into present time and into the fulness of your personhood. Here are a few suggestions.

1 Celebration

Affirm your presence in the world, your potent embodied and embedded relationship with other presences in the world. Celebrate your personal power, your capacities, developed abilities, achievements. Celebrate your passionate engagement with people and places, your interests, interactions, friendships, intimacies. And so on.

2 Openness

Affirm your openness to wider reaches of being which embrace this world, and to the immanent, interior depths within you. See spiritual expression below.

3 Creative thinking

Think aloud on the frontiers of your thinking on any topic which fascinates and engages you.

4 Problem-solving

Address a challenging issue which confronts you, with the excellence of your resourceful intelligence.

5 Project the future

Boldly imagine and express positive possibilities for yourself and the world in 5, 10, or 15 years' time. Imagine extraordinary possibilities for the world in 200, 500 or 1000 years' time.

6 Life-style planning

Creatively consider the various domains and social roles in your life, the relations between them, envision potentially fruitful developments and changes, then set some realizable goals and plan relevant actions to achieve them.

SPIRITUAL EXPRESSION

This is a form of empowerment whose primary purpose is stated in the first item below. The other two purposes are secondary and supportive. All three interweave.

1 Celebration

To affirm and expressively manifest you as a spiritual presence in connectedness with other presences in our world. A spiritual expression is a declaration like 'I am open to Being', 'I feel the presence of the whole', 'I manifest divine life', 'I am a galactic citizen', 'I abide in the free attention of the universe', but it is in your words, in your terms, in language that awakens you to unfurl your spiritual identity. Explore the declarations standing, with fullness of voice, posture and gestures. See no. 9 in Chapter 8 (pp. 109–110), and the section on Primary theatre in Chapter 8 (pp. 112–115)

2 Transmutation

See the whole range of transmutative methods given in Chapter 8 (pp. 107–111).

3 Catharsis

To discharge the fear that walls off wider forms of awareness, the embarrassment and fear that hide your spiritual identity from other people, the grief, fear and anger laid in by religious oppression and trauma; primary distress, the tensions of the human condition (see pp. 243–244).

FOLLOW-UP AND COMMUNITY BUILDING

1 Confidentiality

What you as client work on in a session or group is confidential to that session or group.

2 Sexual attraction

If it occurs between those who first meet as co-counsellors, make it verbally explicit, counsel on it and discharge on it, rather than act on it.

3 Reaching out

Reach out, with a telephone call or a visit, to those who may need attention and a session but be too distressed and shutdown to ask.

4 Possible activities for a local community include:

4.1 Regular co-counselling.

4.2 On-going groups.

4.3 Intensive co-counselling workshops.

4.4 Rotating client marathons.

4.5 Specialist workshops: transpersonal, couples, families, sex, creativity, etc.

4.6 Community counselling centres.

5 Co-counselling International (CCI)

CCI is a federation of independent co-counselling communities worldwide, with international workshops held regularly in the USA, Europe and New Zealand.

REFERENCES

Blake, R. and Mouton, J. (1972) *The Diagnosis and Development Matrix*. Houston: Scientific Methods.

Boud, D. (ed.) (1988) *Developing Student Autonomy in Learning*. London: Kogan Page.

Boud, D. and Miller, N. (eds) (1996) *Working with Experience: Promoting Learning*. London: Routledge.

Buber, M. (1937) *I and Thou*. Edinburgh: Clark.

Capra, F. (1983) *The Turning Point*. London: Fontana.

Cross, K.P. (1976) *Accent on Learning*. London: Jossey Bass.

Cunningham, I. (1988) 'Interactive holistic research: researching self managed learning', in P. Reason (ed.), *Human Inquiry in Action*. London: Sage. pp. 163–81.

Das, B. (1953) *The Science of Emotions*. Madras: Theosophical Publishing House.

Egan, G. (1990) *The Skilled Helper: A Systematic Approach to Effective Helping*. Pacific Grove, CA: Brooks/Cole.

Flavell, J. (1963) *The Developmental Psychology of Jean Piaget*. New York: Van Nostrand Reinhold.

Gendlin, E. (1981) *Focusing*. London: Bantam Press.

Goleman, D. (1995) *Emotional Intelligence*. New York: Bantam.

Grof, S. (1976) *Realms of the Human Unconscious*. New York: Dutton.

Grof, S. (1998) *The Cosmic Game*. Albany, NY: State University of New York Press.

Handy, C. (1985) *The Gods of Management*. London: PAN Books.

Heron, J. (1974) *Course for New Teachers in General Practice I and II*. Guildford: University of Surrey.

Heron, J. (1977a) *Behaviour Analysis in Education and Training*. London: British Postgraduate Medical Federation, University of London; and Guildford: University of Surrey.

Heron, J. (1977b) *Catharsis in Human Development*. London: British Postgraduate Medical Federation, University of London; and Guildford: University of Surrey.

Heron, J. (1988) *Cosmic Psychology*. London: Endymion Press.

Heron, J. (1992) *Feeling and Personhood: Psychology in Another Key*. London: Sage.

Heron, J. (1996) *Co-operative Inquiry: Research into the Human Condition*. London: Sage.

Heron, J. (1997) 'The politics of transference', in R. House and N. Totton (eds), *Implausible Professions: Arguments for Pluralism and Autonomy in Psychotherapy and Counselling*. Ross-on-Wye: PCCS Books. pp. 11–18.

Heron, J. (1998) *Sacred Science: Person-centred Inquiry into the Spiritual and the Subtle*. Ross-on-Wye: PCCS Books.

Heron, J. (1999) *The Complete Facilitator's Handbook*. London: Kogan Page.

Heron, J. and Reason, P. (2000) 'The Practice of Co-operative inquiry', in P. Reason and H. Bradbury (eds), *Handbook of Action Research*. London: Sage. pp. 179–88.

House, R. and Totton, N. (eds) (1997) *Implausible Professions: Arguments for Pluralism and Autonomy in Psychotherapy and Counselling*. Ross-on-Wye: PCCS Books.

Houston, J. (1987) *The Search for the Beloved*. Los Angeles: Tarcher.

Hyde, L. (1955) *An Introduction to Organic Philosophy*. Reigate: Omega Press.

International Coach Federation (2000) http://www.coachfederation.org/natureof-coaching.htm

Jackins, H. (1978) *The Human Side of Human Beings*. Seattle, WA: Rational Island Publishers.

James, W. (1890) *The Principles of Psychology*, vols 1 and 2. New York: Holt, Rinehart and Winston.

Kitselman, A.L. (1953) *E-Therapy*. New York: Institute of Integration.

Koestler, A. (1964) *The Act of Creation*. London: Hutchinson.

Koestler, A. (1978) *Janus*. London: Hutchinson.

Kolb, D.A. (1984) *Experiential Learning*. Englewood Cliffs, NJ: Prentice-Hall.

Langer, S.K. (1988) *Mind: An Essay on Human Feeling*. Baltimore, MD: Johns Hopkins University Press.

Macmurray, J. (1957) *The Self as Agent*. London: Faber and Faber.

Maslow, A.H. (1970) *Motivation and Personality*. New York: Harper and Row.

McMahon, E. and Campbell, P. (1991) *The Focusing Steps*. Kansas City, MO: Sheed and Ward.

Postle, D. (1991) *Emotional Competence*. London: Wentworth Institute.

Rackham, R. and Morgan, T. (1977) *Behaviour Analysis in Training*. London: McGraw-Hill.

Reason, P. (ed.) (1988) *Human Inquiry in Action*. London: Sage.

Reason, P. (ed.) (1994) *Participation in Human Inquiry*. London: Sage.

Reason, P. and Bradbury, H. (eds) (2000) *Handbook of Action Research*. London: Sage.

Rogers, C.R. (1959) 'A theory of therapy, personality, and interpersonal relationships, as developed in the client-centred framework', in S. Koch (ed.), *Psychology: A Study of a Science*, Vol. 3. New York: McGraw-Hill.

Rogers, C.R. (1980) *A Way of Being*. Boston: Houghton Mifflin.

Schon, D.A. (1983) *The Reflective Practitioner: How Professionals Think in Action*. London: Temple Smith.

Spretnak, C. (1995) 'Embodied, embedded philosophy', *Open Eye*, California Institute for Integral Studies, 12 (1): 4–5.

Torbert, W.R. (1991) *The Power of Balance: Transforming Self, Society and Scientific Inquiry*. Newbury Park, CA: Sage.

Torbert, W.R. (2000) 'The practice of action inquiry', in P. Reason and H. Bradbury (eds), *Handbook of Action Research*. London: Sage. pp. 250–60.

Washburn, M. (1995) *The Ego and the Dynamic Ground: A Transpersonal Theory of Human Development*. Albany, NY: SUNY Press.